INTREPID'S
FIGHTING
SQUADRON 18

INTREPID'S FIGHTING SQUADRON 18

FLYING HIGH WITH HARRIS' HELLCATS

MIKE FINK

NAVAL INSTITUTE PRESS
ANNAPOLIS, MD

Naval Institute Press
291 Wood Road
Annapolis, MD 21402

Library of Congress Cataloging-in-Publication Data

Names: Fink, Michael (Researcher/historian), author.
Title: Intrepid's Fighting Squadron 18 : flying high with Harris' Hellcats
  / Michael Fink.
Other titles: Flying high with Harris' Hellcats
Description: Annapolis, MD : Naval Institute Press, [2024] | Includes bibliographical
  references and index.
Identifiers: LCCN 2024026086 (print) | LCCN 2024026087 (ebook) |
  ISBN 9781682473214 (hardcover) | ISBN 9781682473221 (ebook)
Subjects: LCSH: United States. Navy. Fighting Squadron 18—Biography. |
  World War, 1939-1945—Campaigns—Pacific Area. | World War, 1939-1945—
  Naval operations, American. | World War, 1939-1945—Aerial operations,
  American. | BISAC: HISTORY / Wars & Conflicts / World War II /
  Pacific Theater | HISTORY / Military / United States
Classification: LCC D790.375 18th .F56 2024 (print) | LCC D790.375 18th (ebook) |
  DDC 940.54/49730922—dc23/eng/20241024
LC record available at https://lccn.loc.gov/2024026086
LC ebook record available at https://lccn.loc.gov/2024026087

∞ Print editions meet the requirements of ANSI/NISO z39.48-1992
(Permanence of Paper). Printed in the United States of America.

32 31 30 29 28 27 26 25 24   9 8 7 6 5 4 3 2 1
First printing

All maps created by Chris Robinson

FOR THE MEN OF FIGHTING 18 AND THEIR FAMILIES

CONTENTS

MAPS

PREFACE

THIS PROJECT BEGAN in 2015 with a humble goal: to create a Wikipedia page for Capt. Cecil E. Harris, the Navy's second-ranking ace of World War II. I first learned about Harris during my time as a volunteer and employee at the Intrepid Museum in New York City, home of the former USS *Intrepid*, which Harris and his fellow flyers in Fighting Squadron 18 called home between August and November 1944. It was hard not to be inspired hearing about Harris' achievements where they happened, walking the same decks he walked almost seventy-five years earlier.

Most of the information I could find came from the Museum, from books, or from the archive of Gerald Krueger, a Navy veteran from South Dakota who dedicated countless hours to spotlighting Harris' deeds. There was very little I could find online. I thought that was a shame, given Harris' outstanding service record and the many sacrifices he made for his country.

One contributing factor was that Harris seriously disliked the spotlight. During interviews with radio broadcasters and newspapermen, he did his best to duck recognition while drawing attention to his wingman, Franklin Burley, and to his squadron mates more generally. When I finished the Wikipedia project, I decided to continue honoring Harris' legacy and character by recognizing the men he served with as well.

This proved to be a daunting task. I did not have much time to reach out to squadron members and their extended families between long commutes, full-time work, and volunteering. Then COVID hit, and everything shut down. I was temporarily furloughed. Suddenly, I had all the time in the world. Across the country, people were similarly stuck at home waiting out the pandemic. I spent day after day cold-calling phone numbers, hoping to find connections to Fighting 18's aviators. When I managed to get through to people, they seemed happy to be speaking with a human rather than a prerecorded message and doubly appreciative that I wasn't trying to sell them anything.

I was born too late to reach many squadron members directly—in fact, I was lucky to reach two, Chuck deMoss and Larry Donoghue—but over the course of this project, I was able to connect with over two dozen squadron families. Children, grandchildren, nieces, nephews, and siblings of squadron members were eager to speak with me about their loved ones' service. They sent me scans of flight log books, personal correspondence, photographs, artifacts, and more. The exchange of information soon became a two-way street as I helped families interpret these materials using official military records.

Many hands made light(er) work. I started blogging about Fighting 18's aviators so the public could learn more about this relatively unknown unit and so families had an enduring, easily accessible account of their loved ones' service. So much material came in from so many families that the collections began "speaking" to one another. Men who served in the same division mentioned each other in letters and took photographs together. Personalities and inside jokes emerged.

I did not originally intend to pull these separate stories into a book. I am not an author by trade. After amassing so much material and becoming so emotionally involved with squadron families, however, anything less felt like a dereliction of duty. What follows is my attempt to create a unified account of the squadron's experience. It is my "thank you" to the men of Fighting 18 for their service and sacrifice, and to their families for keeping these memories alive for future generations.

ACKNOWLEDGMENTS

FIRST AND FOREMOST, I would not have been able to complete this work without the more than two dozen squadron families who assisted my research. There are so many individuals to credit here that I must limit the list to direct contributions to research. Even then, I am sure I will miss someone, so I apologize in advance for any oversight and for the brevity of the recognition below. I am sure I will have the opportunity to thank you personally when all is said and done.

Thank you to Jennifer Almquist; Tamie Amerman and Eric and Scott Peters; the late Laura Barrera; Claire and Kelea Brownell; Jackie Case; Patti Cashman; Steve Cevoli; Linde Cheema; Judi DuPont and the late Fred DuPont; Thomas Dyke; Janis Grizzard and the Ziemer family, especially VF-18 pilot Bill Ziemer's brothers, Howard and Arthur; Rebecca and Tom Harris; John Herlihy; Kate Johnstone; Joel Keels and the Keels family, especially Orean and Lillie Earle Keels-Fincher (may her memory be a blessing); Valerie Lasser; Barbara Liese; Betsy and Tommy Mayer; Stephanie Mendenhall; Scott, John, and William Murphy; Michael Naughton; Kent Newsome; Brian and Pit O'Maley; Karen Rennemo; Anita Scheckter; Cindy Schilder; Teresa Sherman and her late sister, Nancy; Marsha Thomas; the late Pam Unternaehrer; Lee Walworth; and Paul Watts.

Special thanks are in order here to Patti Cashman, who facilitated and participated in my oral history interview of her father, the late Capt. Larry Donoghue, in 2021. Except for the late Cdr. Chuck deMoss, Larry was the only member of the squadron I was fortunate enough to speak with directly and the only one I met face-to-face, even if COVID necessitated that our meeting be over Zoom. It was an experience I will truly never forget.

I am indebted to a handful of historians and authors as well. A hearty thanks to Greg Fletcher for being an early champion of this project and for carefully reviewing my manuscript. *Intrepid Aviators* served as a major inspiration for this volume, and your knowledge of Air Group 18 proved invaluable. Thank you also to Barrett Tillman and Bob Gandt for your encouragement and support of the Fighting 18 project. Your books are part of the reason I became interested in naval aviation history in the first place. Thank you to Stan Fisher and Leonard Heinz for reading over the manuscript and providing critical feedback to improve the work. Thank you to Woody Aurentz for sharing Charlie Mallory's diary, a vital source. Thank you to the late John Prados for helping to instill confidence in a burgeoning researcher. And thank you to Tom Cutler at the U.S. Naval Institute and Ian Toll for being willing to take my research about the Sibuyan Sea searches seriously despite my status as a relative nobody.

Thank you to those close to me who helped take some of the weight off and forgave my absentmindedness while I tried to fit all the disparate pieces of my research into a finished product. Thank you especially to my mom, to my partner Lindsey, to Patrick Masell, and to Jacob Hebner and his pal Peter D'Arpa. Whether it was a homecooked meal, a hug, or reading drafts and providing feedback, you can be sure it helped and was appreciated.

Finally, thank you to the Intrepid Museum, my home away from home. To Ben Levinsohn for encouraging me to volunteer; to Annette Melendez for seeing something in me during my job interview; to Mike Murtagh and Dylan Cupolo for helping me improve my craft; to Danielle Swanson for bearing with my research requests; and to Louise Gormanly, Alexis Marion, and Susan Marenoff-Zausner for their patience with me as I wrestled with the work-book-life balance. This work simply would not exist without the Museum and the important memories it preserves for future generations.

OFF THE COAST
OF LUZON

KLAXONS BLARED aboard USS *Intrepid*. The 1MC—the ship's main public address circuit—crackled to life at 1215. Hundreds of speakers simultaneously broadcast a message throughout the massive aircraft carrier: "General quarters, general quarters. All hands man your battle stations." This was not a drill. Radar had picked up Japanese aircraft nineteen miles outside the fleet.[1] A Mitsubishi A6M Zero fighter could close that distance in less than five minutes.[2] *Intrepid* and its sister carriers began slewing through the water, churning up white ribbons of wake as they zigzagged evasively. Around them, the two dozen ships making up the carrier group's defensive screen formed concentric circles to provide 360 degrees of anti-aircraft cover fire.

Nearly three thousand officers and enlisted men jumped into action at the sound of the general quarters (GQ) alarm. Sailors ran down corridors, swung through hatches, and leapt up steep ladders to reach their assigned stations. *Intrepid* was almost nine hundred feet long, but after months of practice, they were at their posts in a flash. They were the last line of defense if enemy planes appeared overhead. They knew that their performance in the coming minutes could mark the difference between life and death—not only for themselves, but for their shipmates as well.

The first line of defense was already airborne. Sixteen aviators from *Intrepid*'s Fighting Squadron 18 (VF-18) had been launched at 0930 for patrol duty. Twelve combat air patrol (CAP) pilots circled above the carrier group at high altitude, maintaining communication with shipboard intercept officers hunkered over radar consoles. Timely vectors from the intercept officers placed

1

CAP pilots between *Intrepid* and threats approaching from high altitude. Four Jack patrol pilots were stationed at low altitude on the perimeter of the group, each with his own quadrant of airspace to monitor.[3] Kamikaze suicide bombers sometimes used the ocean's surface to avoid radar. They crept sight unseen toward the fleet at wavetop altitude before pulling up into steep climbs. By the time they were detected, it was already too late. To combat this tactic, Jack pilots coordinated with screening ships and with airborne bomber crews in radar-equipped planes to sniff out hidden threats. This defense system was vital to the survival of the fleet as it continued providing strategic support for the invasion of the Philippines.

Aboard *Intrepid*, directly under the flight deck in ready room four, Lt. Harry Cropper stopped hammering away at the keys of his teletype machine and looked up at the blaring speaker on the bulkhead. This was the day's third alarm, and it was barely noon.[4] Cropper then swept his gaze down to the pile of paperwork on the desk next to him. He didn't have time for yet another interruption. A handful of fighter pilots playing acey-deucey in the ready room were annoyed to have their game interrupted but didn't have a compelling excuse to stay: their orders were to evacuate whenever the GQ alarm sounded. They shuffled by Cropper as he continued his summary of strike 2A, the first strike of the day.

Harry H. Cropper was a thirty-three-year-old lawyer from Wicomico County, Maryland, with piercing gray eyes, pale skin, and soft features. His credentials were exemplary. Cropper was a Princeton graduate, was secretary of his local bar association, and had worked for the assistant attorney general of Maryland before the war.[5] His service as VF-18's air combat intelligence officer (ACIO) perfectly suited his skills as a litigator. Lieutenant Cropper had to interview pilots after their missions, essentially cross-examining them using available evidence such as gun camera footage to corroborate their stories. After sifting through the information, he produced a report that, to the best of his knowledge, reflected the actual impact of the mission.

Cropper's job had gotten busier with each passing day as the squadron shot down more and more planes. Lt. Cecil Harris was leading the pack. Earlier that morning, Harris had destroyed three enemy aircraft over Nielson Field, on the outskirts of Manila, pushing his score to twenty-three. He was an "ace" more than four times over.[6] All the minutiae of these encounters had to make their way into Cropper's reports. How much fuel and ammunition were expended? When, where, and how did the engagement take place? In addition to damage inflicted on the target, were squadron aircraft damaged or lost? Were pilots missing in action? Strike 2C, the third strike of the day, was set to be launched shortly. Strike 2B, the second strike, would land after 2C left. That meant more planes, more pilots, more work. Cropper fixed himself to his seat and continued typing, hoping that the ship would quickly secure from GQ.

Cdr. Wilson Coleman was busy making sure air group personnel cleared out of the gallery deck.[7] He strode purposefully down the passageway, stopping at even intervals to peer inside his squadrons' ready rooms for signs of life. He popped his head into ready room four. A chalkboard and maps were positioned at the front, lecture hall style. Neat rows of desks with leather chairs stretched almost to the back of the room. The only things that clearly gave away the room's purpose were hooks along its perimeter draped with aviators' helmets, goggles, flight suits, and life vests. Despite the alarm, Lieutenant Cropper was still there at the teletype.

Coleman, in his measured Alabama drawl, asked Cropper if he was leaving. Cropper looked up from the teletype and replied that he would be along in a little while. He was determined to put a dent in his paperwork. Coleman had gotten the same reply from other Air Group 18 ACIOs during his sweep of the gallery deck. It likely made him feel a bit uneasy.

A month earlier, Commander Coleman had been stationed aboard USS *Franklin* as commanding officer, or "skipper," of Fighting Squadron 13 (VF-13). He and his men had been deployed since late July 1944 and had seen their fair share of combat together. All of that came to a screeching halt on 30 October when a kamikaze carrying a 250-kilogram bomb dove through the ship's flight deck, causing a massive explosion that claimed the lives of fifty-six officers and men.[8] Most of the men killed or wounded in the attack had been in the gallery deck. With *Franklin* temporarily out of action, Coleman received a promotion to commander, air group (CAG) and was transferred to *Intrepid* to take over its three squadrons: Fighting (VF), Bombing (VB), and Torpedo (VT) 18. He was now responsible for the well-being of hundreds of men. Coleman vowed that the lessons of *Franklin* would not go unlearned. One of his first orders as CAG was for all air group personnel to evacuate the gallery deck as soon as GQ sounded.[9]

The gallery deck was the most vulnerable area inside an *Essex*-class carrier. It was suspended directly beneath the flight deck, which was made of teak and pine wood. Like the flight deck, the gallery deck lacked armor protection in order to lower the ship's weight and center of gravity. There was no compelling reason to keep air group personnel in such a vulnerable area while under attack. Commander Coleman's orders required his men to take shelter in the wardrooms beneath the thickly armored hangar deck. It gave them the best chance of survival if the worst came to pass.

Despite any misgivings Coleman might have had about his ACIOs staying behind, his ready rooms were mostly empty, and the stragglers had promised to get belowdecks when their work was done. The CAG bid Cropper goodbye and turned out of ready room four, leaving the former lawyer to his reports. Fortunately, the situation overhead seemed to be improving. CAP pilots splashed two bogies before they could attack *Intrepid*. There was finally an opportunity to go on the offensive. The third strike of the day, strike 2C, was ready and waiting to take off on its mission targeting Japanese cargo vessels off Luzon. It was absolutely essential to get the thirty aircraft of strike 2C off the deck as soon as possible. If *Intrepid* was attacked again, their fuel and ordnance could explode with devastating consequences. The carrier ceased zigzagging at 1223 and turned into the wind for launch.[10]

Three enemy bombers appeared overhead five minutes later, forcing the flight deck crew to suspend operations after just one *Intrepid* fighter, piloted by Lt. Cecil Harris, made it airborne. Harris had been launched first to deliver a bag of aerial reconnaissance film to USS *Hancock*. Lieutenant Harris cruised toward the neighboring carrier with his flaps and wheels down. He wasn't going to land—just approach as slowly as possible to keep from overshooting his target. He waited until his Hellcat was nearly floating over the deck. At the last second, right before Harris was ready to drop his cargo, *Hancock* suddenly lurched out from under him. They weren't supposed to ring up speed until after he'd delivered the film! Then *Hancock*'s gunners started firing into the air around him.

Harris rolled his Hellcat away from the ship. Looking back over his shoulder, he could see rounds from *Hancock*'s gunners pour into an enemy plane. It was one of the three that had interrupted flight operations on *Intrepid*.[11] Smoke and flames erupted from the kamikaze as it disintegrated under the assault. Its bomb tumbled harmlessly into the water. What was left of the plane rained down on *Hancock* from amidships almost to the bow on the port side, leaving a trail of burning fuel in its wake. Crews extinguished the fires before they could do significant damage.[12] The other two planes seemed to vanish as quickly as they had appeared. The attack was over in ten minutes. CAP patrols, Jack patrols, and shipboard guns were keeping the enemy at bay for the time being. Once things settled down, deck crews aboard *Intrepid* operated with their usual efficiency to get the remaining twenty-nine aircraft aloft. The last plane of strike 2C departed at 1244.[13]

Lt. George Race felt increasingly uneasy about remaining in the gallery deck. The morning GQ alarms had been well spaced out—twenty minutes of adrenaline punctuated by a couple hours' respite before the next alarm. Now three alarms had gone off in the span of less than an hour. In fact, as soon as the last plane from strike 2C cleared the deck, ships on *Intrepid*'s starboard and stern quarters began firing at incoming bogies. It seemed like an endless procession of enemies approaching from all sides, and they appeared to be making it progressively closer to the carriers.

As ACIO for the whole air group, Lieutenant Race was responsible for pulling individual squadron reports into big-picture intelligence summaries and briefings. These were not only for Commander Coleman but also for Capt. Joseph Bolger, the ship's skipper, and Adm. Gerald Bogan, the carrier group commander who made *Intrepid* his flagship in October. Like Cropper, Race had initially stayed behind to wrap up the morning's work. It didn't matter that he wasn't finished, though; some sixth sense urged him to drop everything and get out of there immediately after the latest attack. Race left his office in the gallery deck, hustling down the passageway past ready room four where Cropper was still working. As he rounded the bend to the radar shop, he bumped into a cluster of air group personnel getting the play-by-play from the ship's radar operators. Enemy planes were now directly above the fleet.[14]

Lt. (jg) Charles "Punchy" Mallory of VF-18 didn't need a radar screen to know what was happening overhead. He was watching the battle from the cockpit of his F6F Hellcat. That would have been fine if he were airborne. Instead, he had left the ship that morning with strike 2B only to turn around minutes later due to an oil leak. Now he was stuck in the hangar pleading with a nearby chief petty officer to get him topside while the last of the planes on the flight deck scrambled into the air. He felt worse than useless. His Hellcat was fueled up and loaded with ammunition—a liability under these circumstances. His options were to get belowdecks with the rest of the air group while the ship's crew tried to rapidly de-gas and disarm his aircraft, or to try get off the ship so he could catch up with strike 2C. The choice seemed obvious to the scrappy young fighter pilot.[15]

Mallory redoubled his efforts working on the chief. When he was told to cut his engine, Mallory goosed it in protest. The chief responded by simply walking away. Fortunately for Mallory, another more sympathetic chief saw what was going on. He pulled the chocks off the Hellcat and had his men position the plane on the aft centerline elevator.[16] The whole platform lurched upward, bringing Mallory to the flight deck in a matter of seconds. From his position in the shadow of the ship's tower, Mallory could see teams of gunners frantically loading, spotting, firing, and reloading anti-aircraft artillery. The whole sky was bruised black with their work. Dark clouds marked the detonation of proximity-fused five-inch shells. Below those angry billowing masses, numerous little puffs of smoke showed where 40-millimeter (mm) shells exploded. Then there were the ever-present flashes of tracer fire from 20-mm guns pouring out hundreds of rounds per minute. The spacing of the tracers embroidered the sky, stitching through daytime blue and smoky black with equal intensity.

Over the course of the preceding months, Punchy Mallory had participated in some of the largest air and sea battles in history. He had taken vital reconnaissance photos of the Leyte area, shot down enough Japanese planes to be an ace twice over, and dived through anti-aircraft fire more times than he could count.[17] Climbing through his own carrier's gunfire, though? Undertaking an unauthorized launch? Well, there was a first time for everything. After a quick scan to make sure the flight deck was clear, Mallory poured on the coal. He checked his instruments to ensure there were no issues with his powerplant and then released the brakes to send his Hellcat surging forward. As he passed by the tower and toward his launch point on the ship's bow, *Intrepid* entered an emergency turn to the right, causing the whole ship to heel steeply to port. Mallory wasn't far enough into his deck run to get airborne, but he was well past the point of cutting his engine for a safe stop.

The determined aviator applied right rudder and aileron to keep his plane from skidding off the opposite side of the ship *as Intrepid*'s turn steepened. His Hellcat slowly veered to port despite his best efforts. It was no use. In the next moment, the wooden surface beneath his wheels vanished, replaced by churning white bow wake and dark blue sea. He was still dozens of yards shy of his planned launch point. Gravity and drag began working against him. Mallory carefully balanced between gaining enough speed to stay airborne and enough altitude to avoid crashing. His Hellcat's altimeter stabilized after a few agonizing seconds. The feeling of freefall subsided, replaced by the comforting weight of gravity pushing him into his seat. His plane began steadily climbing. Mallory had survived takeoff, but he wasn't out of the woods yet.

Hellcats from nearby carriers blew past Mallory as he desperately climbed out of artillery range. They were locked onto the tails of inbound enemy fighters. One Zero went down in a mass of smoke and flames, leaving a slick on the ocean's surface. A second was on its way down as well, not out of control due to battle damage but in a rapid descent aimed directly at the aft end of *Intrepid*'s flight deck. Mallory watched with a mixture of disbelief and horror as the enemy fighter crashed nose-first into the ship, right next to the elevator he had ridden topside moments earlier. Its bomb broke through the wooden flight deck into the gallery deck below, where it exploded in ready room five.[18]

Lieutenant Cropper was still working on his reports next door in ready room four. When the bomb hit, the thin bulkhead shielding him from the blast bowed under intense heat and pressure. A spray of shrapnel shot from room to room with no regard for the flimsy surfaces dividing them. Any man unlucky enough to be in its path was grievously injured or killed outright. A blackboard went flying into Cropper and his teletype, sending him to the floor in a heap. He coughed and shook his head. The impact left him dazed. His skin burned.

His eyes watered from the smoke. All that was left of his shirt was the right sleeve.

He had to move fast. Shoving the blackboard aside, Cropper picked himself up and, still coughing and rubbing his eyes, shambled out of the wreck. He knew he needed medical attention. The battle dressing station in the captain's cabin wasn't far; he could receive emergency treatment there. Despite the knock he had taken, Cropper still knew the way through the labyrinthine ship: out to the catwalk, across the flight deck, and down the starboard side passageway, hopefully into the waiting arms of Lt. Cdr. John Fish, the air group's flight surgeon.

Lieutenant Race was heading toward the battle dressing station as well, though not due to injury. The bomb's blast had spread smoke and flames throughout the aft end of the ship. He wanted to get as far away from their source as possible. His earlier instinct to evacuate had paid dividends. Race felt the blast as a "sickening jolt" but was otherwise spared from harm. He only realized the true extent of the damage when he saw Harry Cropper stumbling past him in the passageway. Race took a close look at him. Cropper's face was cut and burned, with shreds of skin beginning to peel off. His eyes were glassy and unfocused. It was a wonder given the way he looked that he'd been able to reach help at all. A corpsman ushered Cropper into the battle dressing station to tend to his burns. Race, without a clear idea of what to do, continued his foray forward through the ship.[19]

The sound of fire quarters alarms rung out. Red tongues of flame licked up through jagged holes in the flight deck, sending columns of smoke skyward like a beacon for eager kamikazes. Lines of men holding hoses worked frantically to beat back the blaze. Down in the hangar, the inferno threatened to envelop fueled, armed aircraft. Damage control teams led by fire marshal Lt. Donald DiMarzo desperately attacked the fires while water curtains and sprinklers drenched them from head to toe. *Intrepid*'s anti-aircraft guns briefly went silent while all hands focused on saving their ship. Incredibly, within just a few minutes, the guns were firing again. Spent shell casings overflowed from the deck edge gun tubs, tumbling down nearly sixty feet into the carrier's churning wake. *Intrepid* wasn't out of the fight just yet.[20]

USS *Cabot* was also being swarmed. One kamikaze crashed into the forward port side of the ship. Its point of impact was marked by a gaping hole in the flight deck and the conspicuous absence of the nearest gun tub, which the plane had barreled through on its way into the ocean. Another Japanese fighter approached from ahead to finish the job. *Cabot*'s forward gunners found the range at the last second. The plane exploded just below them, sending shrapnel pinging off their enclosure.[21]

The attack was relentless. As soon as one raid was beaten back, another took its place. A kamikaze spun into the water near USS *New Jersey*, Third Fleet's flagship, where Adm. William Halsey watched the smoke rising from his carriers with mounting concern. *Intrepid* alone had now expended over ten thousand rounds of ammunition in its fight for survival.[22] How long could his flattops withstand such an all-out assault?

Halsey got his answer a few minutes later. At 1259 another bomb-equipped Zero bore down on *Intrepid*. As the ship's guns opened up on him, the Japanese pilot fired back, raking the stern of the carrier with a spray of bullets that sent men scrambling for cover. *Intrepid*'s gunners found their mark a second later. The whole plane lit up in a flash from the hits. Despite their Herculean effort, the flaming wreck of the plane kept coming. Momentum carried it the rest of the way to the ship, where it pancaked onto the flight deck with a sickening crunch. Most of the plane—including the bomb it was carrying—punched straight through the gallery deck into the hangar below. Damage control crews were still there dealing with fallout from the previous attack.[23]

Lieutenant Race had managed to work his way safely through the gallery deck and was on his way topside with a group of Sailors when the second bomb went off. The whole ship shuddered from stem to stern, nearly throwing him off his feet. Acrid black smoke poured up around the group. Some doubled over, retching from the fumes. Though they were forced to claw their way blindly up steep ladders, all hands remained composed, moving swiftly until the procession spilled out into the open air. Race steadied himself on a rail at the deck's edge. A moment later, a huge geyser of water erupted thirty yards away—a near miss from another enemy plane. The ship's guns were silent. *Intrepid*'s only defense was the thick cloud of smoke surrounding it.[24]

There was no way the ship could land aircraft with its flight deck in shambles. The seventy-five Air Group 18 planes aloft at that moment had to find new homes. Most landed on neighboring carriers *Ticonderoga* and *Essex*. When there was no space left on nearby flattops, the remaining aircraft were routed directly to Tacloban field on Leyte. It was a sobering experience. The field was muddy with rain and swarmed by orphaned aircraft and refugee crews.[25]

Punchy Mallory was one of the pilots routed to Tacloban. As soon as night fell, Japanese bombers began attacking the field. Some flew as low as three hundred feet. Mallory was initially more impressed by friendly anti-aircraft fire than the bombers. The incessant boom and flash of the guns sweeping over the field reminded him of Fourth of July fireworks. As enemy raids continued throughout the night, however, Mallory felt increasingly exposed. Coconut trees were his only shelter from the bombers and the driving rain. The attack continued until 0130. By the next morning, he had acclimated a bit. Mallory dug a foxhole, ate off a tin plate, and slept like a log despite the continued appearance of heckler aircraft. A day later, on 27 November, Mallory and his squadron mates bid farewell to the Army boys. They were heading back to see what had become of their ship.

Their journey started with a lengthy six-hundred-mile flight to Peleliu. It was one step closer to home—at least for most of them. Lt. (jg) Franklin Burley's Hellcat would not start. He was forced to stay behind for another round of canned rations and raids while he waited impatiently for mechanics to fix his plane. Those who made it to Peleliu found the island much more accommodating than Leyte. The men swam, watched movies, and spent time swapping stories with Marines before sacking out for a good night's rest. The next morning, they hurriedly ate and donned their flight gear. It was another four hundred miles to the fleet anchorage at Ulithi Atoll, where they would be reunited with *Intrepid* and the remainder of their squadron.[26]

Plane after plane roared down the crushed coral runway into the serene blue sky above Peleliu. Lt. (jg) Harold "Pop" Thune was one of the last to take off. He waited patiently as his squadron mates slowly shrank into the distance ahead. When it was finally his turn, Lieutenant Thune released his brakes and began bouncing down the makeshift strip. The work of clearing, paving, and otherwise improving the airfield was still under way since it had only been captured a few months earlier. As a result, the edges of the island's intersecting runways were littered with rough deposits of coral. Thune's Hellcat continued to pick up speed.

Just before he could get his plane airborne, one of his tires burst, yanking his plane hard to the side. He barreled off the runway directly into the coral rubble.

Thune's plane ground over jagged debris until a piece punctured its external belly fuel tank. In seconds, the Hellcat was wreathed in flames. Pop Thune's airborne squadron mates craned their necks trying to spot signs of life in the plane, but all they could see was the crash cart racing down the runway to extinguish the fire. Lieutenant Commander Murphy led the rest of his men onward to Ulithi. It was likely a somber flight. He had lost over a dozen young aviators during his time as skipper of Fighting 18. Now he would have to add one more to the list, this time from a senseless accident. That night, Murphy was greeted by an unexpected guest in the barracks on Ulithi. It was Pop Thune. He had miraculously managed to extricate himself from his burning plane on Peleliu, got bandaged up and discharged from the infirmary, and soon thereafter hitched a flight to Ulithi to reunite with his squadron.[27]

By 29 November most pilots had made it back aboard *Intrepid*. They were exhausted but happy. Admiral Halsey had ordered the ship to return to Pearl Harbor along with its air group. They were finally going home after their trial by fire in the Pacific.[28] Since beginning strike operations on 6 September 1944, just eighty-five days earlier, Fighting 18 had recorded 176.5 enemy planes destroyed in aerial combat. That was a rate of more than two per day, earning the squadron the nickname "Two-a-Day 18" in newspapers nationwide. Fighting 18 produced thirteen aces, hunted down Japan's biggest battleships, and scored bomb hits on everything from cargo ships to carriers. At the same time, fourteen pilots were listed as missing in action, and another had been sent home due to the severity of his injuries. Fighting 18 had experienced victory and loss commensurate with the most successful Navy squadrons in history, including those with multiple deployments under their belts.[29]

That is why it came as such a shock when Fighting 18 was ordered off *Intrepid* on 30 November. Rather than going home with the rest of the ship's air group, the squadron was assigned duty aboard USS *Hancock*, which was taking *Intrepid*'s place as flagship of Carrier Task Group 38.2. The Navy decided it needed the squadron to continue holding the line against the kamikaze menace.[30] Reactions ranged from disbelief to outrage. Franklin Burley had just made it back to the fleet after being stranded on Leyte. When he heard the news, he blew his top. He immediately confronted squadron executive officer Lt. Clarence Blouin to protest the decision. In the heat of the moment, Burley must have said something out of line. He was put in hack for ten days as punishment.[31]

Attempts by Admiral Bogan and other high-ranking officers to intercede on Fighting 18's behalf failed. The orders were set in stone. It was an emotional moment for the bomber crews that had flown countless hours under the squadron's protection. They couldn't let Fighting 18 go without a proper send-off. The men had purchased nearly a year's supply of alcohol in Hawaii that had gone almost untouched during their time aboard ship. They decided they should put a dent in it with one last hurrah in honor of the fighters. John Forsyth of VB-18 figured that the ensuing party was among the most raucous thrown in the history of the Navy.[32] By the end of the night, members of VT-18 were drunkenly singing the fight song they had written before the air group's first strike, way back on 6 September 1944: "We're all for you, Zoomie Boys. We know you'll be true, Zoomie Boys. So go give 'em Hell and be sure all's well so the 'Torpeckers' [torpedo-bombers] won't be annoyed!"[33]

When morning arrived on rubber legs and pounding headaches, the fighters picked up their bags and disembarked. They tried to mask their emotions with machismo and humor. John Mayer galloped down the gangplank with two cigars in his mouth and all his flight gear on. Thomas Rennemo had the brim of his ballcap turned up at a wild angle. He was so busy waving to his former shipmates that he missed a step and practically fell into the boat ferrying the squadron to *Hancock*. And just like that, they were gone.[34]

A week later, on 7 December 1944, Mallory jotted down his feelings in his diary. It had been exactly three years since the attack on Pearl Harbor. On that date, he had been in the dorms at West Virginia University with his future wife. This year he spent the day sunbathing on *Hancock*'s flight deck in the vastness of the Pacific.[35] What would next year bring? The way things were going, was he even going to live to see another year? And how exactly did he get here? These were the kinds of questions Punchy Mallory and his squadron mates in Fighting 18 likely asked themselves as they waited for their turn to go home.

CHAPTER 1

CROSSING PATHS AND EARNING WINGS

FATE HAS AN INTERESTING WAY of bringing people together across space and time. Men who lived around the corner from one another before the attack on Pearl Harbor met not due to proximity but because of events that happened thousands of miles away. They had all sorts of ideas about where their lives were headed before the war. Some were already in service, some were still in school, and others had their professional careers uprooted for the sake of the nation.

Paul Amerman was an outgoing, energetic young Brooklynite attending Principia College in Elsah, Illinois. Over 6 feet tall and 188 pounds, the blonde-haired, blue-eyed Paul was the quintessential athlete: He lettered in football, was a mainstay on the track team, and was a talented baseball all-rounder. As if that weren't enough, he participated in a dazzling array of extracurricular activities, including serving as class vice president.[1] Even as a freshman in 1941, it was clear Paul was going places.

Edward Ritter grew up six blocks away from Paul Amerman on Linden Boulevard. His brown hair and ruddy complexion were complemented by cobalt blue eyes that stood out from his dark features. Rather than his eyes giving him a look of intensity, however, Ed's slightly round, expressive face gave him a friendly, inviting air. Like Paul, Ed stayed fit. He spent much of his free time at the local YMCA exercising and boxing, but his foremost pursuit was art. Ed attended Pratt Institute to develop his craft while working for Abraham & Straus, a major New York City department store, as a commercial artist and photo retoucher.[2] After work and school, Ed continued his artistic endeavors at home. He would stuff some tobacco into his pipe, furrow his brow, and set to work with pen and brush portraying life in the Big Apple.

Ed was ice skating with some friends when he first heard the news about Pearl Harbor. The whole city seemed to be in an uproar. Although the attack was shocking, dark clouds gathering on the horizon in the preceding years— from Adolf Hitler's invasion of Poland to the fall of Paris—meant that many fighting-age men had already planned for the possibility of military service.

Ed knew early on that he wanted to be a fighter pilot. It wasn't because of the glitz and glamor associated with air combat. It was because if he made a mistake or got unlucky, only he would be killed. He couldn't stand the thought of embarking a crew whose lives were wholly in his hands. Ed went to see Army Air Forces recruiters in early 1942 to start his journey into the cockpit. At the time, it was his only option. The naval aviation cadet, or V-5, program still required applicants to be at least juniors in college, and Ed was only a sophomore.[3]

In a major setback, Ed failed the Army's pilot aptitude test, seemingly botching his chance to fly. Shortly afterward, the Navy realized it needed more pilots to feed its training pipeline. It was missing out on qualified aviators because of outdated education requirements. A few months later, in April 1942, the Navy opened V-5 recruiting to high school seniors and above. Ed now had a second chance to earn his wings, and this time he wasn't going to let the opportunity slip through his fingers. The determined young New Yorker passed the Navy's test. On 8 May 1942, Ed officially enlisted. A month later he was shipped off to the University of North Carolina, Chapel Hill, for preflight training.[4]

Almost simultaneously, Paul Amerman was heading for a different pre-flight training facility at the University of Iowa. Despite growing up around the corner from each other, entering naval aviation cadet training a month apart, and both heading to Pensacola to earn their Navy "Wings of Gold" around the same time, Paul Amerman and Ed Ritter may not have crossed paths before serving together in Fighting Squadron 18. They had different upbringings, careers, and social circles, and the naval aviation pipeline they both entered in mid-1942 had just undergone a massive expansion. This was not only because the Navy loosened education requirements after Pearl Harbor but also because legislators and aviation advocates worked tirelessly in the immediate prewar years to embed flight training in schools across the country.

The Civilian Pilot Training Program (CPTP) was an effort by the Civil Aeronautics Authority to bring America firmly into the age of flight. The program provided funding for local flying services willing to serve as training facilities for nearby schools. Students could then enroll in flight training with the promise of a private pilot's license if they passed the course. CPTP proved immediately popular. At the end of 1939, less than a year after the program's launch, 435 colleges and universities were offering CPTP courses, training 9,350 students in the basics of flight.[5]

Roughly a year after the program's inception, in October 1940, CPTP came to Northern State Teachers College (NSTC) in Aberdeen, South Dakota. By this time, the "civilian" part of CPTP had become of secondary importance. From September 1940 onward, individuals enrolled in the program had to sign a pledge to enter military aviation if they were deemed fit for service. That did not seem to dissuade students at NSTC. Ten boys showed up on the first day of registration to secure a spot in the course. The name at the top of the list read "Cecil Harris."[6]

Cecil Elwood Harris was born 2 December 1916 in rural Cresbard, South Dakota. He grew up on a sprawling plot of farmland surrounded by fields of waving wheat and dozens of horses. Unfortunately, his coming of age coincided with devastating times for America's agricultural community. Cecil was thirteen years old when the United States plunged headlong into the Great Depression and seventeen years old when Dust Bowl storms ravaged his home state. Crops were destroyed, farmers lost their livelihoods, and bankrupted families fled South Dakota in droves. The Harris farm survived these natural and manmade disasters, but Cecil, preparing to graduate from high school, was already thinking about making his way in the world.

It was the mid-1930s. "Times were pretty hard then," he recalled in a 1968 interview.[7] Many farm families couldn't afford to send their children off for a proper education. Cecil felt lucky he could attend high school in the first place and wanted to do his part to solve this problem. He enrolled at NSTC in 1936. In a year's time, he was out in the vast countryside armed with a teaching certificate and textbooks. He taught seventh grade in rural South Dakota for a few years before returning to NSTC to finish his bachelor's degree.[8]

For Cecil, CPTP was the fulfillment of a boyhood dream. His parents overruled him in high school when he showed an interest in joining the Army Air Corps. Without their written consent, he could not enlist, but now he was old enough to sign on the dotted line.[9] Cecil secured his private pilot's license by the end of the year. He enlisted in the Naval Reserve's V-5 program in March 1941, shipped off to Naval Reserve Air Base Minneapolis in June, and was then forwarded to Naval Air Station Jacksonville, Florida, to complete cadet training.[10]

Another farm boy, Wesley Keels, took CPTP at Brevard College, a small two-year school nestled along the banks of the French Broad River in western North Carolina. Wesley was raised in a sharecropping family where he and his seven siblings picked cotton and soybeans to help supplement the household income. The plot of land they worked was so far out in the sticks that they didn't have a phone line.[11] It was a tough upbringing, one that gave Wesley a stout frame well suited for manual labor. As it had with Cecil Harris, the rigors of farm life prompted Wesley to strike out into the wider world. The family couldn't afford to pay for Wesley's education at Brevard, so he got a job with the Ecusta Paper Corporation to pay his own way.[12] After completing two years of engineering courses and a summer CPTP course in 1941, Wesley secured his private pilot's license and the opportunity to undertake naval aviation cadet training. He enlisted in the Navy in early February 1942. By 30 March 1942 he was at Naval Reserve Air Base Atlanta undergoing primary flight training.[13]

Wesley's work ethic carried over into training, including classroom instruction. His notebooks exhibit a clean cursive hand and carefully sketched diagrams covering everything from the physics of flight to Japanese ship recognition, all the way down to basic Navy nomenclature. A wall or partition was now a bulkhead. The floor was the deck. Left, right, front, and back were port, starboard, bow, and stern. There were all kinds of new rules and regulations to follow. Wesley carefully underlined one of them: "#6—*Never unsheathe a sword in the Wardroom.*"[14] After completing training in Atlanta, he was transferred to Naval Air Station Jacksonville for more advanced flight training. He must have done as well in the cockpit as he did at his desk. He earned his commission in January 1943.[15]

Most of the future members of Fighting Squadron 18 underwent naval aviation cadet training between 1942 and 1943. Many shared similar experiences in terms of their time in the air and their social lives. The most complete record of training comes from Bryant L. "Wally" Walworth, who recorded his experiences in a journal his sister gave him for Christmas in 1942. Bryant was a clean-cut young man studying plant science at the University of Illinois when the war broke out. He had thick, dark eyebrows, deep brown eyes, and a slightly aquiline nose. Like many of his peers, Bryant was athletically gifted. Even though he was of average height, he shined on the basketball court. His clever play at guard carried his team to the University of Illinois intramural championships in 1941.[16]

Because of how far along he was in his collegiate studies, Bryant was deferred from service until after graduation in the summer of 1942. Agronomy was the family trade. His father, Edward, taught the subject at the university, and Bryant himself had just wrapped up six weeks teaching agriculture in a local school before heading off for aviation training. The superintendent of the school wrote him a letter in July 1942, saying, "Was very glad to know just what you decided to do in regard to military service and I think you have enlisted in a department which has a future inasmuch as it is the air force that will eventually settle this conflict."[17]

Though Bryant was sure there was a bright future ahead for pilots, that wasn't his reason for selecting flight duty. He did not see himself as a career aviator; he didn't really love to fly, for that matter. What motivated him to join the air forces was the ability to contribute directly to the war in a manner he could see and experience tangibly. It didn't hurt that such an assignment allowed him to sleep with a roof over his head instead of in a foxhole, or that he could expect to eat proper meals instead of subsisting on canned rations. Those were factors for many enlisting in the Navy. Bryant felt that flying was the best option available to him, so he took it.

Ironically, the young plant scientist had hay fever and was prone to seasonal allergies. Bryant made the mistake of telling this to Army Air Corps recruiters during the early phases of his interview. They immediately lost interest in him. Like Ed Ritter, the Navy wound up being his fallback. When Bryant talked to a Navy doctor about his hay fever, the doctor simply said, "It doesn't seem to bother you. Don't tell anybody that you've got it." Sure enough, he didn't mention it and was cleared to begin training. His hay fever never recurred.[18]

The first half of Bryant's diary is a post facto account of his experiences during the summer and fall of 1942. He reported to Lambert Field in St. Louis, Missouri, on 30 July for ground instruction and elementary flight training. Instead of the glamor portrayed in patriotic media, he experienced the bureaucracy of military life: "On that memorable first day I started, what so far has been a never ending wait in long lines. We waited for a physical, we waited for clothing issue, we waited for chow etc."[19] On the bright side, Bryant crossed paths with a cadet named Al Earp who was from his hometown. They became fast friends, sticking together almost to the end of training even as they moved from base to base.

Bryant's class consisted of fifty men with no prior experience in service outside of, perhaps, the Boy Scouts. When they first tried to respond to basic commands such as "about face," the group turned in as many different directions as humanly possible. Bryant noted in his diary, "We were a sorry looking mess."[20] After a month of practice, however, they had drill running smoothly. The rest of their time was spent in classrooms refreshing their math skills, learning the physics of flight, practicing navigation problems, and memorizing the ins and outs of aircraft powerplants.

The difficulty of training increased exponentially a month later when Bryant headed out of the classroom and onto the field for his introduction to the N3N biplane, a tandem-seat trainer built by the Navy itself. Ensign R. F. Richards was his first instructor. Richards sat in the front seat operating the controls while he spoke to Bryant, sitting in the rear seat, through the Gosport, a simple tube connected to the trainee's helmet. Ensign Richards took Bryant up a mile or so over the field before letting the student take the reins, coaxing him through shallow turns and attempts at holding the plane straight and level. When they landed, Richards turned to Bryant and said, "Well, Walworth, that was just a get-acquainted flight. Tomorrow we really get to work."[21]

He wasn't kidding. The next day, Richards was on Bryant's case, upbraiding him for every little mistake even though it was only his second time in the air. It was hard to take the endless criticism, but his instructor also made sure to have serious, encouraging conversations with him, including some real insight into what he was doing wrong and how he could fix it. Without such stern treatment, Bryant wasn't sure he would have earned an "up" on his solo check flight later in the week, advancing him to the next section of the syllabus.

The stages of flight training were designated by letters. "A" stage was the first twelve hours of tandem flight with an instructor before soloing to prove you could take off and land by yourself. "B" stage was a gradual increase in difficulty. Cadets perfected the A stage maneuvers while their instructors added in some new ones, like "S" turns and small field procedure. These lessons helped trainees learn to account for wind speed and direction, and to more precisely land their aircraft. On his final B check, Bryant's instructor talked through what he did right and wrong for about fifteen minutes after they landed. At the end of the chat, according to Bryant's diary, "he said, 'Well! Walworth that wasn't a bad flight. I believe it was worth an up.' I managed a 'Thank you sir,' and floated out of the hangar on angel wings. I was the happiest boy in camp that night."[22] He had made it through elementary training.

For the next seven weeks, Bryant spent almost all his time in classrooms or gymnasiums. The cadets didn't do any flying during this period of physical and mental conditioning. As tiring as this phase of training might have been, there was still time for a social life. Bryant attended several United Service Organizations dances and a few parties in St. Louis, though he didn't drink. He went on a few dates, but his life was transient at this point. On 23 October Bryant packed his things, had afternoon chow, got paid, and received his next orders. He and Al Earp spent the weekend at home in Illinois before boarding the train to Saufley Field, Pensacola, Florida, for intermediate flight training. The pace and danger of training were about to increase exponentially.[23]

Flying resumed along with stepped-up ground school subjects. After a couple of months away from the controls, "it was just like beginning all over again."[24] Bryant's instructor started with A stage procedures to ease him back into things, then introduced "C" stage. This is when practice became truly exciting, especially for the fighters-to-be. They learned loops and snap-rolls: maneuvers that involved going upside down and pushing the limits of their aircraft. Nosing up and over in a loop, Bryant could feel his plane fall off at the top, not quite carrying through the full arc of the circle he was making through the air. He recovered before his plane spun out. The feeling of freefall was exhilarating. Each time he practiced, he got a better feel for his aircraft. Soon he was executing Immelmanns like a pro, combining a half-loop and half-roll to quickly gain altitude and reverse direction.[25] Bryant remembered his C stage instructor fondly. He bought him a cigarette lighter for the holidays as a token of appreciation.

Christmas 1942, when Bryant received his diary, coincided with "D" and "E" stages, where he learned formation flying with his fellow cadets. The new year brought with it a new plane, the Vultee SNV Valiant, and a new field assignment at nearby Ellyson.[26] The Valiant was much closer to the kind of aircraft Bryant and his fellow cadets would fly in combat. It had a two-way radio, enclosed cockpit, variable pitch propeller, and single-wing design, unlike the vintage-looking N3N biplane. The Valiant also tended to shake severely at stall speed and whine annoyingly when the propeller entered higher pitch, causing trainees to dub the plane the "Vibrator."[27]

In addition to flying more advanced aircraft, more advanced procedures—including flying by instruments and at high altitude—were introduced in these final stages of training. Familiarization with instrument flying started with the Link Trainer, which allowed cadets to practice safely on the ground. This was a godsend for many, including Bryant, who stalled and spun out on his first time in the Link. High-altitude flying and oxygen procedures also entered rotation. Pilots were flown up to 30,000 feet as passengers to experience breathing through masks. Bryant's mask didn't fit properly on his first trip up. As he watched Earth shrink into the distance six miles below, he slumped over in his seat due to lack of oxygen. A flight surgeon hurriedly worked to get his mask hooked on, and Bryant shot back up once his air supply was restored.[28]

Bryant and Al, who had been through training together since July 1942, finally parted ways in February 1943. Al was headed for a VB assignment, while Bryant headed for operational training with a VF squadron. Bryant traded his SNV for a new plane, the North American Aviation SNJ.[29] It was a big upgrade; the SNJ was faster and more maneuverable than its intermediate training counterpart and, perhaps most importantly for fighter training, was equipped with two forward-firing guns.[30] The SNJ was well suited to its role as an advanced trainer, especially since the final phases of training focused on stunt flying, night flying, and gunnery.

Bryant greatly enjoyed air combat and gunnery practice at Barin Field, one of Pensacola's many outlying training facilities. Cadets only needed to average four hits on the tow sleeve to pass. Bryant's average was 9.5. In mock combat with his instructors, Bryant won every fight starting from the altitude advantage and lost every fight when he was the low man. He went two for two against Joe Chrobuck, one of the other cadets in his group. He had come a long way from worrying about washing out in St. Louis. Now he was holding his own, not just against fellow cadets but against his instructors as well. His perseverance paid off. Bryant Walworth earned his Navy Wings of Gold and was commissioned as an officer on 20 April 1943. After a brief trip home to see family for Easter, he headed back to Florida for his next adventure.[31]

Even after they finished cadet training, newly christened ensigns went through one last course of instruction, called operational training, to finish polishing their teamwork and gunnery skills and to introduce them to aircraft being used on the front lines. For fighters, that was the F4F Wildcat. Bryant and Joe Chrobuck were assigned to Flight 65 in Green Cove Springs, Florida. These groups were smaller and more tightly knit than the ones formed during cadet training. In addition to Chrobuck and Walworth, there was a Marine Corps aviator named Tom Sorensen, who Walworth bunked with; a Louisiana farm boy named Franklin Burley who held a degree in agriculture from Louisiana State University—surely he and Walworth talked shop between training hops; and last but not least, none other than Paul Amerman.[32] Once they had gotten to know one another, they all went by more familiar nick-names. Bryant was "Wally" on account of his last name, and Amerman was "Boot," apparently short for "Bootnose."

Their operational training unit (OTU) leader was Lt. Carlton Starkes. To say the men looked up to Starkes was an understatement. He was already a highly decorated war hero and fighter ace, having served with Fighting Squadron 5 (VF-5) during the battles of Midway and Guadalcanal.[33] According to Bryant's training reports from this period, his time with the OTU significantly refined his flying skills. After sixteen additional hours of navigation practice, his marks were raised from "fair" to "excellent." Though he had no prior training, two courses in communications operations and procedure—a total of twenty-four hours—earned him excellent marks. In Starkes' estimation, Bryant could stand to be a bit more aggressive but was "exceptionally dependable,"[34] an important trait in a squadron mate whether they were leading you into battle or sticking to your wing.

This phase of training was marked by highs and lows. The men spent a few weeks in May operating out of St. Simons Airfield in Georgia. A barrier island north of Green Cove Springs, St. Simons was billed as "Georgia's all-year playground."[35] The men were surrounded by scenic marsh vistas and quaint beachside homes. They had liberty every night, meaning they could spend a great deal of time at the Cloister, a swanky resort hotel conveniently located just up the road from the airfield. Joe Chrobuck got married in a little chapel on nearby Sea Island, with Bryant Walworth as his best man and Lieutenant Starkes giving away the bride.

The serenity of their nights on St. Simons was punctuated by the dangers of the intensive gunnery training they underwent during the day. Each time they went up for practice, the men all put a quarter in a pot to serve as an incentive for taking home the high score. Whoever proved most accurate on the day won the pot and had some extra spending money at the Cloister.

One week into their stopover at St. Simons, the men of Flight 65 took off early for gunnery practice off the Georgia coast. The sun was still low in the sky as they buzzed angrily around the tow sleeve. They were practicing overhead runs, diving straight down on the target with their guns blazing before pulling up and away to give the next man in line his turn. Bryant had just finished his pass and was waiting at altitude while his roommate, Tom Sorensen, angled his F4F Wildcat down toward the banner.

Sorensen flew closer and closer, waiting until he was too close to miss the target before diving beneath it. He misjudged the angle slightly—just enough to clip the banner's tow cable. The impact sent Sorensen's plane spinning out of control. It fell six thousand feet down to the water below. As soon as his Wildcat struck the waves, it was gone. There was no sign of Sorensen.[36] Bryant was shocked. After landing, he had to fuel back up and go on another practice hop; there was no time to mourn his lost roommate. Finally, when the day's syllabus was over, Bryant went back to his room to inventory Sorensen's effects so they could be sent home to the pilot's grieving family.

Training with the OTU ended a month later, on 23 June 1943. Walworth, Amerman, and Burley were assigned to the same squadron and given two weeks' leave before reporting to their next duty station in San Diego, California. Being sent to the West Coast meant that they were likely heading for Hawaii soon. They knew based on their orders that this might be their last opportunity to see family and friends before shipping out.

As they made their way cross-country, another OTU wrapped up its syllabus. This group was led by Lt. Gordon Firebaugh, a venerable aviator who engaged in the first battle between American carrier pilots and Japanese land-based fighters in August 1942.[37] Firebaugh's seven freshly graduated cadets included three men headed for duty with Fighting 18: William Ziemer, James Newsome, and John Herlihy.

William C. Ziemer hailed from Tom's River, New Jersey. He was a handsome young man, six feet tall with a square jaw and thick blonde hair. Bill had earned an academic and athletic scholarship to Lafayette College on account of his grades and his football prowess. He was captain of Lafayette's freshman football team in 1940 and was promising enough that the coach of the varsity team put him in as part of the lineup during his sophomore year.[38]

The Ziemer family was all in on the Navy. Bill's father, John, had been at the Battle of Vera Cruz in 1914 aboard cruiser USS *Chester* and later served as a civilian aircraft inspector at Naval Air Station Lakehurst. All five of John's sons followed in his footsteps during World War II: John Jr., or "Jack," was a Seabee; Ernest was an aviation chief machinist's mate; William was an aviator; Howard was an aviation machinist's mate who later became an officer and pilot; and the baby of the bunch, Arthur, finished boot camp in 1945, serving as a radarman aboard destroyer USS *Noa*.[39]

James M. "Buck" Newsome Jr. was also destined for the military. His father served in the Army, and James enrolled in the Citadel, a military college in his native South Carolina, which ensured he would enter service upon graduation. Buck Newsome was over six feet tall with a prominent brow and cleft chin that gave him a rugged look despite his slender frame. During his time training under Lieutenant Firebaugh, Newsome formed close relationships with Bill Ziemer, or "Ziem" as the guys called him, and with John Herlihy, who carried his high school nickname "Chesty" with him into training.

Herlihy was a Massachusetts native with broad shoulders, a round face, and a winning smile. His high-school yearbook forecast where the seniors would be ten years after graduation. His entry read, "Chet has entered in the automobile races and comes out first in them all."[40] The yearbook editor wasn't far off, except Chesty Herlihy was running races at much faster speeds, and with much higher stakes, than those envisioned in the safety of prewar America. He was also doing it within five years, not ten.

Together, Bill Ziemer, Buck Newsome, and Chesty Herlihy received orders to San Diego for squadron assignment. More than a year of training had paid off with coveted fighter billets and frontline service with the fleet. They were about to meet Walworth, Amerman, and Burley in their assigned squadron. It was not yet called Fighting 18, though. The Navy's needs were constantly changing as the war situation evolved throughout 1943, requiring deployment schedules, squadron duties, and personnel to shift unpredictably as the men waited to find out what the war had in store for them.

CHAPTER 2

BECOMING
A SQUADRON

FIGHTING SQUADRON 18 WAS ESTABLISHED in late 1942 as VGS-18, short for heavier-than-air (V) escort (G) scouting (S) Squadron 18.[1] The unit was so named because it was earmarked for service aboard escort aircraft carriers, the Navy's smallest flattops. These ships were more lightly armored and much slower than their larger siblings like *Intrepid*. As a result, escort carriers picked up a grim nickname based on their Navy designation: instead of carrier (C) heavier-than-air (V) escort (E), CVE purportedly stood for "Combustible, Vulnerable, Expendable."[2] Despite these drawbacks, escort carriers could be produced quickly and in large numbers. That meant invasion forces could now have their very own flattops for extended air support duty while the faster fleet and light carriers conducted strikes deep into enemy territory, paving the way for the next big hop across the Pacific.[3]

There wasn't enough space aboard escort carriers to have a full air group with separate squadrons, so VGS-18 operated a mix of torpedo bomber and fighter aircraft. Pilots drilled at Naval Air Station (NAS) Whidbey Island in Washington State through the first few months of 1943. Weather conditions in the Pacific Northwest were atrocious. Besides being generally unpleasant, cloud cover, rain, and the chill air slowed training to a crawl.

On 1 March 1943 the Navy redesignated all VGS squadrons VC, with the C standing for composite.[4] This was a change in name only: the squadrons continued to operate a mix of fighter and torpedo aircraft. Throughout this training period, men made firing passes on tow sleeves in F4F

Wildcat fighters to test their gunnery proficiency, while others practiced torpedo runs in TBF Avenger torpedo bombers. By the end of March 1943, VC-18 was getting increasingly proficient. The Navy decided to move the squadron to Ream Field at San Diego's NAS North Island to be closer to the action.[5]

The difference between NAS Whidbey Island and NAS North Island was night and day. The squadron had nearly coin-flip odds of flying through rain on any given day at Whidbey. At North Island, about a tenth of an inch of rain fell throughout May and June 1943 combined.[6] The men undoubtedly were happy for the change from temperamental Pacific Northwest weather to year-round Southern California sun.

In early May pilots undertook gunnery practice with ships of the fleet, including drills with destroyer USS *Frankford*. Carrier landing practice was likewise emphasized throughout the month, though the men were eased into this challenge. Before they attempted to land on a ship at sea, pilots learned how to put their planes down on a carrier-sized patch of ground as part of field carrier landing practice. These touch-and-go landings were no substitute for the real thing, though. Starting 30 May, VC-18 pilots practiced flight operations from the deck of the brand-new escort carrier USS *Prince William* (CVE 31). VC-18's commanding officer, Edward Link, logged the first launch in the ship's history.[7] On 1 July 1943 the squadron conducted bombing practice on destroyer USS *Trathen* and destroyer escort *Harold C. Thomas*.[8]

Pilots trained throughout July while new additions to the squadron began to arrive from naval air bases across the country. Ensign Bryant Walworth flew commercial from New York to San Diego in late July 1943. He had only just completed operational training.[9] Lt. Frederick "Freddy" Wolff, on the other hand, had been a flight instructor since 1942. He took his last student up on 5 August 1943 before receiving orders to VC-18. He arrived in San Diego later that month.[10] The two most significant arrivals for the squadron were Lt. Cecil Harris, a recently returned combat veteran, and the Grumman F6F Hellcat, a new frontline fighter that further tipped the scales in the Allies' favor. Both proved integral to the squadron's experience in training and in combat.

THE COMBAT VETERAN

Cecil Harris completed advanced carrier training in May 1942, within days of the Battle of the Coral Sea. Given that the the Battle of Midway followed shortly thereafter, it seemed likely he would soon be fighting the Japanese. But Harris wasn't going to the Pacific—at least not yet.

He was initially attached to VGF-27, an escort carrier fighting squadron heading for the Mediterranean aboard USS *Suwannee*.[11] VGF-27 was assigned to provide air support during Operation Torch, the Allied invasion of French North Africa. While fleet carrier fighting squadrons attacked enemy aircraft, escort carrier fighting squadrons performed supporting roles patrolling airspace or strafing anti-aircraft artillery with their machine guns. It was thankless but vital work, less glamorous than dogfighting but potentially just as dangerous.

On 8 November, the day of the invasion, Harris was flying combat air patrol over the fleet as wingman to his squadron's commanding officer, Lt. Cdr. Thomas Wright. Vichy French pilots refused to bring the fight to the carriers, so there was no chance for air combat. They anticipated hours of boredom. On the bright side, the lack of enemy planes gave Harris and his commanding officer a chance to hunt bigger game. The largest battleship in the French navy, *Jean Bart*, was lying stationary in nearby Casablanca Harbor while French destroyers hurriedly fled the harbor for open water. Harris dove repeatedly on the ships with his Wildcat's guns blazing.[12] In two years' time, he'd be taking on even bigger ships halfway around the world.

When its job off the African coast was complete, *Suwannee* headed for duty in the South Pacific. Despite this long-anticipated change of scenery, the next few months were equally dull. Day after day, Harris and company flew convoy escort missions through waters seemingly abandoned by the Japanese. Then, on 6 March 1943, the squadron got exciting news. VGF-27 was needed on Guadalcanal, code-named Cactus, to reinforce the island's defenses. Cecil Harris was about to get a taste of life in the "Cactus Air Force."[13]

The chief yeoman of VF-27 (the squadron dropped the G when they moved ashore), E. C. Simmons, volunteered to join the aviators as a member of the squadron's shore-based detachment. He kept a log of his experiences on

Guadalcanal. Reading excerpts from that journal, one wonders why anybody volunteered for such duty. He probably asked himself the same question while sitting in his soggy, mosquito-infested tent, listening for the drone of Japanese bombers. One story sums up his overall experience: "We made fudge—took it off fire and put in tent to cool. [Washing Machine] Charlie came. Dropped a bomb on bomber strip. . . . Big fire. . . . he came back. Got some more good hits. . . . Shrapnel flew in center of us—very lucky no one was hit . . . would have killed anyone it hit. T'was serious but comical the way everyone fell into their [fox] hole. I went in on my back. Plenty muddy–not much fudge ate."[14]

A week after this incident, on 1 April 1943, eight men from VF-27 were chosen for flight duty as part of a larger force of forty planes attacking targets on the Russell Islands. Harris was in one of these divisions alongside three of his buddies, Claude Frazier, Willard Sweetman, and Douglas Lebow.[15] They had spent the past month flying three hours a day, almost every day, without much to show for it. In all that time, Harris never had the opportunity to engage even a single Japanese plane. In a reversal worthy of the date—April Fools' Day—forty Mitsubishi Zero fighters were waiting to intercept Harris and company.

In the wild air battle that followed, Harris accounted for two of six enemy planes shot down by VF-27 and returned to Guadalcanal without incident. What happened to the other men in his division better illustrates the carnage of the fight. Frazier was forced to crash-land his Wildcat. The plane was so full of holes that it looked like a sieve. Sweetman landed without incident, then fainted due to blood loss from wounds sustained during combat. His whole cockpit was mangled by enemy cannon fire. Worst of all, Lebow was forced to bail out far from base. He'd been close with Harris since the squadron first came together in 1942. His condition was unknown.[16] It's hard to imagine a tougher introduction to air combat after a long stretch of uneventful patrol missions.

Throughout his service with VF-27, Harris' fitness reports consistently marked him out as a "natural pilot" of "outstanding moral and military character" who was "well liked both by officers and men in the squadron."[17] These reports by his commanding officers list him as outstanding when compared with men of equal rank. Harris therefore came to Fighting 18 as the squadron's most experienced combat veteran, as well as a man who could lead his fellow officers by example. Harris' experience losing good friends in VF-27 also ensured he would go above and beyond to help his new squadron mates survive their encounter with the Japanese.

THE PLANE

The second important event was the arrival not of a person, but of a machine: the Grumman F6F Hellcat. The plane's predecessor, the rugged and battle-tested Grumman F4F Wildcat, was a capable aircraft that held the line against Japan's frontline fighters in the early days of the war. By late 1943, however, it was overdue for replacement. Grumman's engineers listened closely to experienced Wildcat pilots and designed the Hellcat according to their needs. In the wake of his successful defense of USS *Lexington* in February 1942, Lt. Cdr. Edward "Butch" O'Hare, the Navy's first fighter ace of World War II, wrote a letter to Grumman employees saying, "You build them, we'll fly them and between us, we can't be beaten."[18] The Wildcat had served him well, but he did have one request for the company's engineers as they contemplated the most integral characteristics of the Wildcat's successor. Lieutenant Commander O'Hare wanted "something that will go upstairs faster"[19]—in other words, something with a greater rate of climb.

Cdr. John "Jimmy" Thach, one of the key tacticians of the air war in the Pacific, similarly told Leon Swirbul, vice president of Grumman Aircraft Engineering Corporation, that the F6F Hellcat needed "more climb and speed."[20] The American design philosophy of armoring aircraft, providing self-sealing fuel tanks, and otherwise weighing planes down with lifesaving features meant that Navy pilots were hard-pressed to duke it out with lightweight Japanese fighters in a turning battle. What they needed was the ability to dive, climb, and sprint faster than their opponents. Put simply, naval aviators needed the ability to fight vertically, on their own terms, instead of on the horizontal, where the Mitsubishi A6M Zero operated at maximum advantage.[21]

What they got more than exceeded their expectations. Whereas the F4F-3 Wildcat had a Pratt & Whitney R-1830 Twin Wasp radial engine capable of generating 1,200 horsepower (hp), the F6F-3 Hellcat sported a much beefier Pratt & Whitney R-2800 Double Wasp putting out 2,000 hp. This new powerplant gave the Hellcat a maximum speed fifty miles per hour faster than the Wildcat, even though the Hellcat weighed almost twice as much as its predecessor.[22] This upgrade allowed Hellcat pilots to adopt radically different tactics from the kind used by Wildcat pilots. Cecil Harris noted, "[The Zero] could still out-turn the F6 of course, but many a time I was able to demonstrate the climbing ability and the diving ability and the straight and level difference between the two airplanes. . . . [B]ecause of the power it had, you could put the nose up . . . shorten your turn or slow your speed down . . . take the nose down, pour on the coal and you'd have your speed right back and you could . . . actually out maneuver them that way."[23]

The Hellcat came with a whole slew of quality-of-life improvements as well. Harold Thune recalled, "In the F4F, to bring the landing gear up, it took 30 cranks. . . . And when we got to the F6, our flight instructor was actually a fellow from Britain. And he had the little brogue, and he then, as the leader, got to fly the F6 before there were many of them out. And his remark when he flew it was—'That's a gentleman's aeroplane.' Because you hit a button and the wheels came up."[24]

The Hellcat's combat debut over the Solomon and Gilbert islands in late 1943 looked promising. Fighting Squadron 9, one of the first units to receive the Hellcat, noted after an air battle in November that "the F6F-3 using combat flaps was able to maneuver effectively with the Zeke [the Allied reporting name for the Zero], that its firepower was much more devastating and that its protection was vastly superior."[25] From late August to December 1943, Hellcat pilots claimed 230 enemy aircraft destroyed in combat for a loss of 30 or fewer of their own.[26]

By the time mid-1944 rolled around, modifications to the Hellcat in the F6F-5 model made the plane even more capable. It had longer range, a higher maximum altitude, a faster top speed, more armor, and greater maneuverability. Water injection provided a short-term powerplant boost in an emergency, allowing pilots to quickly leave their opponents in the dust. In addition to the Hellcat's usual armament of six Browning .50-caliber machine guns and up to one thousand pounds of ordnance, the F6F-5 could be outfitted with rockets for increased ground attack capability.[27] In short, this meant that Fighting 18 was getting one of the premier fighter aircraft of World War II and, more importantly, one that was considerably more capable than their average opponent's.

The arrival of Harris and the Hellcat presaged a bigger change for VC-18. On 15 August 1943, the squadron was redesignated VF-36.[28] This change wasn't in name only, as with the switch from VGS to VC, but instead represented a change in mission and function. Gone were the Avengers; gone were coordinated raids on ships using a mix of torpedo and fighter aircraft. The newly christened VF-36 was slated to head out to the Pacific as a land-based, independent fighting squadron. With no need for torpedo bombers, the squadron's Avenger pilots were transferred to other units in October 1943.[29]

In their place, nearly thirty fighter pilots were added to bring the squadron up to full strength. A dozen men from Composite Squadron 30 (VC-30) were transferred to VF-36, including VC-30's executive officer (XO), Lt. Edward "Murf" Murphy.[30] He was the oldest and most senior of the new arrivals. Lieutenant Murphy had served in the pre–Pearl Harbor days as part of USS *Ranger*'s Scouting Squadron 42, an outfit that earned a commendation for over six thousand hours of flight operations, including more than four thousand carrier landings, with no major accidents.[31] As VC-30's XO, Murphy was essentially the squadron's disciplinarian. He was responsible for enforcing the rules and maintaining order. To remain impartial, he had to keep his distance from the men under him.

The rank-and-file pilots in VC-30 came over to their new squadron with strong friendships already established. Some of these were based on similar dispositions or unique physical characteristics. John "Snuffy" Mayer and Thomas "Squawkie" Rennemo were two of the squadron's most animated characters, exemplifying the "fighter jock" stereotype. Mayer had a round face, button nose, and eyebrows that always appeared slightly arched, giving him a boyish, mischievous look. Rennemo was four years Mayer's senior, with lighter features and a more angular face. You could tell they were ready to get into trouble if they turned up the brims of their ballcaps or cocked back their dress covers.

Edgar "Snipo" Blankenship was a long-faced Arkansan whose deep-set eyes, big ears, and perpetually sleepy smile made him VC-30's comic relief. Noel "Big Tom" Thompson was accurately named for his six-foot, three-inch frame, though gangly Frank "Spider" Foltz had him edged out by at least an inch. Spider had to go through pains to convince the Navy he was suited to shipboard life given his towering height, but he would not take no for an answer.[32]

Friendships also formed because of similar backgrounds and shared interests, whether the men came over from VC-30 or had been with the squadron since the VGS-18 days. Frederick Tracy, Robert "Frog" Hurst, and Robert "Dave" Davis were all talented musicians who brought their instruments with them as they traveled from base to base. Tracy specialized in brass and woodwinds. The 1942 yearbook for his alma mater, Boston College, recalled the sound of his "hot and then sometimes sweet" clarinet. Hurst likewise played multiple instruments, but he was inclined toward guitar. Davis rounded out the bunch with his violin. All three later took part in jam sessions in the torpedo squadron ready room aboard *Intrepid*.

Harold "Pop" Thune wasn't crazy about jazz or big band music. The lanky, clean-cut South Dakotan preferred country. His tastes were hard to accommodate in cosmopolitan San Diego, and he sorely missed the sounds of home while training on the West Coast. Fortunately for Thune, the squadron's commanding officer, Lt. Cdr. Everett Link, sent flight surgeon John "Doc" Fish to San Francisco to bring back some records. Music played an outsized role in maintaining squadron morale. As it turned out, Doc Fish hailed from Kentucky. He brought back some country records as part of his haul. Thune recalled almost seventy-five years later, "While you were out there ... thinking of home ... you wouldn't realize how [meaningful] that was."[33]

Some of the men also got married while they had the chance. Lt. (jg) Robert "Flaps" O'Maley was attended by his close friend in the squadron, Lt. (jg) S. Wells "Mac" McGurk. After breakfast at the Biltmore Hotel in Los Angeles, O'Maley and his bride, Genevieve, were wed at the historic Cathedral of St. Vibiana on 26 September 1943. They left the very same day for their temporary accommodations at the Hotel del Coronado, close to Naval Air Station San Diego.[34]

Training intensified after the new fighter pilots arrived. Bryant Walworth recorded in his wartime diary, "We, of course, had the usual number of ground loops while we were flying from-to. . . . We were lucky not to lose any pilots but we did have accidents. Buck Newsome bailed out of No. 10, my plane, about 12 miles out to sea for the first one. Buck O.K.; plane lost. A couple weeks later Ziemer and Bales had a mid-air collision at about 700 feet. Luckily both pilots got out. How I'm not sure but they did. Both planes were lost."[35]

This proved to be the norm. According to the October 1943 war diary from the Western Sea Frontier, "Plane crashes again highlighted the Frontier's activities, involving five incidents which contributed to a costly day in both personnel and planes."[36] These accidents involved not only Navy but also Marine and Army personnel. By the end of the war, aviation fatality statistics bore out the dangers of training: more than 25 percent of fatalities were attributable to training and ferrying aircraft, whereas only about 24 percent of fatalities were due to air combat with enemy forces.[37]

Carrier qualification, or "carrier quals" for short, was the final stepping stone to deployment. On 18 November 1943, sixteen F6F-3 Hellcats were loaded onto USS *Copahee* (CVE 12) in advance of the squadron's last big test. Remarkably, that same day, eleven SBD Dauntless dive bombers from Bombing Squadron 18 (VB-18) were also loaded aboard *Copahee*. Though neither squadron knew it at the time, the two were going to be brought together as part of the same air group the following year.[38]

USS *Copahee* was laid down in June 1941 as a cargo ship, but the war situation necessitated that it be converted into an aircraft carrier in 1942.[39] *Copahee* was a CVE, or escort carrier, like the squadron had originally been training to board. Such ships were well suited for ferrying aircraft and personnel or for providing air support during landing operations, as *Suwannee* had done during Operation Torch. For training purposes, however, an escort carrier's short flight deck provided a razor-thin margin of error.

Pilots needed to show they could consistently land aboard *Copahee*, which required catching the arresting cables strung across the after portion of the ship's deck. Daily operational remarks from *Copahee*'s war diary show just how dicey carrier quals could be. On 21 November alone, the log notes, "Conducted flight operations with VF-36 squadron. Made a total of 56 take-offs and 51 landings. . . . Unloaded 7 F6F-3 damaged aircraft of VF-36 squad-ron."[40] In Bryant Walworth's estimation, "Our qualifications weren't so hot."[41]

Lt. Robert "Brownie" Brownell was scheduled to take his carrier quals on the squadron's last day aboard *Copahee*. He was eager to clear this final hurdle on his way to the Pacific. Lieutenant Brownell had been waiting for what seemed like ages to secure his spot in a fighting unit. On Christmas Eve 1942, he wrote a letter to a detail officer in the Bureau of Aeronautics, some-one whose role involved filling vacancies and distributing personnel, virtually begging the Navy to transfer him to the front: "For over eighteen months I have had shore duty . . . flight instructor duty. Because of this my moral [sic] is very low. With the beginning of the war I have made every effort to get orders to the fleet. I am writing you in the hope that you can help me get these orders. Orders to a carrier based fighter squadron. Fighters anywhere. No one has ever wanted to get in this war more than myself."[42]

Now it was finally his turn to test his mettle. Landing procedure called for pilots to do a flyby around the ship before turning for their downwind leg. Brownell started his approach on *Copahee*'s starboard side, passing by the escort carrier's short, thin superstructure as he continued beyond the bow. After making his turn in front of the ship, he began flying downwind on its port side, crossing back toward the aft end of the carrier as it steamed through the water. All the while, Lieutenant Brownell adjusted his Hellcat's flaps, changed the pitch of its propeller, rolled in trim to keep its nose level, moved the landing gear control lever down to extend the wheels, and flipped the switch to drop the tailhook. Failure to properly execute any one of these motions before landing could result in catastrophe. He also took care to roll back his canopy and lock it open. He needed to be able to get out in a hurry in case of emergency.

On his turn to enter the final approach behind the carrier, Brownell descended to about 150 feet over the water. He now had to split his atten-tion between the landing signal officer (LSO) on *Copahee*'s deck edge and the instruments in his cockpit displaying his airspeed and altitude. The LSO held paddles that he waved to indicate Brownell's position relative to the ship. They looked like tennis rackets strung horizontally with broad, colorful ribbon. If the LSO stabbed his paddles downward toward the deck, the pilot was too low and needed to pull up. If he held his paddles with his arms sticking up to the sky, the approach was too high. Brownell adjusted his control stick, watching for the LSO's arms to drop straight out from his body, parallel to the deck. That meant he was flying level.

If all went according to plan, the next signal from the LSO would be a "cut," a slashing motion across his chest that meant Brownell could cut his engine and land. The other signal he might receive—one Brownell dreaded—was a wave-off. If the LSO started waving his paddles over his head, crossing them in an "X" motion, it meant the deck was fouled or the approach was poor. Brownell would have to circle back for another attempt, limiting his chances of qualifying and exposing him to rebuke from his commanding officer. A wave-off was a very public failing grade.

Brownell struggled to keep his plane centered as he let down toward *Copahee*. The LSO moved his paddles this way and that, doing his best to straighten Brownell out as his Hellcat rocked side to side. His approach was high and fast, but acceptable. The LSO cut a paddle across his chest. Brownell cut the throttle in response. He held his breath as the deck rose up to meet him. At the last second, his Hellcat yawed to port. It slammed down hard, catching the number four wire at an angle before skidding off the side of the ship.[43]

Brownell and his Hellcat tumbled into the water with a jolt. Fortunately, the plane landed belly-down. Brownell was miraculously uninjured. He treaded freezing-cold water for eight minutes until destroyer USS *Crane*, on plane guard duty, sent a boat over to rescue him.[44] Despite his close shave, Brownell remained undeterred. He knew exactly what he had signed up for and wasn't about to let a little hiccup derail his hard work. He got into the cockpit of another Hellcat, finished making his required landings, and advanced along with the rest of the squadron.

Fighting 36 was finally ready to head to Hawaii two days later. The men boarded light carrier USS *Cabot* (CVL 28) for the uneventful trip from San Diego. *Cabot* seemed luxe compared to *Copahee*. The light carrier was more than one hundred feet longer, had space for nearly twice as many men, and could make the trek from the West Coast to Hawaii in a fraction of the time. Fighting 36 arrived without incident on 30 November, disembarking on Ford Island before flying to Hilo.[45] They were just in time to gain experience with an even bigger carrier: USS *Yorktown* (CV 10). The squadron was going to get a second dose of carrier qualifications.

Yorktown embarked planes from Air Group 10, VF-36, and VB-1 and VT-1 for qualification flights on 16 December. Fighting 36 performed much better during this round than they had aboard *Copahee*. In fact, not a single fighter crashed throughout the course of the day's 198 total landings. They were no doubt greatly assisted by the expansive flight deck of the new carrier, which was nearly three hundred feet longer than *Copahee*'s.[46]

The last major change for the squadron before the new year was an important personnel shift. The skipper, Lt. Cdr. Everett Link, was transferred out of VF-36 to command Air Group 24 aboard USS *Belleau Wood*. Link had run the squadron since the VC-18 days. Rather than bringing in an outsider this late in the game, the decision was made to promote executive officer Lt. (now Lt. Cdr.) Edward Murphy from within. Murphy had big shoes to fill. Though he had spent some time with the fleet, his predecessor was a Naval Academy graduate with years of command experience and a particular style the men were used to. Now, seemingly at the end of their training syllabus, they were being thrown a curveball.

In Murphy's place, Lt. Clarence "Blue" Blouin was promoted to XO. Lieutenant Blouin had dark, wavy hair and dark features. He hailed from Whitinsville, Massachusetts, a town built around one of America's oldest textile factories. His parents were French-speaking immigrants from Quebec who had worked at the factory for decades. Like Bill Ziemer, Clarence Blouin came from a family closely tied to the sea services. Of his three brothers, two were Navy officers and another was an officer in the Coast Guard. Leadership seemed to run in the family.

Blouin was a "Mustang," an enlisted man who had worked his way into the officer corps. He started flight training in the late 1930s and conducted patrols in the northeastern corridor between Quonset Point, Rhode Island,

and Newfoundland in the period immediately before the attack on Pearl Harbor. He had all the requisite skills and experience needed to succeed in his new role as XO of VF-36.

The waning days of 1943 provided an opportunity for the squadron to get situated in Hawaii and to acclimate to new leadership. Sports helped reinforce teamwork and friendly competition. Softball and basketball were perennial favorites. Cecil Harris picked up the nickname "Speedball" for his pitching prowess, while fellow South Dakotan Pop Thune played catcher. "I don't recall that we ever lost to the enlisted men," Thune told interviewers in 2017.[47]

Given how many exceptionally tall pilots VF-36 boasted, basketball was, unsurprisingly, the most popular sport. The most talented big men were Spider Foltz, a member of the 1940 Florida Amateur Athletic Union champion basketball team, and Big Tom Thompson, who played center for Adams State Teachers College in Colorado. VF-36 also had one of the best guards in college basketball to anchor their team. Pop Thune played for the University of Minnesota before enlisting in the Navy. He ended his tenure there as co-captain, leading the school to a winning record in the Big 10 conference.[48]

Ed Ritter preferred to pass the time documenting his experience through art. Black-and-white photographs of his squadron mates didn't capture the green island foliage or the colors of aviators' flight gear: the canary yellow of their "Mae West" life vests, their khaki-colored flight suits, and the thick canvas straps connecting to their parachute packs. So Ed used his skills as a photo retoucher and his palette of paints to hand-color pictures between training assignments. He knew their easy life in Hawaii would not last forever. When the squadron went into combat, these images of simpler times would serve as emotional support. As it turned out, combat was closer than any of them expected. Fighting 36 did not even finish its training syllabus before the men were sent out to learn the ropes.

CHAPTER 3

LEARNING THE ROPES

THE YEAR 1944 DAWNED with the Allies firmly on the offensive in the Pacific. Carrier assaults on an unprecedented scale were about to penetrate deep into Japanese territory in the central Pacific, from the Marshalls to the Carolines and all the way to the Mariana Islands. To assist in this effort, pilots in VF-36 were assigned temporary additional duty with various fleet units. Some ferried aircraft, others were loaned to carrier fighting squadrons, and still others had land-based duty on tiny islands in the Solomons.

The most prominent target in the next phase of operations was Truk (today known as Chuuk). The enemy base was shrouded in mystery. Command staff and pilots alike thought of it as Japan's Pearl Harbor, a sort of "Gibraltar of the Pacific." When he learned his carrier was heading for Truk, Lt. Cdr. Philip Torrey, commander of Air Group 9, recalled, "My first instinct was to jump overboard."[1] He must have been envisioning scores of anti-aircraft batteries, legions of fighters, and battleships bristling with massive guns. If the battle-hardened leader of an entire air group felt that way, imagine what the novice fighters of VF-36 were thinking.

The Navy allocated 9 carriers embarking more than 560 planes to the attack on Truk, which was codenamed Operation Hailstone due to the enormous amount of ordnance earmarked for the base. Unlike strikes on the Marshall Islands just weeks earlier, the goal of the attack on Truk was not to seize a new fleet anchorage: it was simply to pound the base so hard that it would be rendered useless for an extended period of time.[2]

In stark contrast to the mystique that had cropped up around it, however, Truk was never developed to its full potential. Even after the Japanese began rapidly expanding its facilities and defenses in late 1943, Truk's major islands sported only a handful of modest airfields, forty fixed anti-aircraft batteries, no major power stations, and no underground fuel storage facilities. Japanese surface ships in the anchorage would have posed a threat, but they had all been moved out of Truk to the Palau Islands where they were safe from the Allies' rapid advance. What remained behind were largely cargo and supply vessels. In other words, an ill-prepared Truk was left to fend for itself in the face of the largest carrier onslaught to date.[3]

However, the attack on Truk was no cakewalk, or "milk run" in aviator parlance. Some pilots encountered significant anti-aircraft fire and dueled with Japanese fighters. Even if the air had been clear and the gun emplacements silent, combat flight duty and carrier operations were inherently dangerous. Some of the men were not coming home.

TEMPORARY DUTY

Lts. Clarence Blouin, Squawkie Rennemo, Harvey Picken, and Lt. (jg) Mac McGurk were all temporarily attached to Fighting Squadron 9 (VF-9) aboard *Essex*.[4] Because this was VF-9's second combat cruise, its veteran aviators— including Hamilton McWhorter, the Navy's first Hellcat ace, and Eugene Valencia, soon to be one of the Navy's top scorers—ran the show. Fighting 9 pilots got first dibs on the best assignments, while the spares from VF-36 were slotted in as needed.

The first day of Operation Hailstone, 17 February 1944, started with fireworks for VF-9. Pilots on the morning fighter sweep claimed twenty-one enemy planes blasted out of the sky at the cost of just one missing Hellcat. On the second strike of the day, strike 2B, another dozen or more Japanese fighters fell. This time, all the *Essex* pilots made it home.[5]

On the third strike, Lieutenant Blouin commanded a four-plane division. The *Essex* Hellcats escorted bombers from their ship and from nearby *Intrepid*. Their mission was to scour the anchorage for targets of opportunity. As luck had it, they flew right over a destroyer that had made it out of North

Pass, one of the few points of ingress or egress from the atoll. With no friendly aircraft to provide cover, the destroyer faced dive bombing and machine gun strafing attacks by dozens of planes. Ammunition clanged off the hull and tore through decking; oil poured out into the water; a small explosion blossomed amidships. Despite the damage Blouin and company heaped on it, when all was said and done, that plucky little ship was still trudging along—albeit back toward Truk, where it likely met its end.[6]

Two hours later, Mac McGurk and Harvey Picken flew with strike 2D, the fourth strike of the day. By then, more ships had spilled out of North Pass in the mad dash away from Truk. Four in particular—two destroyers, a cruiser, and an oiler—were about fifteen miles beyond the coral fringes of the atoll when McGurk, Picken, and the rest of the fighters began circling overhead. They stayed over the ships for two hours, first raking them with their guns, then observing as the *Essex* and *Intrepid* bombers scored multiple bomb hits on their quarry.[7]

On 22 February McGurk and Picken were joined by Rennemo and Blouin as part of a photographic mission over Saipan. The Navy needed to gather as much intelligence as possible on the Marianas, the next stepping-stone in the island-hopping campaign. This important recon mission was perhaps the last one these four men flew together. The next day, something went wrong while McGurk was returning from routine CAP duty. On final approach to the carrier, his plane lurched awkwardly, crashing into the sea just behind the ship. McGurk was either killed on impact or died after his plane sank beneath the waves. This tragic loss occurred only five days before Air Group 9 was relieved and sent back to Hawaii.[8] Flaps O'Maley was no doubt devastated to hear the news about his groomsman.

It wasn't all fleet carriers for the men of Fighting 36. There were also light and escort carriers. Pilots on these ships did not typically receive the same level of notoriety as their counterparts on the big flattops. Their squadrons contained fewer men and fewer planes and were more frequently assigned less glamorous duties like CAP and ground attack. They had fewer opportunities to rack up big scores than the men of Fighting 9. Nevertheless, they played an important role in the Pacific and exhibited no less valor than their peers.

Ens. Ed Ritter and Lt. Frog Hurst were assigned to Fighting 30 aboard light carrier USS *Monterey*. Ritter flew as part of the initial fighter sweep over Tinian on 22 February. He took off at 0600 into overcast skies as part of a group of twenty-three Hellcats from multiple ships. The clouds cast a thick and unbroken blanket starting at eight thousand feet, meaning that the strike had to rely on dead reckoning and instruments to determine when they should descend over the target.[9]

Ritter's division was one of two leading the charge through the clouds. Speeding toward the ground at more than three hundred knots, his altimeter steadily unwound without any change in the cover until finally, at the last moment, the airfield below materialized. Ritter pulled out of his dive at perilously low altitude. His leader was gone. The other division was nowhere to be seen. That left Ritter and fellow flier Ens. Walter King to fend for themselves.

The two were out of position to hit aircraft parked along the runway, but as they roared overhead, they took full advantage of the lack of airborne opposition. They charged their guns, strafing a control tower and buildings lining the field. Smoke and flames erupted where they found their mark. At the end of his run, King heard a transmission over the radio. The leader of the second division was broadcasting his position and orders to join up. Though Ritter and King were able to rendezvous with another pilot responding to the radio call, the division they were supposed to meet was nowhere to be seen. The prospect of getting everyone back together for a coordinated attack was becoming increasingly dim.

Ritter circled around the southern tip of the island where there was a patch of clear sky. He soon saw the lumbering forms of Avenger torpedo bombers heading up the west coast, looking for a hole in the clouds to start their bombing runs. The Avengers were unescorted, so Ritter and the other two Hellcats headed out to provide them with protection. It may not have been part of the original plan, but at least this was doing something productive.

Ensign King spotted two Japanese fighters below him steadily gaining altitude. They seemed intent on intercepting the Avengers. He and the newly arrived Hellcat broke away from Ritter to engage the threat. The Japanese pilots never had a chance. Approaching from above and behind, King and his new wingman quickly shot down the two interlopers.

Ritter, now completely alone, spotted a solitary enemy fighter off to his right trying to sneak away at low altitude. He didn't want to go on a wild goose chase. Instead, he broke right and sent a quick burst of bullets hurtling in the direction of the plane, which he identified as either an A6M Zeke or a Nakajima Ki-43 Oscar, an Imperial Japanese Army fighter that bore close resemblance to the A6M. As he snapped back to the left to reconvene with King, Ritter saw the enemy plane begin to lose altitude. It did not smoke or show any other signs of damage, but it continued steadily downward until it slammed into the water.[10] That moment made Ed Ritter the only member of Fighting 36 to score in air-to-air combat during this temporary duty period.

While Truk and Saipan were assaulted by fleet and light carriers, a more modest assemblage of ships was quietly carrying out anti-submarine and CAP duty to the east. Maloelap Atoll had been considered one of the most important enemy air bases in the Marshall Islands a few months earlier. The airfield on Taroa in particular represented a threat to the invasions of the Gilbert Islands in November 1943 and the Marshall Islands in early 1944. As a result, Taroa was subjected to a combined Army–Navy–Marine Corps bombing campaign that left the little island in shambles by February. While there did not seem to be any operational aircraft left on Taroa, attempts by Japanese forces on the ground to repair its runways and facilities required the Navy to continue hitting the beleaguered island throughout the month.

Ens. Noel Thompson and Lt. Anthony "Tony" Denman were both assigned to CAP flights and strikes on Taroa as part of VC-66 aboard the escort carrier USS *Nassau*. They arrived on 12 February with replacement aircraft and orders to stick with the squadron until its return to Pearl Harbor. It may have been a letdown to receive this assignment while other members of the squadron got placed aboard fleet carriers like *Essex*. Even worse, VC-66 was flying FM-1 Wildcat fighters, a step backward from the F6F Hellcats Thompson and Denman had already become accustomed to. They couldn't have been too upset, though. They were finally getting a chance to put their training to the test.[11]

There was a feeling of awe aboard *Nassau* as the little carrier made its way into the new fleet anchorage at Majuro Atoll. Ships of all shapes and sizes filled the radiant blue lagoon with a "tremendous collection of floating power" as far as the eye could see.[12] That was no easy feat, given the size of the lagoon. Thompson and Denman must have been stunned by the scale of the operation. What they were witnessing was the establishment of a new base of operations for the Navy's push across the central Pacific. The combination of massed carrier airpower, full logistical support, and proximity to enemy bases gave Task Force 58, the fast carrier task force under Adm. Raymond Spruance, an unprecedented degree of mobility and striking power.

Thompson and Denman spent most of their time on CAP and snooper anti-submarine patrol. They were itinerant aviators, and even if they had been full-fledged members of VC-66, opportunities for strike duty aboard an escort carrier were far more limited than at the tip of the spear with the fast carriers. They did, however, have at least one opportunity to try their luck as fighter-bombers.

On 16 February the two men participated in a strike against Taroa airfield. Their Wildcats were loaded with two bombs: a one-hundred-pound general-purpose bomb and a one-hundred-pound incendiary. Though the island was already a wreck from two years of attacks, anti-aircraft fire—from the chatter of machine guns to the booming thump of heavy artillery pieces—remained intense. Pilots were stalwart in the face of heavy fire. One plane had a round tear through its starboard wing, severing the wires that charged its guns and armed its bombs. The pilot had to return to base with his payload. Even with this one Wildcat out of the fight, the remaining seven pilots each logged hits with their general-purpose bombs: two on a barracks, four on assorted buildings, and one on an "elbow pier" that looked like a bent arm extending from the shoreline.[13] The bombing campaign against Taroa continued long after Thompson, Denman, and *Nassau* moved on. By the time Japan surrendered the following year, more than 4,378 tons of ordnance had been dropped on the island, an average of 5.5 pounds of explosives per square meter.[14]

In early March 1944 Thompson and Denman were transferred back to Hawaii to finish training with VF-36. They were "indoctrinated in the business of war"[15] after facing down gunfire, dropping bombs, and making harrowing carrier landings on the tiny deck of an escort carrier. The next day, Blouin, Rennemo, and Picken arrived from *Essex*; Ritter and Hurst returned from *Monterey*; and the rest of the men—Robert Morris from *Yorktown*, Flaps O'Maley from *Enterprise,* and others from all manner of carriers—filtered back to Hawaii. They had a bit more experience under their belts and a renewed sense of purpose. They were ready to get out there in a squadron of their own, where they'd have opportunities they were denied as replacement pilots.

Lieutenant Blouin had one last responsibility to take care of before he could get back to work with Fighting 36. He had been the only squadron member present when Mac McGurk was killed. McGurk's father had a whole host of questions about the incident and was desperate for information. Blouin reached out directly to the family with two letters detailing the tragic event:

> As he came into the final approach . . . the landing signal officer reports that he was too low and he signalled [*sic*] for Mac to go around again. . . . Mac was either slow at answering this signal or . . . his propeller was probably in high pitch. . . . At the very last possible moment to avoid hitting the ship, there was a loud roar from his engine and the plane was seen to stand almost straight up when she rolled over on her back and went into the water. . . . [A] destroyer searched the spot thoroughly but found no sign of Mac.[16]

Blouin enclosed a squadron photo of VF-36 taken in late 1943 and some words of comfort: "Your loss is shared by every one of us in the squadron, for we all thought very much of Mac."

The letter meant the world to John McGurk. He wrote back,

> Thank you from the bottom of my heart and for Mrs. McGurk, too. . . . The lad was a great pal to me and I've an idea we were much closer

than the average Father and son because we shared our fun, our miseries and I even tried to share his Navy experiences with him but the Service wouldn't have me and my greatest regret is that I couldn't be with him at the end. . . . We shall always remember however, and with thankfullness [sic], that he DID get into action against the enemy and was able to score even in a minor capacity.[17]

Blouin's first letter, penned on 5 March 1944, was one of the last acts made by squadron personnel before VF-36 was redesignated yet again. The squadron would henceforth be known as Fighting 18 (VF-18). Instead of deploying to an island in the Pacific for land-based duty, it was being folded into Carrier Air Group 18 (CVG-18), which lacked a fighting squadron due to a confusing series of events. There had been a prior VF-18 that served as part of Air Group 17 aboard USS *Bunker Hill*. This was due to VF-17 testing out the new F4U Corsair fighter, which needed further modifications before it was deemed suitable for carrier operations. VF-17 was detached from its air group for land-based duty and replaced by the first VF-18, leaving CVG-18 without a fighting squadron when it reformed.

Ensign Walter Passi was no doubt elated to learn about the change of plans when he returned to the squadron at the end of March. Pilots attached to the big carriers had mostly glowing reviews of life at sea. Passi's experience with the land-based VF-40 could not have been more different. Five days after reporting to the unit, on 8 March, Passi and his fellow flyers were forced to move from their base on Bougainville Island to neighboring Treasury Island due to shelling by enemy forces. In fact, the squadron had moved from New Georgia to Bougainville, Bougainville to Treasury Island, and Treasury Island to Green Island in the brief period that Passi was attached. He was tired of mosquitos, stifling heat, shelling, and always sleeping in different bunks.[18]

The men of newly designated Fighting 18 were in the right place, at the right time, to avoid the difficulties of life ashore. They were being assigned to one of the Navy's newest, biggest, and most advanced aircraft carriers to play a central role in the drive across the Pacific. That future was still months away, however. Fighting 18 needed to train with its new air group while they waited for the arrival of their assigned ship: USS *Intrepid*.

USS *INTREPID*

USS *Intrepid* (CV 11) was put into commission half a year earlier, on 16 August 1943. In the ship's designation, "11" indicated its hull number, marking it out as the eleventh carrier ordered by the Navy.[19] *Intrepid* was an early member of the *Essex* class, which boasted more ships than any class of fleet carriers ever built by any country. These ships were emblematic of the huge strides that had been taken since USS *Langley*, the Navy's first carrier, entered service in 1922. Early carrier designers had to account for naval treaties constraining size and armament in the interwar period. They also had to learn as they built, leading to changes in design philosophies that are evident in the marked differences between ships like USS *Ranger*, the Navy's first purpose-built carrier, and the *Yorktown* class that did much of the fighting in the early phases of World War II.[20]

The first *Essex*-class carriers, including *Intrepid*, were ordered in the summer of 1940. Their flight decks were longer and wider than the *Yorktown*-class ships. They were also heavier than their forebears but sported more powerful propulsion systems capable of making them just as fast. And perhaps most importantly, their survivability was greatly enhanced by increased armor, more effective damage control equipment, and more anti-aircraft guns.[21]

It took time for orders, appropriations, and resources to come together in actual construction. *Intrepid*'s keel was not laid until 1 December 1941, just six days before the attack on Pearl Harbor. After that event, it was apparent that ships like *Intrepid* were needed urgently. But building an 870-foot-long ship that displaced 36,380 tons fully loaded wasn't an overnight affair. Only through significant advancements in production techniques, and an all-hands effort at Newport News Shipbuilding in Virginia, was it possible to finish *Intrepid* from the ground up in an incredible seventeen months. The underlying design of the ship showed how much the Navy had learned in less than two decades of carrier operations, and its construction demonstrated how quickly the nation's industrial base could respond to the military's needs.[22]

After *Intrepid*'s commissioning, the ship conducted a shakedown cruise in October 1943 to acquaint its new crew with air operations, general quarters drills, anti-aircraft artillery operation, and all the other integral components of operating a state-of-the-art aircraft carrier. Many crew members either hadn't been to sea at all or had never worked on a carrier. Once the ship's captain, Thomas Sprague, was satisfied that everybody was up to speed and working efficiently, *Intrepid* could finally head through the Panama Canal to bring the fight to the enemy.

The trip proved to be a rocky one, figuratively and literally. When *Intrepid* passed through the Gaillard Cut—a narrow, serpentine section of the canal bisecting the Continental Divide—a shear in the water drove the slow-moving carrier toward the looming cliffs. The starboard side of *Intrepid*'s bow scraped across the channel wall before its course could be corrected. Though the collision only caused minor damage, it was an inauspicious start to the ship's service. *Intrepid* reached Pearl Harbor on 10 January 1944, in time to pick up Air Group 6 for strikes on the Marshall and Caroline islands.

Intrepid's Air Group 6 achieved a great deal of success between 29 January and 17 February. Lt. Alexander Vraciu became the ship's first ace on its first day of combat operations after shooting down three enemy bombers in a single flight (having downed two enemies during his previous deployment). During the subsequent assault on Truk, *Intrepid* contributed 846 sorties, destroying planes in the air, seriously damaging installations on the ground, and sinking numerous cargo ships on the water. Then, just after midnight on 17 February, an aerial torpedo launched by a nighttime snooper struck the after starboard quarter of the ship. The explosion and ensuing flooding killed eleven men and injured another seventeen. It also seriously damaged the ship's rudder, making *Intrepid* extremely difficult to steer.[23]

Intrepid needed major repairs. In fact, the ship couldn't even stand out of Pearl Harbor without the addition of a jury rudder to help keep it on course during the long trip to Hunters Point, California. The jury rudder was installed on 5 March, the same day Fighting 18 received word they were becoming part of Air Group 18.[24] Now they just had to wait until May, when repairs were supposed to be finished and *Intrepid* was scheduled to head out on its second combat deployment.[25]

AIR GROUP TRAINING

Becoming part of a larger air group meant undergoing new phases of training to account for new responsibilities; it meant meeting a whole new cast of characters in VB-18 and VT-18; and it also meant that skipper Murphy, still easing into his role as commanding officer of Fighting Squadron 18, was now subordinate to the CAG. Murphy's new boss was Cdr. William Ellis, a tall, patrician-looking North Carolinian with a no-nonsense attitude that had served him well in his previous commands. He expected those under him to perform their duties intelligently and efficiently.

Commander Ellis was a Naval Academy graduate with an extensive pedigree. He earned his commission almost ten years before the United States was dragged into war, having served with scouting and fighting squadrons aboard some of the Navy's most famous carriers, including USS *Enterprise*. During Operation Torch, he commanded VGF-26 aboard USS *Sangamon*, sister ship of *Suwannee*, where Cecil Harris was busy logging his first strikes. Now Ellis was being given his own air group to look after.[26]

The CAG's principal responsibility was ensuring the effective operation of his air group as a singular unit. Starting in March 1944, Commander Ellis led all three squadrons in massed attacks on practice targets around the air group's home at Hilo to prepare pilots and aircrews for their coming deployment. Nobody was used to coordinating this many aircraft all flying together, nor had they yet established who was really in charge on these exercises. As a result, the first attempts at teamwork by Air Group 18 felt like the blind leading the blind. These touch-and-go affairs earned Commander Ellis a playful nickname from his men: "El Gropo." A combination of his name, Ellis, and function (Gropo, like group commander), the moniker was also a way to poke fun at the CAG's navigational skills—or perceived lack thereof.[27]

The men trained hard during these first few months to get up to speed as quickly as possible. It wasn't just their survival that counted on it. The Second Marine Division was training at nearby Camp Tarawa for the upcoming invasion of the Marianas. Flying close air support for ground forces required communication with target coordinators, rapid interpretation of gridded maps of the landing beaches, and careful attention to the position of friendly forces.

The aviators had a great deal of respect and admiration for the boots on the ground. The Marines sweated it out with limited accommodations and had to experience the bloody truth of war face to face. Pilots and air crews were usually removed from all of that. They knew how good they had it, relatively speaking.

Edgar Blankenship and some of the other men in Fighting 18 swapped stories, jokes, and drinks with the Marines between joint training exercises. Blankenship reckoned he cut a sharp figure in his leather flight jacket and a Marine's campaign cover—the circular-brimmed, four-dented hat usually seen on drill instructors in movies. He snapped photos of the Guthrie brothers, two men he seems to have been especially close to, and got a group photo of the men in their barracks reminiscing about old times.[28] This particular group of Marines, the 3rd Battalion, 6th Regiment, 2nd Division, was slated to land on Saipan in mid-June.[29] They would likely hit the beaches before *Intrepid* was ready for combat. But that didn't matter: what did matter was making sure Fighting 18 and its sister squadrons were ready to support troops on the ground—no matter who they were—when their deployment coincided with the next phase of the island-hopping campaign.

In addition to group navigation and close air support, Fighting 18 practiced attacking VB-18 aircraft off the coast of Hilo. These simulated war games came as close to the real thing as possible. Pilots pushed their Hellcats to the limit in steep dives, quick turns, and close, high-speed passes by VB-18's Helldivers. On 5 April, a month to the day since Fighting 18 had joined its new air group, tragedy struck. Lt. (jg) John Forsyth of VB-18 was flying as part of a twelve-plane formation with his wingman, Ens. Chester "Chet" Rolka. They were part of a three-plane "V" in a line of four Vs trailing off to the right.

Fighting 18's Hellcats came zooming down from above to practice combat maneuvers. Six fighters bore in from the right, while six others simultaneously attacked from the left. They pressed the attack so close that it made Forsyth and his fellow bombers "as nervous as cats. . . . I wanted to get on the radio and back them off from the chicken game."[30] The bombers did their best to hold steady in the face of this onslaught.

Forsyth winced as he watched one of the Hellcats barrel toward him. The pilot was Ens. Jackson Vliet, one of the younger, newer additions to Fighting 18. It was immediately clear to Forsyth that Vliet was on a collision course with his wingman. Rolka tried to slide over to make room for the eager young fighter. As Ensign Vliet realized what was about to happen, he jammed his stick forward to dive out of danger, but it was already too late. His plane's wing hit Rolka's at the root. Both wings sheared off from the violence of the impact. Forsyth could only watch as the two planes spun into the water below, leaving behind an oil slick and flames, but no sign of life from either Vliet or Rolka. Two more members of the air group were dead before they had even deployed. Practice was called off for the rest of the day.

The plan of the day for 10 April 1944 is indicative of an average day of training for Fighting 18. As usual, the schedule had been drawn up by Lt. Cecil Harris under the supervision of skipper Murphy. Four-man divisions were assigned names corresponding to different colors—red, green, black, blue—making them easy to identify on the plan of the day. The red and black divisions had the day off. Paul Amerman, serving as the duty officer, also dodged flight assignment. The rest of the squadron reported to the ready room at 0800 to listen as Harris and Murphy went over the schedule.

Executive Officer Blouin and Lieutenant Brownell's divisions started with gunnery, conducting live-fire exercises with their inboard guns. Ens. Arthur "Moe" Mollenhauer pulled the tow sleeve. Having to slowly run a banner in your wake while your buddies zoomed by you, firing just behind your tail, was nobody's idea of a good time. While those two divisions honed their accuracy, another two, led by Harris and Lt. Harvey Picken, practiced dive-bombing runs on rock targets. Getting a handle on dive angle and release altitude was important, even if the exercises lacked moving targets or anti-aircraft fire like they would face in combat. Finally, three sections of pilots comprising six Hellcats mounted a mock attack on VB-18.

All of this took place in just an hour and a half, after which the pilots reviewed their work, enjoyed a short breather, and then rotated assignments. Some of the morning gunnery pilots swapped to attack, while the morning attack divisions had their Hellcats loaded with ammunition for gunnery. The day was rounded out by recognition training in the afternoon and night flying starting at 1845.

Night flying was easily the most dangerous element of training. There was a reason that separate night fighting squadrons, designated VF(N), were specially trained and deployed by the Navy. In fact, plans for Fighting 18's tour of duty aboard *Intrepid* called for a separate detachment of night fighters to serve in the period between sundown and sunup. But contingencies needed to be in place regardless. All pilots participated in night training to keep their instrument flying skills honed for foul weather operations or in case evening strikes ran late.

The plan for night training on 10 April started with section tactics. Wingmen needed to practice communication with their section leaders and join-up in situations where their only visual references were tiny lights on the wingtips and fuselage of nearby planes. Altimeters, artificial horizons, airspeed indicators, and gyrocompasses took over in lieu of the pilots' usual senses. They relied on these instruments to guide them through the uniform darkness to their leaders. Afterward, the two separate sections making up a full four-plane division practiced grouping up. Adding more aircraft to the mix increased the danger. In the dark, it was especially difficult for pilots to maintain adequate distance between one another without the group coming undone. In training, they were close to land if a pilot became lost. Deployment would be a different story. Thousands of square miles of empty ocean would not forgive such mistakes.

CHAPTER 4

DEPLOYMENT DELAYED

BETWEEN TRAINING ASSIGNMENTS on the Big Island, the men had plenty of opportunities to explore Hawaii. The Hilo Yacht Club pool was a favorite hangout for lazy days close to the air station. Going farther afield, there were opportunities for fun on the beach and private estates opened to officers. A photo taken after a spearfishing expedition featuring Robert "Growler" Gowling, Paul Amerman, Punchy Mallory, Donald Watts, and Frog Hurst shows the men with goggles on their heads, spears in one hand, and make-believe fish in the other.[1] The sport must have been harder than they anticipated. On a private ranch, squadron XO Clarence Blouin, Chesty Herlihy, and Buck Newsome rode horseback with lassos to practice roping cattle and went on hunting trips with Snipo Blankenship and the rancher's dogs.[2] There were also larger journeys by the whole air group to heavily forested streams, where cool waters and shady banks provided an escape from the heat.

Outings like this helped reinforce friendships and served as a release valve after long days of dangerous training exercises. Some of the trips were downright spiritual. The Star of the Sea Painted Church was a fitting place for the men to contemplate their future. Colorful frescoes completely covered the wooden church's vaulted ceiling. Above the altar, a painting of Mary holding baby Jesus stood out against a cerulean backdrop. Mary and Jesus were centered over the altar, framed by a large gold star in the middle of the oceanic scene. Star of the Sea, or Stella Maris, served as both a title for Mary and another name for Polaris, the North Star, whose guidance had aided sailors since ancient times.[3]

Letters home were also an integral part of squadron morale. Robert O'Maley, who had married in Los Angeles in 1943, wrote to his wife in May 1944 that he was eager for deployment: "The sooner we go to sea the sooner we get home. I hope I get to see you around Christmas time." O'Maley wrote home to mark important events like his wife's birthday or their eight-month wedding anniversary. He did not like to boast or write about his experiences in the squadron, even if such topics would have made an exciting read. He prefaced explanations of his role in Fighting 18 by saying, "I am just an ordinary fighter pilot who is going to get back to his wife in one piece."[4]

O'Maley was one of Fighting 18's section leaders, putting his responsibilities in the middle between the young ensigns taking orders as wingmen and the division leaders responsible for four-plane units. He had seen some amazing things during his temporary additional duty aboard USS *Enterprise* in early 1944: the devastation of Tarawa after its capture by the Marines, the verdant beauty of Palau from thousands of feet above. O'Maley was recommended for an Air Medal for participating in the first Truk raid, but he brushed the possible award off: "They must be recommending anybody these days. . . . Burnett got recommended also. He deserves it more than I. . . . His plane got shot up."[5] O'Maley was probably also thinking of his squadron mate and wedding attendant, Wells McGurk, who was killed in flight operations aboard *Essex*. If his letters were self-effacing, it was because he knew what some of his squadron mates had already sacrificed for their country.

On 5 June the air group relocated to Naval Air Station Kaneohe to finish training. VB-18 was assigned the Curtiss SB2C-3, the newest version of the Helldiver; VT-18 got a final infusion of pilots, bringing the squadron's complement to twenty-seven; and in early July, VF-18 pilots began logging hours in F6F-5 model Hellcats with increased ground attack capabilities, water injection systems for emergency power, and spring tab ailerons that allowed for greater maneuverability than previous models.[6] All signs pointed to the air group boarding *Intrepid* sooner than later. There was just one snag: The carrier was still suffering complications from the torpedo hit in February.

Intrepid left Hunters Point Naval Shipyard on 9 June to meet its new air group in Hawaii. Repairs appeared to be completed. Three days later, just northeast of its destination, the ship lost all steering control. Though steering was shifted to secondary conn at the aft end of the ship, it froze there as well. *Intrepid* had to limp into Pearl Harbor under partial power for yet another period in drydock.[7] By the time the carrier was fixed up enough to stand out of Pearl Harbor, it was earmarked for important transport duty. *Intrepid* departed on 23 June 1944 to deliver Air Group 19 to the front and subsequently to bring back injured Army and Navy personnel from the fleet anchorage at Eniwetok.[8]

That was the last straw for some of the eager young aviators in Air Group 18. Orders had been issued and rescinded; schedules were changed at the last second; new aircraft, like F6F-5s and SB2C-3s, were introduced one day and gone the next, replaced by planes even older than the ones pilots had been flying at the start of the year. Griping reached an all-time high. William Ellis, the air group commander, had to step in. The same day *Intrepid* steamed out of Pearl Harbor, he drafted a letter to all hands addressing their complaints as frankly and firmly as possible: "These things are exasperating. Yet fortunately, a majority of the Air Group accepts them in stride knowing that military matters do not and never will run smoothly on schedule. . . . Air Group Eighteen will move up into combat soon enough. In the meantime let every man condition himself physically and mentally . . . for the job ahead."[9]

This was solid advice. Some of the most difficult training exercises were still on the horizon. Nighttime field carrier landing practice (FCLP) was added to the syllabus in July. These touch-and-go landings were conducted in the dark to simulate carrier landings at night or in foul weather. Night flying required pilots to put absolute trust in their plane's instruments. Their body's sense of motion could become confused without visual reference—a problem their plane's altimeter did not have. But the altimeter still had to be cross-checked against other instruments to ensure level flight, pitch, and heading. Even though night flying duty aboard ship would be assigned to separate detachments of specially trained pilots, it was important for everyone to develop at least a passing familiarity with instrument flight.

Lt. Freddy Wolff was unequivocally one of the toughest guys in Fighting 18. He had a rough upbringing in Buffalo, New York, after losing his mother at a young age and falling in with a bad crowd. He ran numbers for local betting rings and boxed to hone his short, stocky frame into a formidable weapon. Fortunately, he was able to forge a better path for himself through sports. His strength on the gridiron and in the ring earned him a scholarship to Ohio Northern University and paved the way for his career in the Navy.[10]

Wolff was also one of the most senior men in Fighting 18. He was designated a naval aviator way back in May 1941. Since that time, he had logged over two thousand hours in various aircraft as an instructor and with the squadron. But even Wolff wrote *"yike!"* [*sic*] in the margins next to his first nighttime FCLP entry in his log book.[11] These were harrowing exercises. Another experienced aviator in Air Group 18, Lt. Leo M. Christensen of VT-18, had nighttime FCLP a day after Wolff. He disappeared after just one touch and go. Lieutenant Christensen had apparently become disoriented while making a turn over the water. Despite rescue efforts that lasted well beyond midnight, there was no trace of either Christensen or his Avenger.[12]

The air group finally received word in late July that *Intrepid* was ready for them. Fighting 18's enlisted men hauled all the squadron's gear aboard ship—only to unload it again after *Intrepid* developed mechanical difficulties on 29 July.[13] The delays were maddening and served as an ill omen for Air Group 18's inaugural combat cruise.

Intrepid finally started toward Eniwetok Atoll on the morning of 16 August—the carrier's first birthday—and reached the anchorage a week later, on 24 August. Eniwetok had been captured in February 1944 as part of the invasion of the Marshall Islands. In the handful of months between troop landings and *Intrepid*'s arrival, the base had developed to such an extent that the Seabees, or naval construction battalions, had to erect Quonset huts on top of existing structures to manage the sprawl. The buildings looked especially tall since the highest natural point of elevation in the whole atoll was a mere fifteen feet. Still, to the new arrivals, the facilities seemed primitive compared to Hawaii. The trees were all stumps from naval bombardment, it was "hotter than hell" on the shore, and all the beer was warm.[14] While the islands themselves may have been unimpressive, the lagoon they guarded wowed all the men aboard ship. At over fifty miles in circumference, Eniwetok Atoll was big enough to contain sixteen carriers and more than fifty surface combatants spread out as far as the eye could see across the vast expanse of the Navy's premier forward operating base.[15]

In early September the fast carrier force underwent a change in command. The Navy used a rotating system to ensure there would be no pause in the ongoing offensive. To accomplish this, one fleet commander planned for future operations ashore while another prosecuted an active campaign at sea. They then switched places. In this case, Adm. Raymond Spruance had just completed a run of operations including Hailstone (the raid on Truk), as well as support for the invasion of the Marianas, which culminated in the Battle of the Philippine Sea. Under Admiral Spruance, the fast carriers were referred to as Task Force 58. Meanwhile, Adm. William "Bull" Halsey had organized

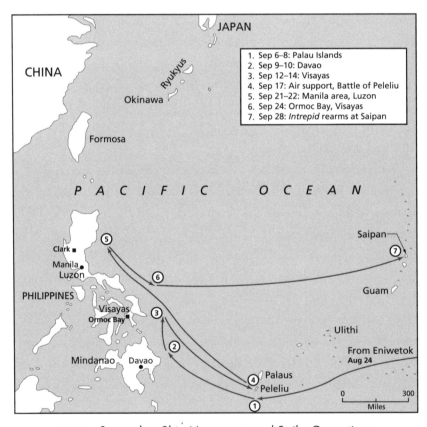

MAP 1. September Ship Movements and Strike Operations

forces for the upcoming Philippine campaign. When he came aboard his flag-ship, battleship USS *New Jersey*, on 24 August, the fast carrier task force was renamed Task Force 38. The ships were still essentially the same, but there was no reason not to complicate the picture for Japanese intelligence officers trying to keep track of U.S. Navy fleet movements.[16]

The first target for Halsey's carrier raids was the Palau Islands, including Peleliu, where the Marines were slated to land on 15 September. For Fighting 18, an eager new squadron ready to test its mettle, strikes on the Palaus from 6–8 September proved a bitter disappointment. Japanese pilots were nowhere to be seen. Only token anti-aircraft fire met Air Group 18's bombing attacks on military installations and anti-aircraft emplacements.[17] This was because *Intrepid* arrived on the scene well after the isolation of the Palaus. Operation Desecrate One, carrier strikes launched in late March 1944, had disrupted Japan's use of the Palaus as a military way station, and by June, U.S. subma-rines enforced a devastating blockade of supply lines.[18]

The effectiveness of the Navy's vise grip on the Palaus is best illustrated by Babelthuap (Babeldoab), the largest and most populous island in the chain. The bloody U.S. Marine Corps invasion of Peleliu, farther to the south, led to nearly eleven thousand Japanese casualties at the cost of over eight thousand casualties on the Allied side. On Babelthuap, over five thou-sand Japanese military personnel and a similar number of civilians died by the end of the war even though the island was entirely bypassed. Instead, months without resupply of food or medicine caused famine and disease on a massive scale.[19]

The flip side of disappointment at not seeing significant action was relief at surviving the first combat missions of their deployment. By the end of the day on 7 September, 194 planes from Air Group 18 had taken off from *Intrepid*'s flight deck. There was not a single personnel loss across five full strikes, and only one plane, a Helldiver from VB-18, was lost in a water landing close to the fleet. It was cause for celebration. There were ample toasts given in the Fighting 18 ready room that night thanks to tiny two-ounce bottles of liquor distributed by flight surgeon Doc Fish. Men gathered in a circle, arms around each other's shoulders, to say something they were thankful for. Lt. John

"Larry" Donoghue was not one of the squadron's pilots and he did not drink, but he was there in the circle nonetheless to share in the moment.

Lieutenant Donoghue was Fighting 18's engineering officer aboard *Intrepid*. He was responsible for overseeing maintenance on the squadron's Hellcats—a function critical to the aviators' performance and safety. Coordinating maintenance and repair was a full-time job. Over the course of World War II, carriers like *Intrepid* averaged five to seven aviation technicians per aircraft. Fighting squadrons embarked more than fifty Hellcats, meaning Donoghue had to work with scores of enlisted men from the ship's air department. He received status reports regarding aircraft availability, compared them with the number of planes scheduled to fly the following day, then organized his workforce to ensure there were enough planes "up" (in flyable condition) to meet the squadron's obligations. He orchestrated the hustle and bustle in the hangar deck while the enlisted men worked around the clock repairing and replacing everything from tires to whole engine assemblies.[20]

Donoghue had wanted to be a naval aviator, but his eyesight disqualified him from flight service. The next best thing to flying was making things fly, so he went to school at the Armour Institute (now the Illinois Institute of Technology) and later got a job working for the Martin Company in Baltimore. He was actually working in an aircraft factory when the Japanese attacked Pearl Harbor. Though he could have been deferred given his role in the defense industry, Larry went down to enlist and was accepted as a specialist thanks to his engineering background. By the time Fighting 18 arrived at Hawaii two years later, he knew the F6F Hellcat inside and out.[21]

When it came time to say what he was thankful for in the ready room, Donoghue immediately thought of the aviators around him. They faced danger day in and day out to fulfill the ship's mission. He was thankful for their selflessness and wanted to reciprocate, so he said, "I'd do anything for you. I'd give you the shirt off my back."[22] The pilots were no doubt thankful for Donoghue, too. His crew ensured their planes had the best odds of making it back from combat. In the spirit of camaraderie, and with a little nudge from the booze, the men around Donoghue decided to take his words literally. They laughed and began tugging forcefully at his shirt, leaving it ruffled and torn by the time their antics were over.

The air group suffered its first combat loss the following day. Babelthuap had been thoroughly worked over on 7 September, leaving little of value to assign to the bombers. Nevertheless, schedules had been set, and there was ordnance to expend. The target for the morning of 8 September was a burning oil dump on the southwest coast of the island. Enemy aircraft were once again completely absent. Anti-aircraft fire greeted the strike on arrival, but as soon as the fighters started strafing, the gunners stopped firing. They apparently thought better of staying at their posts in the face of such an onslaught.[23]

Three of the torpedo bombers joined up above the fuel dump, circling before entering their bombing runs. Lt. Ben Riley went down first, releasing his two-thousand-pound bomb on the target. He nosed his plane back up and dipped a wing to circle so he could observe the other two planes as they made their passes. Lt. (jg) John Savage was next. He was determined to plant his bomb square in the middle of the dump. Riley watched Savage glide steadily downward, proceeding lower and lower in a shallow twenty-five-degree approach.

A two-thousand-pound general-purpose bomb could unleash a terrific blast, especially on a volatile target like a cache of ammunition or fuel. Savage's bomb tumbled out of his Avenger's internal payload bay, lightening the plane by nearly a ton. Riley watched his squadron mate pull up to regain altitude, but he was well under one thousand feet. Before Savage could claw his way skyward, the bomb exploded beneath him, carrying away the empennage of his plane. The tailless Avenger spun in close to the shore, leaving a slick of hydraulic fluid and debris marring the blue-green expanse just beyond the mangrove trees. The crash claimed the lives of Lt. (jg) Savage and his two crewmen, Aviation Radioman Second Class Albert "Bud" Rybarczyk and Aviation Ordnanceman Second Class Ora Sharninghouse Jr.[24]

This accident could have happened to any pilot, and they all knew it. Dive Bombing 18 had lost its original skipper, Lt. Cdr. Harlan Dickson, when he pressed his dive too low during a training exercise in California. He had previously earned Navy Crosses at Coral Sea and Midway, making him one of the most experienced and highly decorated men in the air group.[25] Target fixation did not discriminate between novices and old hands.

Savage, Sharninghouse, and Rybarczyk were eulogized as some of the best men in Air Group 18. They were grieved in that quiet, stoic way required of fighting men in the middle of a deployment. Their friends surveyed belongings to ship home to grieving families and rededicated themselves to the task at hand as both distraction and vengeance. Savage would no longer be seen in ready room chairs scrawling notes before a mission; Sharninghouse's and Rybarczyk's bunks in the air group's enlisted berthing spaces were empty. They would not be the last to fall by the wayside.

Intrepid's carrier group, Task Group 38.2, moved farther west a couple days later. Despite inching ever closer to Japan's inner defensive perimeter, strikes against Mindanao in the Philippines did not trigger a response by Japanese air forces. This was due in part to the absolute devastation visited upon Davao by *Intrepid*'s air group. On 9 September photo reconnaissance flights by Lt. (jg) Redman "Beetle" Beatley of VF-18 gave the fighters such clear images of enemy airstrips and parked aircraft that pilots were assigned specific planes to destroy on follow-up strikes.[26] At dawn the next morning, VF-18 pilots swarmed over Matina aerodrome outside Davao, pressing home strafing runs as low as three hundred feet in the face of intense anti-aircraft fire. They destroyed or seriously damaged at least sixteen planes.[27]

Through it all, the only enemy Fighting 18 encountered in the skies over Mindanao was a solitary Mitsubishi Ki-46 Dinah reconnaissance plane that showed no interest in engaging. Ens. William H. Murray and Lt. Harvey Picken sprung on the enemy before he could escape into cloud cover, riddling his aircraft with .50-caliber bullets. The plane went crashing to the ground shortly thereafter. It was the squadron's first confirmed kill.[28]

The Fast Carrier Task Force climbed its way up the Philippine archipelago from Mindanao to the Visayas, inching closer to the Japanese home islands. Air operations continued on 12 September, but no Japanese planes were encountered to the east where Task Group 38.2 was assigned. By this point VF-18's frustration with the situation was palpable: "Many operational airfields were indicated, strong air opposition was anticipated. . . . Results were disappointing; just as they were at Davao. Although a likelier looking field than San Pedro, Tacloban also proved disappointing. There was no air opposition."[29]

The most action VF-18 saw that day was the "Battle of Samar Sea,"[30] which took place in a small body of water on the west coast of Samar Island just south of the San Bernardino Strait. The label "battle" was applied jokingly. Punchy Mallory and Moe Mollenhauer were scheduled to break off from the main body of strike 2D to fly a photographic mission, but when the weather became uncooperative, they shifted gears, looking instead for any targets worth attacking. It didn't take long for them to find one.

A convoy of wooden vessels composed of eight merchant ships and four small boats was headed south through the Samar Sea, prominently flying the Japanese flag. Raymond Coll, a reporter embedded aboard *Intrepid* at the time, interviewed Moe Mollenhauer about the event shortly after it happened:

By luck we spotted this convoy sneaking down the coast toward Leyte and we swooped down so low we could see the vessels were loaded with trucks, tractors, etc. Boy, did we let 'em have it with our 50s. Those bullets really ripped 'em apart. We were flying so low we barely skimmed the water. I'll never forget the speed boat that was leading the procession. I let him have it and literally cut the boat in two. It was a great show. There was a lot of valuable . . . material that went down that day. When I cut that speed boat in half I was thinking of my brother-in-law Gary Wiedner of Maywood, Ill., a Seabee who was killed by strafing while going ashore at Saipan.[31]

Two *Intrepid* fighters encountered enemy aircraft on 12 September, but these pilots were not members of Fighting 18. The men in question were assigned to Night Fighting Squadron 78 (VF[N]-78), Detachment 2. The unit was comprised of a handful of aviators led by Lt. William H. B. Millar. As would be expected of a leader in one of the most challenging and dangerous branches of aviation, Bill Millar was an extraordinary young man. The New Jersey native received Montclair High School's award for "a sound mind in a sound body," reflecting his participation in Latin and science clubs and on the varsity soccer and track teams. Millar received a scholarship to Princeton for his academic performance, graduating in 1941 and going right into naval aviation cadet training that summer.[32]

Because of the operational plan for September, Lieutenant Millar and his men did not fly at night. Instead, they were being used to staff "lifeguard" combat air patrol duty over submarines rescuing downed pilots, or to augment the basic CAP missions flown by VF-18. To date it had been limited, boring, even frustrating work. The lifeguard radio frequency was almost always crowded with unnecessary chatter that made coordinating with the subs difficult. The lack of radio discipline was especially galling to the lifeguard CAP pilots given the time-sensitive nature of rescue operations.[33]

On 12 September, though, Lieutenant Millar and his wingman, Ens. Donald Matheson, got lucky en route to their station off the southern coast of Leyte. A Yokosuka P1Y Frances bomber appeared below them at two thousand feet. Millar quickly radioed Matheson to bracket the bomber with him, and together the two poured long bursts of gunfire into the plane. Millar scored the first hits, causing the Frances' port engine to explode. The plane wavered and lost altitude but continued determinedly heading east as Ensign Matheson tore into its tail and fuselage. Before it could clear the east coast of Leyte, the Frances disappeared in a massive fireball either from crashing into the ground or from the detonation of its payload.[34]

While Fighting 18 griped about the unexpected absence of Japanese planes in the Leyte/Samar area, pilots in Task Groups 38.1 and 38.3 encountered dozens of them to the west over Cebu Island. Fighters from *Lexington* and *Essex* racked up impressive numbers during their predawn sweep and initial strikes. VF-15 Cdr. David McCampbell, the Navy's future Ace of Aces, was only one of a handful of pilots to score three or more kills that day.[35]

Ens. Thomas Tillar, a fighter pilot with *Hornet*'s VF-2, started 12 September with considerably worse luck. His Hellcat was hit while mixing it up with Zero fighters over Cebu. Oil sprayed out over his windshield, obscuring his view. He looked down at his instruments and was unsurprised to see the needle on the oil pressure gauge dropping like a stone. He was losing altitude and speed as his division headed out over the water. There was no way Tillar could make it back to the fleet. He'd have to make a water landing near Leyte.[36]

Despite the shaky start, Tillar splashed down without a hitch and climbed into his life raft. The current brought him to Apit Island, where he was greeted by friendly Filipinos offering food and shelter. Things were now looking up. Before he was rescued by a SOC floatplane later that day, a guerrilla fighter told Tillar that while some Japanese forces remained on Cebu, there was virtually no presence on neighboring Leyte. He committed this tidbit to memory and mulled things over as the SOC brought him back to its home base, the cruiser USS *Wichita*.[37]

Fighting 18 faced its first real challenge the following day, 13 September. Strike 2A launched at around 0610 to destroy aircraft and installations on northern Negros Island. *Bunker Hill*'s Air Group 8 led the way in and was the first to encounter the hornet's nest of enemies covering the target area. Dive Bombing 8 (VB-8) observed more than forty Japanese planes;[38] the Air Group 18 action report pegs the number as high as fifty-three.[39] Whatever the final count, fighters had their work cut out for them protecting their bomber comrades.

VF-18 division leaders for this strike were Lt. James Neighbours and Lt. Cecil Harris. Neighbours and his wingman, Ens. Leonard "Woody" Woodward, acted as close support, flying ahead of the Helldivers and Avengers to disable anti-aircraft guns—or, at the very least, to draw fire away from the bombers. Harris' division of four Hellcats flew close cover behind the bombers to protect them from enemy fighters intent on intercepting the strike. His wingman, Lt. (jg) Franklin Burley, and the other two men in the division had never engaged in air combat. In fact, most of the men in Fighting 18 had not yet encountered an enemy plane in the air.

As the strike group crossed over the eastern shore of Negros Island, a Zero fighter crept up from below the clouds, attempting to pounce on the formation from behind. Harris was the first to spot it. His division attacked right away, forcing the enemy to prematurely break off his run on the bombers. The Zero pilot hit the deck, diving away into the long blanket of clouds from which he had come, but Harris and company were not about to give up the chase. They came down hot on his heels. When the four pilots broke out into the clear, they were directly over Fabrica airfield, plunging rapidly toward fifteen Japanese fighters. They had just enough time to make quick passes at the enemies as they descended from twenty-five hundred feet down to five hundred feet.[40]

By the time they pulled out of their dives, enemies were all around them. Wingmen protected their leaders as best they could, picking Japanese pilots off their buddies' tails, but it was difficult for the novice pilots to stay glued to their leaders. Burley told a reporter,

> I took my regular position for a section run. I must have been a little over-anxious, because I passed Harris and had to pull out first. So I lost sight of him. But I saw several Zekes below me, and I initiated an attack all by myself, which was very stupid. I got on one Zeke, fired at him, and saw my tracers hit him. Just then, I gave a worried glance over my left shoulder and saw a Zeke sitting on my tail. Immediately I remembered the voice of Harris, back at Ream Field, screaming "Join up." The Zeke on my tail blew up, and a Hellcat whistled past. It turned out to be Harris.

Lieutenant Harris downed three more enemies in the melee—all A6M3 Hamp variants of the Zero—running his day's score to four.[41]

Neighbours and Woodward had a worse time of it. They were supposed to have another division helping them and should have had their assigned targets swept by a foregoing flight of eight fighters. Neither of these things happened due to confusion on the part of the *Bunker Hill* group. As the action report detailed, "8 VF from *Intrepid* were assigned to fighter sweep which was to cover airfields located on Northern Negros Island. Upon making rendezvous with planes from *Bunker Hill* and *Cabot*, strike leader from *Bunker Hill* directed our 8 VF to accompany 4 VF from *Bunker Hill* in sweep over Bulan Field located in Southeastern Luzon. As a result of this decision strike 2A which was launched immediately after sweep arrived over Negros with only meager cover."[42]

The *Bunker Hill* report makes no mention of a change in plans, stating simply that *Intrepid* fighters were sent to Luzon. It does, however, provide additional information concerning the understaffing at Negros Island: "Lt.

Cronin's division which was scheduled and briefed for the Negros area, went to the Legaspi area instead."[43] These locations were more than 150 miles apart and on completely different islands.

If the VF-18 report is taken into consideration alongside the VF-8 report, a full twelve fighters originally allocated to the main strike body at Negros went to southern Luzon instead. This was particularly problematic as the myriad fields on Negros were not yet well-documented with photo intelligence. Neighbours and Woodward now had the outsized job of protecting eighteen bombers against an entire airfield's worth of anti-aircraft guns.

They dove repeatedly on the field, flying headlong into withering medium-caliber fire—anything from 20-mm cannon fire, which can punch a hole in a plane, to 50-mm high-explosive shells capable of blowing a plane completely apart.[44] In the midst of the action, men from both Fighting and Bombing 18 saw Neighbours dive to 1,500 feet, right into the teeth of blazing Japanese artillery. As soon as the pilot leveled out for his strafing run, the guns found their range. His comrades watched as flak blossomed behind the zooming plane, chasing progressively closer until the black puffs of smoke finally caught their quarry. A direct hit to the Hellcat's tail blew it off the fuselage. The plane spun crazily toward the ground, crashed, and exploded. Woodward radioed Neighbours, hoping beyond hope he had made it out. His message was greeted with silence.[45]

Ensign Woodward was now a division unto himself, the lone fighter shepherding *Intrepid*'s bombers back home. Suddenly, he heard someone calling for help. It was a Hellcat pilot from another carrier whose plane was badly damaged. An enemy Ki-43 Oscar fighter was hot on his tail, looking to finish him off. Woodward caught sight of the chase and quickly banked down from above, whipping himself around to take the Oscar head on. As he opened fire with his .50-caliber machine guns, the Japanese pilot tried to nose his plane up and away from the arcing rounds. It was a costly mistake. Woodward pulled up hard in pursuit, raking the belly of the Oscar with gunfire until the plane began trailing fire and fell away toward the ground. Almost at stall speed after executing the quick pull-up, Woodward spotted another Japanese fighter heading his way. He decided he had had enough excitement for one day. Woodward firewalled his throttle, easily pulling away from the enemy to rejoin the bombers on their flight back to *Intrepid*.[46]

On 13 September, the squadron had its first taste of air-to-air combat. By the end of the day, VF-18 had its first ace in Harris, suffered its first combat fatality with the loss of Neighbours, and performed admirably as a part of its air group. According to VT-18, their fighter escort prevented enemy aircraft from interfering with strike operations.[47] One Avenger and its three-man crew were lost to anti-aircraft fire, but the toll could have been worse if not for Neighbours' gallant strafing. In addition to aerial victories, strike 2A beached a ship and damaged eight others, cratered one runway and damaged two more, and damaged or destroyed six Japanese bombers on the ground. All told, it had been a successful introduction to war.

Members of the ship's company were surprisingly well-informed about the squadron's activities. Even those belowdecks, farthest removed from air operations, managed to eavesdrop on the excitement. Warrant Officer Richard Montfort wrote in his diary on 13 September, "Our source of news is pretty good. We have our radios tuned in on the fighter commander and hear all the orders to the pilots. Also in the engine room one of us puts on a headset and plugs into the JA circuit which is the Captain's circuit and get all the dope that is passed on to him."[48]

As *Intrepid* moved southeast for a return to the Palaus, leaders at the Octagon Conference in Quebec laid out plans for the remainder of the year. At the start of the conference, on 12 September, the combined chiefs of staff reaffirmed a target date of 20 December 1944 for landings in the Leyte-Surigao area.[49] The chiefs happened to meet the same day Ensign Tillar went down. The pilot's rescue and subsequent stay aboard *Wichita* allowed him to fully brief Rear Adm. C. Turner Joy about the lack of Japanese forces on Leyte. His report bubbled up the chain of command until Rear Adm. Joseph "Jocko" Clark finally ensured it reached Admiral Halsey. Ensign Tillar's account was fully in keeping with the overarching intelligence assessment that Leyte was "wide open."[50] This was all the information Admiral Halsey needed to propose a dramatic increase in the pace of operations.

The new plan called for skipping less strategically important islands like Yap and avoiding more difficult landings at sites like Mindanao, where the Japanese were funneling in reinforcements. Leyte was a logical alternative, since the decision to invade the Philippines had already been set in stone in late July 1944.[51] Adm. Ernest King, the commander-in-chief of the U.S. Fleet and Chief of Naval Operations, was at that moment attending the Octagon Conference alongside President Franklin D. Roosevelt. He quickly received the good news from Admiral Halsey and coordinated with Gen. Douglas MacArthur regarding next steps. When it came time to discuss the progress of the campaign in the Pacific on 15 September, King outlined favorable reports by Halsey and his counterparts in the Army's Fifth Air Force, then made the announcement that they were going to "advance the date of . . . operations by about two months."[52]

The combined chiefs were enthusiastic. Gen. George Marshall felt that if they could move up the dates of future operations this way, it would limit Japan's ability to respond to operations in Burma scheduled for late 1944. General Henry "Hap" Arnold, in command of the Army Air Forces, reported that Japan's air forces were in shambles. According to the notes taken during his statement, General Arnold went so far as to say that they had "neither the will nor the wherewithal to act offensively."[53] The conference made it a done deal. Troops would land on Leyte on 20 October to keep Japan firmly on the back foot.

While Yap and some of the other islands originally planned for invasion could now be bypassed, landing forces had already been assembled for the invasion of Peleliu. It was too late to call things off. *Intrepid* revisited the Palau Islands on 17 September to strike Peleliu and Angaur in support of freshly landed troops. To help burn the dense jungle foliage shielding Japanese positions from prying eyes, VF-18 turned their planes' external fuel tanks into napalm bombs. Napalm was a new weapon as yet untested in the Pacific theater, and instructions on how to use it reached the ship just two hours before takeoff. Results proved disappointing: Only those bombs dropped on Angaur exploded on impact. The rest of them had to be strafed repeatedly to start fires.[54]

One particular pilot had nerves of steel and ice in his veins on this mission. With the guns on the ground quiet for the time being, Lt. (jg) Isaac Wesley Keels Jr. nosed down into his glide path determined to put his bomb exactly where the air coordinator assigned him. He held to his thirty-degree approach as the sky faded from view and the earth rushed up to meet him. Most other pilots were releasing anywhere from one thousand feet to four hundred feet. Keels let his altimeter unwind all the way to a mere one hundred feet—practically treetop level—before dropping his payload and yanking back on the stick.[55] The explosion of his belly tank and the sight of a Hellcat whipping foliage with propeller wash was likely a welcome sight for the infantrymen on the ground. Keels was no doubt pleased, too. He had picked up the nickname "Red Lightning" at Brevard College for the way he raced his Ford Model T around campus.[56] If only his classmates could see how fast he could push a Hellcat!

As it turned out, problems with ordnance were just one variable out of many—including poor visibility due to uncooperative weather and duplicate claims by air groups—that caused Navy planners to greatly overestimate the damage done by naval and aerial bombardment. The factor that most limited the Navy's efficacy, however, was the fact that the enemy had fundamentally changed their island defense strategy starting with the Battle of Biak in mid-1944. Before that point, the Japanese either fought the Allies at the beachhead or launched massed banzai charges to slow their advance. At Biak, the Japanese instead decided to heavily fortify interior positions, hoarding resources so they could meet the Allies on their own terms.[57]

Marines landed at Peleliu on 15 September anticipating a hard-fought but short battle. They were correct on the first count, but due to the new Japanese defense strategy, they found themselves mired in grueling combat that lasted over a month. The 1st Marine Division suffered a whopping 56 percent casualty rate as they fought tooth and nail, sometimes in direct hand-to-hand combat, with determined Imperial Japanese Army infantryman.[58]

While the Marines duked it out on Peleliu, Task Group 38.2 withdrew to refuel. There was a special significance to the upcoming missions that made men simultaneously eager and anxious, whether they were among the ship's company or part of the air group. *Intrepid* was going to participate in the first carrier strikes against Luzon since Japanese forces seized control of the Philippines in early December 1941.[59] After missing out on the Marianas and the Battle of the Philippine Sea, this was finally an assignment that felt like an integral part of the war effort. They were striking Japan along its last line of defense, along an axis whose control determined the final course of the war in the Pacific.

CHAPTER 5

ESCALATION

SITUATED AT THE NORTHERN END of the Philippine archipelago, Luzon is the country's largest and most populous island. It had been home to American military installations since the end of the Spanish-American War. By the eve of the attack on Pearl Harbor, it was a nexus of U.S. Army Air Forces power. This toehold in the Pacific wound up collapsing rapidly in the face of Japanese strikes. Attacks launched against Far East Air Forces bases on 8 December 1941 destroyed nearly one hundred aircraft on Luzon.[1] The ensuing lack of air support greatly aided Japanese invasion plans, hastening the fall of Gen. Jonathan M. Wainwright's forces. By the time *Intrepid* arrived on the scene almost three years later, those same bases, which together accounted for more than a dozen airstrips dotting the island from top to bottom, were an integral part of Japan's air defense network. Strikes by Task Group 38.2 on 21–22 September 1944 were intended to knock the biggest of these facilities, the former Clark Field, out of commission.

The whole air group expected *Intrepid* to come under attack from Japanese planes any day. Despite the looming danger and the recent memory of 13 September's aerial melee, VF-18 pilots remained eager for a fight. Lt. Cecil Harris later said in a 1945 interview, "Every time I see an enemy plane I get scared . . . But I figure there are so many enemy planes in the air, the more I knock down, the less I have to worry about."[2] In other words, the best defense was a strong offense.

Punchy Mallory abided by the same logic. He was aggressive and adept at air-to-air combat. He could lead a target just right, calculating the proper angle of deflection needed to score a hit regardless of his plane's position relative to his opponent's. Mallory had a good deal of practice before coming to the squadron. He grew up with rifle in hand, learning how to track and hunt game in the woods of his native West Virginia.[3] He was one of several high-scoring fighter pilots who attributed their success to their rural upbringing.

The strike plan for 21 September called for Hellcats from Fighting 18 to sweep Clark Field, shooting down patrolling fighters in the air and burning those planes unfortunate enough to be caught on the ground. Subsequent strikes would include the full roster of dive bombers, torpedo planes, and their fighter escort to deliver the knockout blow. Men on the sweep rose before 0400 to meet this busy schedule. They chugged strong coffee and wolfed down steak and eggs before their mission briefing in the ready room. They were scheduled to launch at 0722. Despite poor weather, all their planes were airborne in a matter of minutes.

CAG William Ellis personally led strike 2A off the deck of *Intrepid* about forty minutes after the sweep departed, bringing his bombers and fighters inland toward Clark Field. Planes took off in driving rain with limited visibility. By the time Ellis' planes made it to the sprawling aerodrome, the weather had started to clear a bit, providing VB-18 with tiny openings in the clouds through which they could pick their targets.

Pilots pushing through the cloud cover into the open air above Clark Field were stunned: it was untouched. The fighter sweep preceding strike 2A must have gotten held up by or lost in the storm. Fortunately, the same torrential downpour that sidelined the fighter sweep also grounded Japanese planes and masked the strike's approach. The weather prevented accurate assessment of bomb damage, but the buildings between Clark's northern and southern fields were built in such close proximity that misses on primary targets flattened those nearby.[4]

Strike 2B came next. Its pilots caught ships at anchor off Luzon before the Japanese could scramble air cover. The morning was going swimmingly. Now all that was needed were reconnaissance photos to assess the extent of the damage inflicted by the carrier groups. It was an important assignment, according to the air group's war history: "Photo missions . . . have top priority. It seems that Beatley, Mallory, and Picken are flying constantly." These intelligence gathering missions were so important to Adm. William Halsey, commander of the Third Fleet, that he issued orders forbidding photo recon fighters from engaging enemy aircraft unless they came under attack themselves. Air Group 18's commanding officer reinforced that order; Ellis told the fighter jocks to "lay off shooting down Zekes, get some pictures."[5]

Lieutenant Picken's three photo fighters, along with escort Lt. (jg) George Eckel, had taken off with strike 2B to do just that. While the rest of the strike continued west to Subic Bay, they broke off for Clark Field to assess the morning's work with their camera-equipped F6F-5P Hellcats. They were given no additional fighter escort, and they were flying right over the biggest air complex in the Philippines after their ship had hurled a proverbial rock at it.

The weather was much improved over Clark Field by the time Picken, Mallory, Beatley, and Eckel arrived, so it was easy for the four men to see that Third Fleet had roused the Japanese from their slumber. Planes had taken off in response to the carrier attacks, including five twin-engine Mitsubishi G4M Betty bombers.[6] The men, with their orders, considered their options. Bettys could carry torpedoes and easily had the ability to reach Third Fleet if the Japanese discovered its location. There was no fighter escort protecting these lumbering land-based bombers, and the photo fighters had the element of surprise in addition to advantages in speed and altitude. They decided their superiors would understand if they paused their picture-taking mission to neutralize the threat.

Mallory dove on the Bettys from behind, causing the formation to cut and run. It was just like flushing a covey of quail from the brush. He went after the first bomber that left the protection of its flock. His Hellcat's six Browning .50-caliber machine guns punched dozens of holes through the thinly armored plane, causing tongues of flame to lick out where bullets struck. Japanese crews nicknamed the G4M *Hamaki*, or "Cigar," because of the plane's shape. The nickname was apt for an entirely different reason: its lack of self-sealing fuel tanks and other defensive measures caused it to go up in flames after just a few hits, leading Americans to dub the Betty the "Flying Lighter."[7]

Beatley, Mallory's wingman, chased the flaming bomber down toward Clark Field. He gave it a few more bursts of gunfire for good measure before leveling off to rejoin his section leader. Meanwhile, Picken and his wingman Eckel were employing the same tactics. Picken raked a Betty with machine gun fire, then Eckel dove on the wounded bomber to deliver the coup de grace. By the time all was said and done, there were four fires burning on the ground, each marking a Betty's point of impact.[8]

There was still more than enough fuel in their Hellcats to complete their photo mission after the turkey shoot. The men split up into two groups, two planes each, to canvass Clark. As the only planes airborne at that moment, they drew significant fire from anti-aircraft guns. For five minutes—minutes that seemed like an eternity—Mallory and Picken weathered flak of all calibers while they took as many pictures as they could of the huge base.

Enemy planes began buzzing through the air around Fighting 18's photo team. Beatley was the first to spot the rising threat. He bent his throttle to catch a Betty being loosely escorted by a singular Ki-61 Tony fighter plane. The Tony's design was so different from other Japanese fighters that it was initially thought to be a license-built German or Italian plane—hence its nickname. In reality it was a homegrown Kawasaki design inspired by an earlier relationship with German engineers.[9]

As Beatley closed in for the kill on the hapless bomber, Mallory, flying on his wing, scanned the area around them. Metal glinted at him from one of the many runways bisecting Clark Base as a handful of Tony fighters scrambled into the air. Mallory shouted a warning through the radio. The four *Intrepid* fighters needed to form up while they still possessed the speed and altitude advantage.

Upon hearing the call, Eckel craned his head to locate the new threat. He saw Beatley gunning down the Betty. That couldn't be what Punchy Mallory was so excited about. Then, out of the corner of his eye, he spied eight more Betty bombers circling above the base. They scattered like bowling pins as Eckel gave chase. He was confident he'd found Mallory's targets. He was so energized by the fighting that he zipped by his prey too quickly, overshooting his first two gunnery runs on two of the fleeing Japanese planes. He doubled back for a third pass, chasing his quarry down to five hundred feet before he finally found his mark. One of the Bettys started streaming smoke as it fell to the ground. The remaining bombers were all spread out now. Eckel joined up on the other men in his division in case enemy fighters appeared. Picken, Beatley, and Mallory were above and ahead of him, flying in the same direction.[10]

Eckel slowly climbed to meet them. As he did, three Tonys—the real reason for Mallory's radio transmission—swooped down from above on the surprised pilot. Quick thinking, fast reflexes, and a powerful engine with an added boost from water injection pulled him out of his predicament before the Japanese fighters could finish him off. Eckel wasn't the only one in danger, though, and his three Tonys weren't the only Japanese fighters prowling the skies above Clark Field.

Beetle Beatley slowly circled over a smoldering wreck that used to be a Betty, confirming his kill while he kept one eye on his section leader. Mallory had just shot down a Tony. Relieved, Beatley checked the space around him to confirm the coast was clear. He quickly looked left and right: just scattered clouds and sky out there. He glanced over his shoulder to check his tail and got "the thrill of his life."[11] Four Tonys were closing fast.

Mallory wasn't about to leave his wingman in the lurch: "I looked down and saw one of our fighters about five thousand feet below the rest of us, boxed in. . . . It was only a matter of seconds before he'd be shot down. I called for a break and went into a dive."[12] Beatley was lucky to be in the care of a "Flying Mountaineer," a West Virginia fighter pilot who could shoot with the best of them. Mallory opened fire on the closest Tony with a seventy-degree deflection shot, expertly leading the target so his gunfire hit the mark right at the enemy's cockpit. The sleek Japanese fighter caught fire and spun off Beatley's tail. One down, three to go.

Beatley and Mallory were now both under one thousand feet and in dire straits. Six more Tonys took off from fields below, more than making up for Mallory's latest victory. Tonys would be in their element in a low-altitude turning fight. The Japanese pilots' strength in numbers, their tactics, and their planes' characteristics combined to give them an edge over the *Intrepid* aviators in their Hellcats.

The two carrier pilots worked furiously. After downing the lead Tony, Mallory scissored past the second plane in line to take potshots at his wingman. He didn't score hits, but he did make the enemy pilot think twice about continuing the engagement. Beatley turned as well, weaving with Mallory to get back into position on his wing. Mallory knew they couldn't keep this up forever. He radioed Beatley to begin climbing.

There was no way the Tonys could keep up. Beatley and Mallory passed them at 12,000 feet despite starting their climb below their adversaries. Their Grumman-built Hellcats roared, Pratt & Whitney Double Wasp engines thrumming with raw power as the sleek blue birds streaked skyward. Eckel saw the pair hurtling through the clouds and joined up. The Tony pilots stayed at lower altitude rather than chasing the trio.[13]

Harvey Picken, the lead photo pilot, duked it out separately with a handful of Tonys. He scored some hits but knew the photo mission trumped combat. Despite his best efforts to behave, however, Picken scored one more on his way out to sea. Cruising over the foothills of the Sierra Madre Mountains, he made out the shape of a lone Japanese heavy bomber flying close to the ground. The Helen, as the Allies dubbed the twin-engine Nakajima Ki-49, didn't stand a chance. Picken shot the plane down even though only one of his six machine guns was working after the big battle over Clark.

The squadron war history's statement "that Beatley, Mallory, and Picken are flying constantly" was no exaggeration. Within an hour and a half of arriving back at *Intrepid*, the three of them (sans Eckel, who was done flying for the day) were in freshly fueled Hellcats, launching with strike 2C to take more pictures of Clark Field. They picked up three more kills, while their escort, Lt. Robert "Dave" Davis, downed one Tony and damaged another. By the end of the day on 21 September, the photo fighters were credited with shooting down fourteen enemy planes. Charlie Mallory had five kills, making him an ace in a day.[14]

The photo fighters had been ordered not to engage with enemy forces. CAG Ellis was livid. Men tended to get Navy Crosses for becoming an ace in a day. Instead, Ellis told Mallory he'd be lucky if he didn't get court-martialed for disobeying Admiral Halsey's—and his own—explicit instructions.[15]

Court-martial was probably an idle threat. Ellis was an experienced leader who knew the effect such an action would have on air group morale. He may have even been secretly thrilled that his fighters were demonstrating such spirit and prowess. Still, his threat conveyed the seriousness of the photo pilots' insubordination.

Over the course of the day, fourteen members of VF-18 claimed a total of 24.5 enemies shot down and a handful more damaged. Losses to the whole air group were three planes and no men, proving the pilots of Fighting 18 were not only competent air-to-air brawlers but also able escorts. Two of the three plane losses were bombers that made it back to *Intrepid*. Art Chauvel in his SB2C Helldiver, returning from strike 2C, slammed into the crash barrier after missing the ship's arrestor wires. Given the damage sustained by his plane, it was a miracle that Chauvel walked away unscathed. His gunner only had a minor concussion. The Helldiver itself was demolished—broken completely in two by its impact with the barrier—and had to be thrown overboard as a total loss. The other bomber was a TBM Avenger. When it landed aboard ship, the plane was inspected, written off, and shoved over the deck edge. A 20-mm shell caused structural damage that was simply irreparable given the limited facilities available at sea.[16]

The third loss was Hellcat bureau number 58216.[17] Its pilot, Boot Amerman, flew with thirty-three other Air Group 18 planes on strike 2D, *Intrepid*'s final strike of the day on 21 September. CAG Ellis was once again strike leader. He brought the bombers and their fighter escort up the west coast of Luzon to the area just south of Lingayen Gulf, where a convoy of Japanese ships had previously been spotted. The eight Japanese vessels encountered there were slow-moving merchant freighters of varying types—ore carriers, tankers, general cargo ships—with displacements ranging from two hundred to eight thousand tons. Though most of these coal- and diesel-powered transports were unarmed, a few had medium-caliber anti-aircraft guns. More importantly, they had protection from the elements. Low-hanging cumulus clouds obscured visibility, forcing bombers to start their dives low.[18]

As usual, Amerman flew wing on Lt. Donald Watts, one of Fighting 18's section leaders. With no air cover protecting the convoy, Watts and Amerman headed down expecting a milk run. They focused on two big ships, each estimated at four thousand tons or more. The sound and fury of two Hellcats blazing away with a combined twelve .50-caliber machine guns punctured the quiet uniformity of the slate-gray day. Helldivers then pushed over, releasing their payload of 1,000-pound armor-piercing bombs as low as nineteen hundred feet. VT-18's Avengers followed shortly behind with two-thousand-pound general-purpose bombs.

Watts and Amerman witnessed the results firsthand. They were still making strafing runs when a bomb hit the aft end of one of the freighters, blowing off its entire stern section. By the end of the strike, the score was one sunk, two probably sunk, and one seriously damaged. Half the convoy was destroyed in one fell swoop.[19]

Boot Amerman struggled to keep up on the return trip to *Intrepid*. He had to wrestle with his controls practically the whole way, from Lingayen Gulf on Luzon's west coast, over the breadth of the island, and out into the Philippine Sea to the east. Despite the convoy's light defenses, some lucky gunner had managed to put a shell close to Amerman's Hellcat. Shrapnel had shredded his wing, and the controls inside were bungled. With his right aileron frozen in the up position, he sweated his way toward the task group. Hopefully Lt. Richard "Rit" Moot, the landing signal officer, would be able to bring him down safely.

On final approach to *Intrepid*, Amerman saw Moot on his platform on the portside deck edge vigorously crossing his paddles over his head—a wave-off. Amerman was under no circumstances allowed to land aboard ship given the obvious difficulty he had controlling his damaged Hellcat. He'd have to put the plane down in the water. Amerman was tired after struggling against the plane's finicky controls for almost two hours. Now he had to maintain enough focus to pick out a patch of ocean, prepare himself for a crash landing, and extract himself from the plane before it dragged him under the waves. While he continued to wrestle with the controls, Amerman squirmed out of his parachute, cut his life raft loose, cinched his safety belt and shoulder straps tight for the bumpy ride, and hoped for the best.

The sea was choppy. If he plowed into oncoming waves, he could flip his plane or be knocked unconscious by the rough landing. He had to time his descent just right. When he spotted an opening, Amerman put his Hellcat into a full stall at sixty knots airspeed and touched down. His landing was as gentle as possible under the circumstances. He quickly climbed into his raft as his plane started sinking; it slipped from view in just thirty-five seconds. Dusk seemed to approach almost as rapidly. Amerman fired his Very pistol to signal nearby ships in the fading light. He was hauled aboard USS *Halsey Powell* in under an hour. The uninjured pilot, exhausted after his ordeal, was returned to *Intrepid* on 23 September when *Halsey Powell* came alongside to refuel from the carrier's reserves. It seemed like a fair exchange.[20]

The danger posed by anti-aircraft fire like the kind that killed James Neighbours and almost claimed Boot Amerman's life was ever-present for aviators. Fighter pilots feared it considerably more than air combat—and for good reason. The men of Fighting 18 had squared off against dozens of enemy planes on at least two separate occasions, had been outnumbered in those fights, and had come through without losing a single pilot. Anti-aircraft fire, on the other hand, could strike sight unseen at any time. A single unlucky hit could mean the difference between a return trip to base and a violent death.

Intrepid's fighters swallowed their fear and continued to fly low during strafing missions, silencing enemy guns so the bombers could do their jobs. On 22 September Air Group 18 returned to Clark Field to give it another shellacking. The wild fighting of the previous day had apparently exhausted Japanese aerial resistance. Planes were left heavily camouflaged on the ground instead of being sacrificed in a futile effort to protect Clark Field.

The first strike of the day arrived over the target just before 0800. VF-18 pilots pressed their luck to ensure maximum damage in their strafing runs. The strike report noted, "Most strafing runs were leveled out at above eight hundred feet but several pilots went right down to the deck. One F6F returning with mud on its wings."[21] The results speak for themselves: sixteen enemy aircraft were claimed destroyed on the ground by VF pilots with another twenty-three damaged. The VB and VT planes claimed four hangars destroyed and personnel and supply buildings seriously damaged.

Ens. Walter L. Passi participated in his very first mission with Fighting 18 that morning. He was one of the pilots who flew low over the field in the face of medium-caliber anti-aircraft fire. When his section leader, Ens. George Naff, started leveling out to strafe a Dinah reconnaissance plane on the ground, Passi broke off to hit his own targets, a pair of Zeke fighters parked side by side in a nearby revetment. Planes were going up in flames left and right all over Clark Field. Japanese ground crews either did not have enough time to empty their fuel tanks, or they had hoped to get the planes in the air later that day. Frog Hurst pulled out of his strafing run at about five hundred feet with anti-aircraft fire zipping all around him. Although he was perilously low, he noticed another Hellcat flying even closer to the ground. Hurst could see that its canopy was covered with blood. The plane soon nosed over and crashed. It was Passi; he had destroyed his target but had pressed his luck too far.[22]

Even though Third Fleet had spent multiple days off the coast of the Philippines in enemy territory, the Japanese offensive response proved just as anemic as its defense. VF(N)-78 Detachment 2 flew morning CAP while Fighting 18 allocated as many pilots as possible to strike duty. Lt. Bill Millar's four-plane division—practically the whole detachment—spotted two Mitsubishi A6M Zeke fighters heading west away from the center of the carrier force. The second section, with leader Lt. William Thompson and wingman Ens. William Herpich, attacked first. Thompson opened up from long range on the Zeke in front, leading his target so his bullets raked along the plane from its engine down to its wing root. The Zeke pilot dove in response, trying to shake the pursuing Hellcats as his plane trailed a tell-tale streamer of smoke. The other enemy fighter entered a steep climb, probably hoping the Hellcats would continue chasing his partner.

Millar and his wingman Donald Matheson did follow the flaming Zeke down. Their corkscrew dive took them from ninety-five hundred feet down to four thousand feet, where the enemy suddenly leveled out. The Zeke was no longer smoking and seemed to be in perfect working order. Its pilot, deciding to fight rather than flee, turned to bring his guns to bear on Millar. Millar was quicker on the draw, though. He fired ahead of the turning plane, forcing its pilot to dive away rather than complete his maneuver. The Zeke disappeared into the clouds below. Millar and Matheson climbed for altitude to get back to patrol duty rather than chasing after their clearly beaten adversary.

Meanwhile, Thompson and Herpich climbed after the other Zeke, which their Hellcats had no problem overtaking. They bracketed the plane and both scored hits that caused smoke to pour from their target. The Zeke rolled inverted and nosed over, diving through the clouds. Since this plane appeared to be out of control when it disappeared from view, Thompson and Herpich got credit for a kill, while Millar had to settle for "damaged" rather than "destroyed" for the other plane.[23]

The final day of strike operations for the month, 24 September, was reminiscent of the first day, 6 September; it was characterized by frustrating assignments with little payoff. Ellis led strike 2A off the deck at 0600 to hit shipping reported in Ormoc Bay on Leyte, but the bay was empty. When Ellis led the strike over a reported troop concentration afterward, the area was abandoned. The only target they found that morning was a "fat freighter" for the torpedo planes to test their five-inch high-velocity aircraft rockets on. With some help from VF-18's Lieutenant Blouin strafing the ship stem to stern, the Avengers scored twenty-three hits, leaving the freighter a burned-out hulk.[24]

The next deck load of planes, strike 2B, was likewise "a disappointing one" for Fighting 18, and strike 2C, which headed to Cebu Island, was even worse: "No worthwhile targets were assigned and none were encountered. . . . The strike was inefficient and generally unproductive."[25] To add injury to insult, strike 2C encountered more anti-aircraft fire than any of the earlier missions that day.

Wally Walworth felt his plane suddenly jostle and shake during strafing runs on strike 2C, but through determination and sheer adrenaline, he regained control of his aircraft. He wasn't sure exactly what had happened, but he didn't think he'd taken a hit—maybe just a close shave. He put the incident out of mind for the time being.

Lieutenant Walworth's fellow pilots could see what he could not: His plane had not only taken a hit, but the explosion had also blown a one-foot hole in the starboard side of its fuselage just in front of the tail. The other side of his aircraft, where pieces of shrapnel punched through, looked like Swiss cheese. The pilots flying beside Walworth kept the information to themselves.

It would only distract him if he knew the grievous damage his plane had suffered.[26]

Walworth's dilemma became clear when he came in to land aboard ship. His plane was slow to respond when he moved the stick. There was a huge amount of play in his controls. His first pass was high and fast, forcing LSO Rit Moot to wave him off. Walworth circled back around for a second attempt, man-handling his bucking Hellcat like a bull rider. Fortunately, Moot saw the hole in Walworth's fuselage as he passed by and knew the plane might not stay airborne for a third attempt. Walworth was still coming in high and fast, so Moot gave him the cut from farther out to account for the difference in speed and altitude.

It was perfectly timed. Wally Walworth caught the number three wire and bounced to a stop. He marveled at the sight of *Intrepid*'s flight deck stretching before him. It was a textbook landing, perhaps the best he'd ever made. When he got out of his Hellcat, Walworth peered through the huge hole in its fuselage. One of the control cables, which were composed of three strands of metal braided together, was shot completely away, and the other one was down to its last pencil-thin strand. Walworth was astounded that he had made it back to the fleet at all, let alone landed safely aboard ship. Moot's cut probably saved his life.[27]

Lt. (jg) William H. "Junior" Sartwelle was not so lucky. Two days prior he had been with Ens. Walter Passi as one of the low-strafing pilots determined to inflict maximum damage on Clark Field. Sartwelle was much loved in the squadron, "a fearless pilot and one of our best men."[28] On strike 2C, the young Texan once more proved his mettle by flying at treetop height over Cebu with his guns blazing. Nobody saw him go down, but given the lack of airborne opposition and his failure to return, it was speculated that, like Passi and Neighbours, Sartwelle was downed by anti-aircraft fire.

The news hit Roy O. "Bud" Burnett Jr. like a sledgehammer. Sartwelle and Burnett had become close during their time in training. Sartwelle was one of the squadron's youngest pilots at twenty years old, while Burnett, eight years his senior, was one of its oldest. Pop Thune remembered that they had formed a kind of father-son bond. The two had much in common. Burnett's father owned and operated Burnett Motors and had done well for himself in Portland, while Sartwelle's father founded Port City Stockyards in Houston, Texas. They both had promising futures ahead of them in their respective family businesses. Sadly, only Burnett went on to realize his American dream.[29]

September had been a month of trial and error leading to some remarkable successes and some bitter disappointments. Fighting 18 pilots received a "very well done" message from the commander, support air, for their role strafing targets at Peleliu and Angaur. Commander Ellis, Captain Bolger, and Admiral Bogan had given pilots a "well done" for their flying in extreme weather on 22 September. Ellis said it was the best work in the worst weather he'd ever seen. On the flip side, their air group had been blamed for hitting a residential area. Even though pilots and crews felt another group was responsible, pointing fingers would not help their case. Morale was also suffering from the squadron's first casualties, from faulty gun camera film causing issues certifying kills, and from an increasingly intensive strike schedule. Charles Mallory wrote in his diary, "These past few weeks of hard strikes have left most of us in need of a little rest."[30]

Intrepid arrived at Saipan on 28 September to replenish its stores and rearm. The layover meant a short reprieve from combat. Air Group 18 had built up a good deal of anxious energy over the course of its first month in action that needed expending. When it was announced there was no shore leave or liberty on the first day at the island, men got their frustration out by playing basketball on one of the ship's aircraft elevators. "What games! They are more like football games than anything else. Luckily not to [sic] many fellows got hurt," Mallory wrote.[31]

Fortunately, the month ended on a high note. The next day, men queued up for hours to get ashore. There were ample opportunities for fun, including "a beer party" and haggling with Marines for Japanese souvenirs. A handful of Fighting 18 pilots, including Mallory, Bill Mufich, Bill Bland, Paul Amerman, and Chuck deMoss, had a pint of liquor to trade. It may as well have been gold on Saipan. They used it to borrow a Jeep from the Seabees. When he got back aboard ship, Mallory wrote, "Did we have a time. I drove up slippery roads at 45 mph in a heavy rain, skidding from one side to the other. Then we drove back over the mountains to see the 2nd Marine Div. boys. They were at Hilo with us."[32]

Intrepid's fighter jocks were genuinely curious about what had happened to their Marine buddies from training. The squadron war history went so far as to say, "In our opinion the Second Division Marines have had the toughest assignments and deserve more credit than any other single fighting unit in the services. . . . We saw some of our friends . . . and were distressed to learn of the death of Colonel Easley, who led the batallion [*sic*] we worked with at Kamuela."[33]

While aboard ship, aviators had dinner service on china, a roof over their heads, and beds to sleep in. They were acutely aware that Marines and other forces fighting their way from island to island lacked all such luxuries. It was not unusual for pilots to have relatives fighting on the ground, either. Moe Mollenhauer's brother-in-law was killed in the Saipan landings. Coming to the island was no doubt an emotional experience for him.

It was only a few days before *Intrepid* was on the move again. Saipan was not destined to be a major way station for carriers. Instead, the newest and closest fleet anchorage was at Ulithi Atoll, about 550 miles due south. Ulithi had only recently been captured when *Intrepid* arrived and was therefore devoid of any creature comforts. The ship's crew and air group grumbled even more than they had at Eniwetok: "Our forces occupied Ulithi . . . several weeks ago, and the Navy adopted it as a base, to our everlasting sorrow. . . . We arrived there and sat around for two days. The ship had no boats and we were unable to get ashore."[34] To make matters worse, the ship arrived just in time for a typhoon to whip the lagoon into "mountainous waves." It was not a good first impression.

On the other hand, the advantages of Ulithi over Eniwetok were immediately apparent to Navy planners. Ulithi was more than a thousand miles west of the previous anchorage. *Intrepid* had to steam for almost a week to get within striking distance of the southern Philippines while operating from Eniwetok. Leaving Ulithi, the ship was able to reach southern Japan in only a few days. It may have been useless as a shelter from rough weather, but Ulithi's "strategic position justified . . . acceptance with its shortcomings."[35]

Securing this anchorage was especially important now that *Intrepid* and the rest of the fast carriers were operating within spitting distance of Japan. In fact, Admiral Halsey's next major target was the Ryukyu Islands, including Okinawa and Ie Shima. These were not far-flung imperial outposts. The Ryukyus had been considered part of Japan since the nineteenth century. An attack on these islands was an attack on the enemy's home soil.

Before leaving Ulithi for these strikes, a few changes were in order for *Intrepid* and Task Group 38.2. At the beginning of September, USS *Independence* had been fully equipped to carry out night operations for the whole task group as part of an experiment. The light carrier had a special night air group, including a mix of twenty-five radar-equipped Hellcats and Avengers that operated in lieu of the smaller detachments aboard *Essex*-class carriers. The experiment proved successful enough that *Intrepid*'s VF(N)-78 Detachment 2 was absorbed into Fighting 18. Lt. Bill Millar and his men had already been flying daytime missions anyway. This change just meant they would now have the opportunity to fly strikes instead of their usual CAP assignments.[36]

More significantly, on 1 October *Intrepid* became the flagship of Task Group 38.2. Adm. Gerald Bogan relocated from *Bunker Hill* to *Intrepid*, along with over one hundred enlisted men and nineteen staff officers responsible for coordinating operations.[37] These officers were fighter directors, intelligence analysts, photographic interpreters, and other specialists synthesizing and disseminating information from the task group's nearly thirty ships.

Adm. Gerald Bogan was born in 1894. He had been an aviator for so long that he previously commanded Squadron One in the late 1920s.[38] Bogan had the look of a fighting admiral. He had a flat face and a flat, broad nose, which he had broken five or six times doing everything from sparring with bouncers to crashing aircraft. He had even fractured his skull falling off the edge of *Saratoga*'s flight deck in the dark.[39] That was not enough to dissuade him from further sea service.

Bogan's rough-and-ready spirit endeared him to the aviators under his command, but he was also notoriously particular. If you did not do things Bogan's way or did not adjust yourself to meet his exacting standards, you could expect to find yourself transferred. If he saw promise in you, though, you were marked out for a successful career in the Navy. Capt. Robert Pirie, Bogan's chief of staff, ended his service as a vice admiral; Cdr. Edward Outlaw, one of Bogan's operations officers, went on to captain *Intrepid* before retiring as a rear admiral.[40] Bogan had an eye for talent.

Pacific storm fronts continued to mask carrier movements in October as they had during the late September strikes on Luzon. *Intrepid* and its task group steamed toward the Ryukyus behind a solid wall of wind and rain. Aboard battleship *New Jersey*, Admiral Halsey's staff officers referred to the typhoon as "Task Force Zero," as if it were part of the Navy's fleet. Between foul weather and the interdiction of enemy search efforts by long-range scouts based out of Saipan, Task Group 38.2 was able to steam within about one hundred nautical miles of Okinawa without detection.[41]

Two and a half years had elapsed since the Doolittle Raid, the first carrier-launched strikes on Japan's home islands. Now the carriers were back and stronger than ever. No enemy aircraft protected the skies over Ie Shima on the morning of 10 October, allowing for extremely effective bombing by Air Group 18. Aerial photographs show barracks lit up by roaring fires sending black streamers of smoke skyward. Two images attest to the skill of VT-18 pilot Lt. Ben Riley, who dropped a bomb directly in the center of an X formed by two intersecting runways.[42]

There was plenty of game on the water as well. VF-18 pilots found surface craft gathered on either side of the Motobu Peninsula, which sticks out from Okinawa's west coast like a big doorknob. Rudy Van Dyke led a division on strafing runs against a wildly maneuvering destroyer in Nago Bay, a major port on the southern side of the peninsula. His Hellcats churned up water and steel until the burning Japanese ship was forced to beach itself. On the other side of Motobu, Lt. Fred Wolff spotted a group of camouflaged cargo ships at Unten Bay, which housed a submarine and torpedo boat base. Wolff's debrief with VF-18 intelligence officer Lt. Harry Cropper allowed later strikes to hunt down and finish these ships off, depriving the Japanese of valuable matériel.[43]

Despite these strikes taking place a mere 250 miles from Kyushu, the southernmost of Japan's four major islands, *Intrepid* pilots flew unopposed throughout the afternoon. The aircraft action reports for the day's strikes contain myriad entries documenting attacks on enemy ships and ground facilities. In all, between the morning fighter sweep and the final strike of the day, Air Group 18 reported sinking, probably sinking, or damaging a total of twenty-five separate vessels.[44]

The carrier task force launched a total of 1,396 aircraft on 10 October and only lost 21 planes.[45] Snuffy Mayer was the only member of Fighting 18 shot down during strike operations. While crossing the western shore of Okinawa over Toguchi Beach, his Hellcat was hit by medium-caliber flak. His radio was disabled, and, more critically, his control cables and tailhook were damaged. Fortunately, his plane was still airworthy. Mayer brought his damaged Hellcat out to the edge of the fleet before making a good water landing and scrambling off the wing of his plane into his raft. In just twelve minutes, destroyer USS *Cushing* scooped the uninjured pilot out of the water. Given the pace of flight operations, however, Mayer was not returned to *Intrepid* until the following morning.[46]

The enemy was now on high alert. In response to the Okinawa strikes, Imperial Japanese Navy (IJN) commanders initiated plans for a "decisive battle" with Allied naval forces. Though the true decision point of the war had long since passed, the *Sho*, or "Victory," plan, committed the bulk of the IJN's air and sea power to one last-ditch effort at stalling the Allied advance across the Pacific. *Sho* was not designed as a decisive battle in the traditional sense of battleships trading gunfire or, more recently, carriers fighting each other from beyond visual range. Instead, its aim was the destruction of Allied landing forces. Japan's biggest battleships would wreak havoc among the auxiliaries, transports, and escort carriers needed to sustain the invasion of the Philippines.[47]

The plan was unpopular with Japanese sailors. It seemed like a waste to send the crown jewels of the IJN on a mission to destroy transports when the enemy carrier fleet was roaming nearby with impunity.[48] On the other hand, the disparity in naval forces between Japan and America had never been greater. The U.S. Navy's fast carrier task force now embarked in excess of one thousand aircraft. American training pipelines churned out new aviators in droves, putting them into combat only after they had received hundreds of hours of training. Japan, meanwhile, was slowly attempting to rebuild its naval air corps after the drubbing it had taken during the Battle of the Philippine Sea in late June 1944, popularly known as the "Great Marianas Turkey Shoot." The quantity and quality of Japanese pilots—army and navy—were in a state of constant decline. The same divergence existed in aircraft maintenance and production as well.[49] There was simply no comparison between Japan's once-touted First Air Fleet, the Kido Butai, and the now vastly superior fast carrier task force.

Sho was supposed to be reserved as a reaction to Allied landings, not as a response to carrier strikes. Japanese commanders needed to accept losses in the Ryukyus and wait for reports indicating the location of invasion forces. However, at the moment the carriers appeared, Combined Fleet commander Admiral Toyoda Soemu was on Formosa (Taiwan) wrapping up a fleet review. The Ryukyu strikes stranded him far from his headquarters with limited ability to direct a response himself. Admiral Toyoda's chief of staff, Shigeru Fukudome, took the reins. He asked for and received permission to commit air forces earmarked for *Sho* to the immediate defense of Formosa and the Philippines. This decision effectively separated the IJN's air and sea forces.[50]

On 11 October *Intrepid* and the other ships in its task group prepared for an extended period of intense strikes against Formosa. *Intrepid* fueled between approximately 1229 and 1412. In the hour and a half the carrier was moored to oiler USS *Mississinewa*, the ship received more than 252,000 gallons of fuel and 56,000 gallons of aviation gas.[51] That evening, Fighting 18's flight officer, Lt. Cecil Harris, drew up the roster for the following day's fighter sweep. Lieutenant Commander Murphy's four-plane division would lead the charge, which meant Harris needed to pick twelve more of his squadron mates for flight duty. He knew from speaking with Lieutenant Cropper, the squadron's intelligence officer, that Formosa was going to be their toughest challenge yet.

Besides lacking the element of surprise, VF-18 would be the first fighting squadron to bomb during the multi-carrier sweep and the first to provide low cover, meaning they'd be the first pilots exposed to anti-aircraft fire. After-ward, their Hellcats would be stuck at low altitude struggling to get back up to speed if—in this case, more likely *when*—enemy aircraft pounced. Despite the danger involved, Harris put his own division down for duty. He had almost single-handedly trained the squadron. He had formed close relation-ships with the men, and his role as flight officer meant he was regularly forced to put them in harm's way. It only seemed right to be with them during their toughest assignment to date.

CHAPTER 6

FIRE OVER FORMOSA

BLEARY-EYED AVIATORS rolled out of bed at 0400 on 12 October. Exhaustion from successive nights riding out storm-swelled seas competed with excitement surrounding the day's strikes. They had been briefed on Formosa all week. It seemed like each update provided some new clue that this was going to be the "big one." Pilots washed, got dressed, and hit the wardroom for chow before their final briefing. The milk was powdered, but the bacon and eggs more than made up for it.[1]

As men finished filtering into the ready room, the excited chatter and jokes faded away. The atmosphere became deadly serious. Pilots took their seats, pulling out plotting boards to transcribe important details written on chalkboards at the head of the room. They logged Point Option, the anticipated location of *Intrepid* at the end of their mission, as well as the ship's YE codes, which helped them decipher *Intrepid*'s bearing using the carrier's radio homing system. The latter was of vital importance in case the ship had to move off its anticipated course while the strike was airborne.[2]

Lt. Harry Cropper kicked off the preliminaries. There was no doubt that after the carrier strike on the Ryukyus, the Japanese had reinforced their air strength on Formosa. It was something the enemy could do continuously with planes from the Philippines and from Japan itself throughout the course of the day. Anti-aircraft fire would be intense. If pilots were forced down over the island, their chances of survival would be poor. Cropper exhorted the aviators to remember their evasion training. Formosa had been under Japanese rule for fifty years. There were no guerrillas sympathetic to the Allies as there were in the Philippines. If captured, they would be imprisoned or worse. In addition to enemy forces, they faced the threat of tropical disease and venomous snakes. Their last challenge was the mountain range dominating the island's interior. Hiking over rugged terrain with limited supplies while avoiding roving Japanese patrols was a nightmare scenario. All of this was a long-winded way of saying, "Get out over the water if you can. Good luck. You'll need it." The room was silent.[3]

Next, Lt. Cdr. Edward Murphy went over the mission parameters and fundamentals. Their primary target was Shinchiku, one of the largest air-dromes on the island. Fighters from *Bunker Hill* and *Hancock* would join up with them on approach. This meant nine full divisions of Hellcats were kicking off the action.[4] Murphy's audience perked up a bit. This is what the pilots wanted to hear about: not the danger Formosa posed to them, but the danger they posed to it. Shinchiku had five known runways and facilities for maintenance, repair, and aircraft assembly. It was likely a main training and staging base.[5] *Intrepid* fighters were assigned to bomb first, and divisions from *Hancock* and *Bunker Hill* would fly cover for them during their bombing runs. At the secondary target, Matsuyama, the roles were reversed: *Intrepid* fighters had cover duty while the other two squadrons bombed.[6]

The skipper wrapped up with the fundamentals. Many of his young pilots had yet to see an enemy plane in the air. It was critical that they maintain discipline in the heat of the moment. They needed to limit radio communication to issues of vital importance, conserve ammunition, and stick like glue to their section leaders' wings. When the briefing ended, a message came blaring over the loudspeaker: "Pilots, man your planes!" Expectation was about to give way to reality. It was time to see what Fighting 18 was made of.

The assigned men sprang from their seats. They tucked their plotting boards tightly under their arms as they shuffled out of the room in Murphy's wake. Continuing single file through the narrow corridors of the gallery deck, they reached the base of the ladder leading up to the flight deck and headed topside. The stale smell of oil and paint and sweat that permeated shipboard life was quickly replaced by salty ocean air. Each man groped his way across the flight deck in the inky predawn darkness. They moved from plane to plane

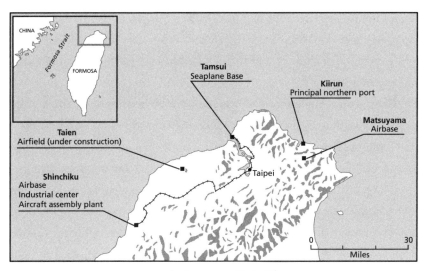

MAP 2. Formosa Air Battle

until they located their assigned mount. Plane captains were standing by for a final nose-to-tail check of the aircraft. In fact, nonflying officers and enlisted men had already been at it for hours. They had to ensure that the Hellcats were airworthy, properly spotted, fueled, and loaded with ordnance and ammunition; that catapults were functioning; and that all the myriad infrastructure that supported these missions was in place to ensure their success.

The Pacific sky was still "as black as the inside of your hat" when flight operations began at 0606.[7] That didn't seem to impede the deck crews, who had all sixteen Hellcats airborne by 0616, an average launch time of less than forty seconds per plane.[8] Lieutenant Commander Murphy took off first. When he cleared the deck, he turned slightly to starboard to avoid the ship's path in case he needed to ditch. Murphy counted to thirty. He had to space out his next move according to the approximate launch times of the planes behind him.

When thirty seconds elapsed, Murphy made a gentle 180-degree turn to port. This was a carefully choreographed affair based on the time it would take for his men to catch up. Murphy's wingman was next. His 180-degree turn was slightly sharper, cutting inside Murphy's trajectory to bring him quickly behind and then roughly forty-five degrees off his leader's starboard wing. The process was repeated until all the *Intrepid* fighters were stacked up in right echelon. After grouping up with the twenty fighters from *Intrepid*'s sister carriers, they proceeded beyond the ships of the screen out over the empty sea.

Bomb-laden Hellcats quickly made landfall, roaring over the heavily forested coastline as they proceeded west. Pilots stayed above 14,000 feet to cross Formosa's mountainous interior until they reached the far side of the range. Then they descended to scan through the broken cloud layer for their target. It did not take long to spot Shinchiku's aerodrome and the rows of barracks laid out near the coast. Murphy led the sweep into the Strait of Formosa before turning around to approach the target from the west. Dawn light twinkled off his Hellcats as they wheeled and turned together in tight formation like a flock of starlings.[9]

Down on the ground, anxious Japanese anti-aircraft gunners waited on high alert, straining their eyes against the horizon. The first radar reports of approaching aircraft were logged at 0610,[10] more than an hour before the sweep appeared. There were about 270 aircraft present on Formosa at that moment.[11] Japanese pilots had plenty of time to get airborne for interception. As usual, it seemed that Cropper's intel was spot-on. This was going to be a knock-down, drag-out fight.

Intrepid's fighters peeled off from the larger group. Pilots pushed their sticks forward to bring their planes into steep dives. Lt. Frank Hearrell's broad view of the coastline and the mountains tunneled down until only the target remained. He was coming in hot over a group of six hangars arranged in an "L" shape between the barracks and the runways. Guns on the ground threw a tremendous amount of flak up toward his Hellcat.

Heavy-caliber shells left black puffballs of smoke where they detonated. Smaller and more frequent medium-caliber cannon fire lit up the morning sky, and the telltale streaks of tracer rounds from machine guns appeared increasingly threatening as Hearrell reached release altitude. The volume and accuracy of these volleys forced several pilots around him to drop their bombs from as high as five thousand feet. It was hard to gauge their success under these circumstances. Hearrell hung in there just a bit longer. He planted his bomb squarely in the middle of the hangar complex before pulling out. He scrambled away from the anti-aircraft fire on the heels of his fellow fighters, getting back into position with his division for the flight to the second target.[12]

There were myriad fields around Shinchiku, including two other naval air stations, five army airfields, and one seaplane base.[13] They couldn't all be neutralized, but Matsuyama airfield warranted the sweep's attention. It was chosen as the secondary target with *Bunker Hill*'s Fighting Squadron 8 on fighter-bomber duty. As the squadrons proceeded east together, all eyes were on the lookout for any metallic glint in the sky, any signs of movement signaling the start of battle.

The weather worsened on approach to Matsuyama. As they passed over outlying Kako airfield, all was quiet. Continuing eastward, the weather below them remained spotty, with an almost unbroken layer of stratus clouds overhead creating a murky ceiling at 11,000 feet. The world between the cloud layers was an almost uniform gray that made navigation difficult. A little break in the cover appeared over Taien airfield. Radios crackled to life. A pilot in *Bunker Hill*'s Fighting 8 spotted what appeared to be twin-engine heavy fighters taking off from the base. Someone in Fighting 18 reported twin-engine bombers, nicknamed Lily and Sally, circling the field as if they were preparing to land.[14] Whatever the identity of the aircraft and their intent, they required the immediate attention of the sweep.

Principal responsibility for dealing with this threat fell to Fighting 18 since they were assigned low cover. Lieutenant Harris led two divisions down to intercept. With his radio giving him trouble, Harris had his second section leader, Lt. (jg) Bill Ziemer, spearhead the charge.[15] Although their eight Hellcats were more than a match for their prey, additional pilots from both squadrons began to leave their stations at intermediate and high cover to get in on the action. They closed rapidly on the bombers. A few minutes later, the dozen or so twin-engine aircraft were flaming wrecks littering the ground around Taien. The hungry young fighters were having a field day.

Only one division from Fighting 8 remained at high cover. It included the squadron's skipper, Cdr. William Collins, and ace pilot Lt. Edward "Whitey" Feightner. They could see some of the action through the clouds below.

Feightner was enjoying the spectacle when his wingman suddenly reported bogeys. The timing couldn't have been worse. A downpour of Japanese army and navy fighters came raining from the clouds above while the majority of the Hellcats were still at low altitude. In a matter of seconds, Collins' division was outnumbered four to one—and that was just the first wave of enemies. By the time all was said and done, reports from the two squadrons indicated between forty and seventy-five fighters bearing down on them. Commander Collins' men had participated in defensive operations during the Marianas Turkey Shoot in June 1944 and had been in combat for months. This was without a doubt the biggest air battle they had ever seen.[16]

Maintaining formation in the face of such an onslaught was impossible. As soon as the attack started, it devolved into single plane tail-chases interrupted by random aircraft appearing out of the blue. Pilots from both squadrons found themselves intermixed in ad hoc sections. Lt. (jg) Ralph Rosen of VF-8 couldn't keep track of Collins but found an *Intrepid* fighter on the tail of an enemy plane. The two weaved past one another taking turns pouring gunfire into the Japanese fighter, until suddenly Rosen felt a jolt. He'd been hit from behind. The enemy in pursuit was still sending tracers zipping over his wings, forcing Rosen to take immediate evasive action. Fortunately, his Hellcat was still airworthy. Commander Collins' experience was similar. He was credited with shooting down five enemies but had his port guns knocked out and returned to the carrier with some extra "ventilation" holes in his Hellcat.[17]

Fighting 18's Chuck deMoss felt like he was watching a movie. Planes were scissoring past one another, firing, exploding, pilots bailing out. He turned toward an enemy fighter for a quick pass and zoomed by several men floating down in parachutes. deMoss thought back to his time as a dive bomber pilot on Guadalcanal. He'd been on the ground during a Japanese aerial attack, utterly powerless to help. That experience shored up his desire to transfer to fighters. deMoss scored two victories during the thirty or so minutes of swirling aerial combat before returning to the ship.[18]

Pop Thune also downed two fighters reported as A6M Zekes. He started out with a run on one from above. The sudden appearance of Thune's Hellcat spooked his opponent, who instinctively pulled back on the stick. If the

Japanese pilot had ducked to the side or turned hard instead of trying to climb, he might have escaped. The second he nosed up, it was all over. Rounds tore into the Zeke as it continued climbing. Its ascent slowed; smoke began to pour out in its wake. It reached its peak, rolled over, and spouted flames as it hurtled toward the ground. Thune climbed back into the fray and quickly shot down another one. The adrenaline was coursing through his veins.

There was no time for celebration. Thune suddenly had an enemy on his tail, and this pilot seemed more adept than the others. Thune rolled out and dove away. Try as he might, he couldn't shake his opponent. He probably thought of Lieutenant Cropper's talk that morning and the odds he faced if he went down in the middle of Formosa. Then he thought of another talk—one he'd had earlier with Lieutenant Harris. As the only man in the squadron with combat experience, Harris naturally fielded many hypotheticals from his fellow flyers. In this case, Thune had asked what to do if he couldn't escape pursuit. Most times, the Hellcat could outdistance an enemy fighter, especially the new -5 model, but what if you were unable to sprint away?

Harris started speaking with his hands in the way fighter pilots do when words won't suffice. He stood shoulder to shoulder with Thune, putting one hand in front of the other in a straight line. His right hand, in front, represented an imperiled Hellcat, while his left hand, hovering a few inches behind, portrayed the Zeke on its tail. Harris suddenly lifted his right hand up in a steep climb. Thune wasn't surprised at the gesture. He'd seen Harris do this before and had practiced it himself in training. In a live-fire situation, though, it meant he'd be bleeding off precious speed with an enemy on his tail. Harris brought his right hand back, smoothly sliding the left into the front position. He nosed the fingers on his right hand down until his hands were once more in line with one another. They had switched places. Thune would now be calling the shots from his enemy's six. He thought about it for a second. His Hellcat would be tougher, its engine stronger, and its armament more powerful than a typical Japanese plane. The risk seemed worth the payoff, but it was a risk nonetheless.

Thune snapped out of his reverie. His gut told him to give it a shot. His left hand tugged back on the throttle control lever, rapidly slowing the flow of fuel to his roaring engine. As it sputtered in protest, he yanked back on the control stick with a white-knuckle grip. Thune's view was suddenly all sky. He kicked hard on his right rudder pedal to skid the plane and held his breath for a moment. His pursuer zoomed by without scoring a hit. As soon as the Zeke passed beneath him, Thune reversed the maneuver. He kicked left rudder, yawing his plane while hammering his control stick forward. The Hellcat sank like a stone until he was back in line with the Japanese fighter. He nudged the throttle forward and immediately felt his Hellcat accelerate. Thune started lining up his shot, but he had already won the duel. His opponent bailed out of the plane rather than continuing the engagement.[19]

Harris and his wingman, Franklin Burley, claimed seven planes between them. It was a testament to Burley's plane-handling skills that he managed to stay on Harris' wing throughout the engagement. It seemed he had fully internalized the lessons from his close call in September, when he tried to go it alone over Negros Island.[20] Harris was credited with two bombers and two fighters, and Burley with three Zekes. One of their opponents was hit by both pilots, making it difficult to determine who should receive credit. The men flipped a coin back aboard ship; Burley won the toss.[21] If fate had ordained differently, Harris would have been an ace in a day. Given how Harris eschewed the limelight, he may have been relieved at the outcome.

The spotlight was firmly on young Moe Mollenhauer, who was credited not only with shooting down five enemy planes but with scoring hits on an additional five as well. It was his first time in aerial combat.[22] Ensign Mollenhauer was one of the hungry young fighters who let adrenaline get the best of them over Taien. He had left his station flying cover to pounce on one of the Betty bombers. It peeled off from the protection of its peers, making a beeline for the coast. Mollenhauer followed it down to two hundred feet with guns blazing. Smoke poured from the wounded plane, and in short order, the Betty crashed into the water. Mollenhauer pulled up to return to his section leader, but the sky above was now filled with enemy fighters, and his leader was nowhere to be seen.

As he climbed, Mollenhauer saw a Zeke on a Hellcat's tail. The chase ran right in front of his nose. He banked, quickly tapping his Hellcat's gun button.

Rounds arced through the Zeke's red *Hinomaru*—or "meatball" as the Allied flyers called it—painted on its fuselage. The plane tumbled away from the battle. Before Mollenhauer could join up with the Hellcat, another Japanese fighter suddenly surged up in front of him. He rolled into position and opened fire. The plane burst into flames.

A fourth enemy approached head-on. Mollenhauer couldn't believe it; it was flying directly into his gunsight. He held down the gun button until streamers began trailing from the enemy plane. Mollenhauer skidded and banked as hard as he could, following the smoking fighter as its pilot struggled to stay airborne. Moe Mollenhauer wanted to see it crash, not just to get evidence for the intelligence officers aboard *Intrepid* but to know that another enemy had fallen as payback for his brother-in-law and lost comrades.[23]

A Japanese fighter saw Mollenhauer's Hellcat descending and decided to make a move. Gunfire started zipping over Mollenhauer's wings. Now his heart was in his throat. He'd been sweating so much his flight suit was stuck to him like a second skin. After what seemed like an eternity of jinking and juking, trying to shake the enemy on his tail, a Hellcat from another carrier finally saw Mollenhauer's predicament and jumped in to knock the Zeke off.

The battle finally started to peter out. The previously crowded airspace was largely empty, but the ground was now littered with burning wrecks. As Mollenhauer regained altitude, he finally found his section leader. They were low on ammunition and fuel, but their work wasn't finished quite yet. They spotted a Japanese fighter trying to sneak away into the clouds. They boxed the pilot in, forcing him out to sea. With his leader holding steady on the far side of the enemy plane, Mollenhauer moved in for the kill. He poured gunfire into the cockpit, causing the Zeke to spin out of control. It was his fifth victory of the day. He was Fighting 18's newest ace and his hometown of Santa Barbara, California's, first ace of the war.[24]

Mollenhauer and his section leader met up with the rest of the flight on the return trip to base. His hands were shaking so badly he could barely hold the stick. Mollenhauer looked around at the number of planes returning to *Intrepid*. He marked at least three absences. The sweep had been a meat-grinder. At any point—from deciding to leave his section leader early on, to following the smoking Zero to low altitude—he could have become one of those missing pilots.

When he finally made it back aboard *Intrepid*, Moe was given a small two-ounce bottle of bourbon to calm his nerves and was debriefed by Lieutenant Cropper. There was a lot he had to recount despite being mentally and physically exhausted from his long flight. As if that wasn't enough, Mollenhauer was then turned over to war correspondents Ray Coll Jr. of the *Honolulu Advertiser* and Philip Heisler of the *Baltimore Sun*. He was the hero of the hour, and they were determined to get the scoop. Mollenhauer remained modest: "They just kept flying in front of me and I just kept my finger on the gun button." In a couple weeks' time, this quote was in dozens of newspapers across the United States.[25]

In stark contrast to Moe Mollenhauer, the pilots who fared the worst were from the divisions originally assigned to destroy the bombers. They were liable to be at the lowest altitudes and traveling at the slowest speeds when enemy fighters pounced. Bill Ziemer and his wingman, Lt. (jg) Egidio "Dibat" DiBatista, were each credited with a bomber kill. When the fight began overhead, they had to climb hard to join the fray. They poured on the coal, using full throttle to bring them from treetop height to eight thousand feet as quickly as possible. Something had to give, though. They rapidly lost speed as their engines worked to overcome gravity's pull. By the time they reached the edge of the fight, they were indicating a mere 120 knots. They might as well have been standing still.

For the Japanese fighters streaming through the clouds above, these two Hellcats were easy prey. DiBatista felt his plane shudder violently as 7.7-mm machine guns and 20-mm cannons found their mark. His Hellcat could survive dozens of rounds from the smaller guns, but each detonation of a 20-mm shell felt like a giant hand forcefully shoving his plane to the side. His head whipped around the cockpit from repeated impacts on the armor plate behind him. Struggling in a daze to evade the assault and maintain control of his damaged plane, DiBatista lost sight of Ziemer. He tried in vain to find his section leader in the moments that followed. A Hellcat blew past him with a

Zero in pursuit. Was that Ziemer? DiBatista got on the enemy's tail. He succeeded in scaring him off, but the friendly plane wasn't his leader.[26]

Ziemer's Hellcat took an even worse beating than DiBatista's. After
being forced to crash-land in a clearing, Ziemer had to run for the relative
safety of the jungle. He hauled his raft and other equipment with him,
bushwhacking for hours while evading enemy patrols. If he could get to the
beach, there was a chance between his dye marker and signaling mirror that
he could alert aircraft overheard.[27] He wasn't the only one shot down. Ens.
Ralph DuPont, one of the youngest men in the squadron, and Wesley Keels,
who had shown his fearlessness bombing the Palaus a month earlier, were
also missing in action.[28]

DiBatista was lucky by comparison. He managed to limp back to the fleet
with his damaged Hellcat thanks to escort by VF-18 squadron mates Buck
Newsome and George Eckel. DiBatista's guns were out of commission, Newsome's were out of ammo, and Eckel only had one working gun left, but their
opponents did not know that. Strength in numbers kept the Japanese fighters
at bay.

Landing aboard ship was out of the question given the state of DiBatista's
plane, and so was a water landing. DiBatista radioed his intent to bail out, jok-
ing with Eckel that he was bad luck: the two did not often fly together given
Eckel's photo duties, but somehow Eckel was there both times DiBatista had
to ditch.[29] DiBatista rolled his plane inverted, hoping he would be dumped
from the wrecked cockpit, but even this proved too much for his Hellcat. It
bucked as he tumbled into the open air, moving just enough to clip his left leg
on the way out. The impact left him dazed but conscious. He opened his chute
and floated down. DiBatista did his best to tread water despite the searing
pain in his leg.[30]

Lookouts aboard USS *Yarnall* saw DiBatista's plane and chute come down
at 0928. The destroyer sped over to throw him a line. He attempted to clam-
ber up the ship's cargo net but fell back into the water every time he tried to
put weight on his left leg. The ship's crew had to use a special stretcher to bring
him aboard. Once he was safely below deck, an examination revealed that his
leg was fractured in multiple places between the knee and ankle. The ship's

medical officer immobilized it. Shortly after *Yarnall* went back to its station, there were reports of a plane in distress. It looked like they had to pluck yet another pilot out of the water. It was a busy day for all involved.[31]

This was the single costliest mission flown by Fighting 18 to date: three pilots were missing in action, and DiBatista was too injured to continue his deployment. *Intrepid*'s Task Group 38.2, which included three fleet and two light carriers, only lost seven fighter pilots in total between 12–14 October. This meant that nearly half of all fighters lost by the task group over Formosa during three full days of offensive operations were lost on this single sweep— and all were from Fighting 18.[32] Their assignment bombing Shinchiku and maintaining low cover had proved deadly.

As poorly as things had gone for *Intrepid*'s fighters, the situation was considerably worse for their enemies. Roughly a third of the Japanese fighter strength on Formosa was wiped out. Among the losses were some of Japan's best remaining pilots, like Warrant Officer Junjiro Ito with Air Group 221. Ito was a veteran of the Battle of the Coral Sea in 1942 and had been attached to fleet carrier *Zuikaku*.[33] The participation of such experienced naval aviators no doubt instilled confidence in Japanese leadership on Formosa. They watched these terrific battles playing out overhead with unbridled enthusiasm. Vice Adm. Shigeru Fukudome, in charge of the lion's share of Japanese airpower for the *Sho* operation as commander, Second Air Fleet, witnessed one such engagement from his base at Takao in southern Formosa. He told Allied interviewers after the war,

> As I watched . . . a terrific aerial combat began directly above my head. Our interceptors swooped down in great force at the invading enemy planes. Our planes appeared to do so well that I thought I could desire no better performance. In a matter of moments, one after another, planes were seen falling down, enveloped in flames. "Well done, Well done! A tremendous success!" I clapped my hands. Alas! to my sudden disappointment, a closer look revealed that all those shot down were our fighters, and all those proudly circling above our heads were enemy planes![34]

The weather worsened throughout the day. To the southeast at Karenko, *Hancock*'s Air Group 7 ran into a low ceiling of rain clouds. Another group heading north to Kiirun (Keelung) encountered "adverse weather conditions" that made target identification impossible.[35] *Bunker Hill*'s Air Group 8 likewise had to make a detour around northern Formosa because of "heavy cloud conditions."[36] The weather system that had made Okinawa a breeze was making things miserable over Formosa.

Air Group Cdr. William Ellis led the twenty-six planes assigned to strike 2A off *Intrepid* immediately on the heels of the sweep. He was target coordinator for the whole task group, meaning he would be focused on the success of not only his own squadrons, but also those of Air Groups 7 and 8. The sky was all clouds down to fifteen hundred feet as the strike approached Kiirun.[37] The weather meant that VB-18 would have to glide-bomb through the clouds at shallow angles, releasing their payloads with much more lead time. Accuracy would be greatly reduced. Even if the bombers managed to hit important installations, the odds of being able to identify them through photographs or pilot reports were slim given the short window they had under the overcast. They might have to select alternate targets, abandoning the primary mission altogether.

That was not going to happen if Lt. Cdr. Mark Eslick had anything to say about it. The skipper of Dive Bombing 18 was determined to make this strike count. Kiirun Harbor was a high-value target. His bombers had been individually assigned specific buildings lining the water's edge, from warehouses on the docks to administrative and industrial facilities. He intended to bring his men down like a hammer on the port, come hell or high water.

Eslick was respected, even revered, by his men. His wingman for this mission, Lt. (jg) John Forsyth, later wrote that "Lt. Comdr. Mark Eslick . . . is a good man, fair and honest. . . . The Navy is his life. He's not a showoff. He's conscientious and he's dedicated to the cause, dedicated to his squadron, dedicated to us."[38] Forsyth had to stick to Eslick like glue no matter the dangers involved. Nevertheless, the tactics adopted for this strike worried him. They were flying up the valley housing Kiirun Harbor instead of across it, leaving them exposed to anti-aircraft fire for the duration of their bombing runs. Forsyth would have preferred to use the hills on either side of the harbor as cover on the way in. He could feel in the pit of his stomach that this was going to be rough.

The weather was so foul that it was difficult to differentiate between dark gray low-hanging clouds and the rapidly approaching slopes of Formosa's towering mountains. It was doubly difficult for pilots to keep visual contact with the planes in front of them. The cloud-blurred silhouettes of nearby aircraft were their only tether to the larger strike group as they proceeded toward the target. The lead plane in the second bomber section momentarily lost sight of the plane in front of him. He banked into a clearing to get back on the missing Helldiver's wing, but it was gone. The first section of dive bombers, comprised of Eslick and five other aircraft, was now proceeding to Kiirun alone.[39]

As the strike came unglued, Commander Ellis ordered his remaining pilots to proceed to the secondary target. They followed the Kiirun River westward until its confluence with the Tamsui. This larger river in turn led to a seaplane base on the coast where the river emptied into the Strait of Formosa. Perhaps the weather was better farther west. Ellis passed command of the *Intrepid* strike group to Lt. Cdr. Lloyd Van Antwerp, the skipper of VT-18, to focus on his responsibilities as target coordinator. The Tamsui strike group now consisted of six dive bombers, eight Avenger torpedo bombers, and five Hellcat escorts.[40]

In addition to the seaplane base, Tamsui was also the site of the Rising Sun Petroleum Company, Ltd., which had started its life as part of the Shell Transport and Trading Company. The western coast of Formosa was rich in petroleum deposits, making oil extraction one of the principal industrial pursuits on the island. Heavy oil brought in via steamship was pumped through iron pipes into a 2,500-ton holding tank at Tamsui or unloaded in barrels for warehousing nearby. From there, it could be distributed via railway across Formosa. Given the Japanese military's monumental consumption of fuel and the increasing difficulty it had securing petroleum as the war progressed, the company was taken over by the Japanese government in 1944. As a result, Tamsui represented an excellent target site, even if it played second fiddle to Kiirun.[41]

The clouds that were smothering northern Formosa retreated to three thousand feet as the strike reached the western side of the island. Van Antwerp could finally get a better lay of the land. The seaplane base and petroleum facilities were situated on the northern side of the river near its mouth. Railroad tracks snaked their way down the coast, forming a clear line between the base and the outlying area. Massive warehouses hundreds of feet long sat on the water's edge just beyond the train station. Following the tracks southeast, the coastline jutted out into the river where Rising Sun Petroleum's fuel tanks and the seaplane base were situated. A 125-foot-wide ramp sloped off into the water at the end of a large runway curling along the uneven shore.

Tamsui appeared relatively tame. There were only a few vessels in the harbor, fewer anti-aircraft batteries than had been reported at Kiirun, and no interceptors rising to meet the strike. Van Antwerp instructed his bombers to take their time and make it count. Hellcats, Helldivers, and Avengers glided down through the cloud layer into the clear skies over Tamsui. As usual, the fighters approached first to bomb and strafe, but it was really VB-18 and VT-18 that stole the show. The six dive bombers with the group each packed a 1,000-pound semi-armor-piercing bomb in their bays, in addition to a 250-pound general-purpose bomb mounted on hardpoints under each wing. Selecting the seaplane ramp, a radio station, warehouses, and a few barges tied up nearby, the Helldivers sped down with devastating effect. Columns of smoke rose where their targets—reduced to burned-out hulks and twisted metal—angrily burned.[42]

Each torpedo bomber carried four five-hundred-pound bombs. When they hit the larger of the two oil tanks, it blew up so fiercely that the surrounding area was instantly blanketed with thick, oily smoke. The fires raged for days afterward, leading locals to dub these strikes the "three-day burning of stinky oil tanks."[43] Warehouses near the train station were leveled by four direct hits. Sections of track and train cars at the adjacent depot were mangled by another bomber. All along the coastline, valuable matériel was going up in flames without any retaliation by the Japanese. The Avenger pilots even took time to hunt down a gunboat and lugger at the mouth of the river after they'd dropped their bombs, strafing with their machine guns as if they were fighter jocks.

Things had gone swimmingly at Tamsui. Van Antwerp's bombers grouped back up, climbing above the broken cloud layer, while Fighting 18's five Hellcats, led by Lt. Rudolph "Rudy" Van Dyke, maintained station overhead. Each of the Hellcats sported six guns that started the day loaded with four hundred rounds apiece. Some ammunition had been expended strafing, but the fighters conserved what they could. They still needed to escort the bombers back over thirty or so miles of enemy territory before they got "feet wet" in the Pacific. Once everyone gathered, the strike retraced its steps to the rendezvous point to join up with the bomber division that had proceeded to Kiirun.

The two separated elements of the strike reached the rendezvous point at almost the same time. Enemy planes were there waiting for them. Sleek Tonys with pointed noses and Oscars, the Imperial Japanese Army's Zero look-alike, swarmed over the ridgeline. Fighting 18 pilots did their best to protect the bombers but were outnumbered almost three to one.

In this case, quality was markedly more important than quantity. *Intrepid*'s fighters probably had hundreds, if not thousands, more hours of flight time than their opponents. Compounding the problem for the Japanese pilots, their planes were simply no match for the Hellcat. Though the Tonys and Oscars could turn tighter and were more maneuverable at lower speeds, the Hellcat could outrun them in level flight and could out-dive and out-climb them with ease. Lieutenant Van Dyke and his men were able to dictate the terms of the engagement through superior skill and technology.

This mismatch showed itself almost immediately. When Van Dyke engaged attacking enemies, they broke ranks and hit the deck. It seemed as if their only concern was getting away rather than pressing their numerical advantage. Van Dyke chased three Tonys down to the treetops one after another, leaving three scattered wrecks in his wake. He quickly pulled back up to check on the Avengers. Enemy fighters were still harassing them.

Van Dyke's men maintained discipline and stuck together. Ens. William Bland picked a Tony off Lt. Fred Tracy's tail, weaving with his section leader to ensure that somebody was always watching his six. Bland scored one confirmed kill and a probable; Tracy was credited with three and a probable. They may have lacked numerical superiority overall, but in separate small battles across the mountainside, they often outnumbered their opponents.

When all was said and done, one Hellcat showed minor damage to a center wing panel from enemy gunfire. That was it. None of the squadron's pilots were injured or lost. Their planes could take a round or two through the wing as if nothing ever happened. Japanese fighters, on the other hand, were nowhere near as stout. The strike report noted with some satisfaction that "Tonys still burn and explode when hit."[44]

While VF-18 duked it out with the enemy, Van Antwerp led his bombers east to clear the island as quickly as possible. The sooner they made it out over the water, the better. Behind each torpedo bomber pilot, in a separate plexi-glass bubble located just aft of the canopy, sat a ball turret gunner operating a .50-caliber machine gun. Gunners steered their motorized weapon mounts side to side, tracking a few determined Japanese fighters. Avenger pilots had to hold their planes steady to keep their gunners' aim true while keeping their eyes forward to stay in tight formation with division leaders. They had to trust their turret gunners to watch their tails.

Somehow, they completed their ridgeline run without losing a single plane. Van Antwerp led his men down below the clouds as the mountains receded behind them. They could use the weather to cover their escape. Anxious pilots slid their planes as close together as they dared in case more trouble showed up. Before they could reach the coast, another dozen Japanese fighters came down from above. These enemies opted for head-on passes as opposed to tail chases. They wanted to avoid the ball turret guns and the smaller ventral guns sticking out from the rear of the Avengers.

Without the maneuverability or speed of fighters, Van Antwerp elected to keep his planes together to concentrate their firepower. According to the strike report, "No TBMs ever flew closer formation than during this attack." Enemies approaching from head-on were met by a combined sixteen Brown-ing machine guns producing an absolute hail of bullets. As the first opponent made his pass, Van Antwerp turned toward him. In unison, his seven trailing Avengers followed suit. The wall of machine gun fire forced the attacker to break off and approach from a different angle.

When the fighters rolled by, turret and ventral gunners made them pay. One Nakajima Ki-44 Tojo fighter approaching from above was hit by a turret gunner. As he passed the formation, a rear gunner scored hits that finished him off. Another fighter started smoking, and part of its wing sheared off. Van Antwerp's strategy was working, but their opponents were unrelenting. The torpedo bombers were under attack for about forty minutes, a veritable lifetime in air combat terms. A few stubborn Japanese fighters even followed them one hundred miles off the coast as they made their escape.

Rudy Van Dyke was the first Fighting 18 pilot to finally make it back to the beleaguered "torpeckers" of VT-18. Lt. (jg) Kenny Barden was overjoyed to see a Hellcat in the mix but increasingly dismayed that the friendly pilot didn't seem to be able to shoot down any of his opponents. What Barden didn't know was that between strafing and air combat, Van Dyke had blown through all his ammunition. There was still something he could do, though. Despite the danger involved, Rudy Van Dyke continued to make passes at enemy fighters. The mere threat of a Hellcat was enough to make his opponents break off their attacks on the Avengers to take cover or fight him head-on. These "dry runs" gave the bombers a break, allowing them to continue their journey back to the ship.[45] Later, Barden wrote in his diary, "From that day on, Rudy . . . was our squadron's nomination for 'Man of the Year.' "[46]

Like the fighter sweep before it, strike 2A returned to *Intrepid* short-handed. Three planes and five men were missing. Fighting 18's Ens. Harry Webster was apparently forced to make a water landing outside the fleet. Nobody saw him go down, and he had not been heard from since. VB-18 lost two Helldivers and their two-man crews during the daring unescorted run over Kiirun. Commander Eslick was among the missing. He had faced withering anti-aircraft fire and interception by determined enemy fighters but still managed to inflict serious damage on dockside warehouses despite the harbor's defenses.[47]

Only three and a half hours had elapsed since the beginning of flight operations that morning. Fighting 18 lost more pilots in that brief period than they had since boarding *Intrepid* two months earlier. Despite this mauling, there were still four missions left to fly that day: a photo reconnaissance hop, a second fighter sweep, and two strikes, all heading to the same targets at Tamsui and Kiirun.[48]

Another VF-18 pilot was almost lost on the second fighter sweep when Lt. Thomas Rennemo got separated from the group after his bombing run. He was intercepted by six Tojo fighters as he headed west, but he had a trick up his sleeve to buy himself some time. Rennemo waggled his Hellcat's wings, a recognition signal friendly pilots often gave to one another.[49] The Japanese planes approached without attacking, giving Rennemo the opportunity to throw the first punch. He opened fire as they zoomed past, but his aim was off the mark. He was now surrounded by half a dozen swarming aircraft. His second attempt proved more successful. He shot one plane down from behind and blasted another head-on before deciding to run for it. His Hellcat easily outpaced his opponents.[50]

In exchange for the lives lost on 12 October, Fighting 18 reported forty-six enemy aircraft destroyed, with an additional eight probables and five at least damaged.[51] There was no way the Japanese air forces could sustain such losses. They had to stop the Allied attacks at their source: at the carriers operating just off the Formosan coast. There was already a group of Japanese pilots earmarked to do exactly that. Their arrival was mere hours away.

CHAPTER 7

ON PATROL AND
IN SUPPORT

ON 12 OCTOBER the order to darken ship rang throughout *Intrepid* at 1825. Hatches leading out onto catwalks were dogged tight. Sailors drew blackout curtains to prevent any sliver of light from giving away their position. As the sun disappeared over the horizon, *Intrepid*'s silhouette began to merge with the twilight sky. Ships of the screen followed suit until the whole task group was swallowed up in the encroaching night. It was time to begin long hours of stealthy loitering off Formosa. Despite the cover of darkness, all hands knew they were in for a bumpy ride after their nonstop assault on the enemy stronghold.[1]

It did not take long for these fears to materialize. Japanese commanders had unleashed the vaunted T Air Attack Force to avenge their earlier losses. The "T" stood for Typhoon, as the Imperial Japanese Army and Navy pilots assigned to this unit underwent special training for foul weather and night-time attack. Though not yet fully proficient, the T Air Attack Force had almost two hundred aircraft at its disposal as well as experienced aviators who could be counted on to find enemy ships through the murk.[2]

Over the course of seven hours, between approximately 1900 and 0200, *Intrepid*'s task group was repeatedly forced to release its anti-aircraft batteries, opening fire and maneuvering radically amidst a nonstop procession of Japanese bombers. Air-dropped flares lit up the night sky, casting reflections off the ocean's surface that painted the scene in a ghostly light.[3] *Cabot*'s combat air patrol pilots fended off the first wave, but Japanese crews continued to trickle in singularly and in small groups, overwhelming the fighters.

One Mitsubishi G4M Betty bomber approached *Cabot* from portside. It was so close to the water that the ship's guns barely required elevation. Tracers stitched through the night sky until finally, at point-blank range, the plane burst into flames. That was not enough to bring it down; the Betty continued on its course, passing only seventy-five feet over the flight deck before beginning to nose down toward the waves. It crashed about three hundred yards off the starboard quarter. According to those watching, the spectacle rated "average entertainment value, 4.0."[4] *Intrepid*'s gunners were no slouches, either. They expended 859 rounds of 40-mm ammunition and over 3,300 rounds of 20-mm ammunition to destroy three more aircraft that slipped through the *Cabot* CAP.[5]

The gun crews were ecstatic. According to embedded war correspondent Ray Coll Jr., gun tub ten, on the portside aft of the deck edge aircraft elevator, was responsible for downing one of these planes.[6] Gun tub ten was unusual in that it was crewed principally by Black men from the mess. The Navy was still segregated, pigeonholing Sailors of color into menial positions, cooking, cleaning, and otherwise serving their White peers aboard ship. But this group of men had been trained to operate anti-aircraft positions during general quarters,[7] and they had just successfully defended their ship. Perhaps this act of bravery and prowess would help change the minds of some of their shipmates concerning the Navy's racial policies. Either way, their services were desperately needed. The T Air Attack Force was far from done with Admiral Halsey's Third Fleet.

Fighting 18 didn't have to provide the morning fighter sweep the next day, a fact for which the squadron's worn-out men were no doubt grateful. They arose to find the weather much the same as the previous day: cloudy over the principal targets and more manageable on the west coast, meaning that Kiirun was again skipped in favor of Shinchiku. It's hard to imagine anybody took issue with that; Kiirun had been a deathtrap. At least at Shinchiku, there might be game to hunt.

While the bombers found plenty of targets there during the morning and afternoon strikes, VF-18 was stuck pulling double duty as fighter-bombers and bomber escorts. They were expected to protect the Helldivers and Avengers en route to the target, leave their ranks to bomb/strafe enemy positions, climb for altitude to protect the bombers during their runs, and then escort them back to *Intrepid* when all was said and done.

As it turned out, the Japanese had already spent the bulk of their air defense the previous day. Not a single enemy plane rose in defiance of these strikes. Shinchiku was, however, still extremely well-defended by ground-based anti-aircraft platforms. They proved alarmingly accurate. One Hell-diver crew was forced to parachute over Formosa after their plane was hit; nearly a dozen other aircraft from across the group's three squadrons were damaged in some way.

Only the stepped-up use of "window" seemed to help draw the Japanese heavy-caliber guns off their mark, suggesting that some of them were radar-controlled. Window, aluminum strips pre-cut to specific lengths based on known enemy frequencies, was used to confuse enemy radar. TBM-1C aircraft could be installed with radar intercept consoles capable of identifying enemy frequencies. This allowed crews to deploy bundles of window based on the specific wavelength detected. Radiomen were given dozens of bundles and instructed to drop a certain number of units at established intervals.

During one strike, which approached the target on a southbound heading with land to the portside, heavy and accurate anti-aircraft fire was encountered during the initial phase of the bombing run. Once window was dropped and the flight banked north, with land to starboard, crews noticed that fire trailed high and behind, as if the guns were still following their initial point of aim. Regardless of the cause, the effect window had on morale cannot be overstated. Feeling that they had an extra level of protection going into their bombing runs provided pilots and crews the assurance they needed to focus on the mission at hand.[8]

Despite the danger posed by artillery, *Intrepid*'s air group inflicted substantial damage to Shinchiku. Fighting 18 XO Lt. Clarence Blouin and Lt. (jg) Edgar Blankenship were singled out for hits on a hangar that collapsed in the wake of their bombing run. There was still plenty of work to be done, however. New airfields were discovered during these missions. Lt. Wilson McNeill of VB-18 found one that didn't appear anywhere on his maps.[9] The pilots of neighboring Task Group 38.3 were given maps of their strike zone indicating only four Japanese fields. By the end of the day, they had determined there were at least fifteen.[10]

What the Japanese lacked in aerial defense over Formosa, they made up for in attack capacity off the coast. Task Group 38.4 was swarmed all over by Betty bombers, whose torpedoes narrowly missed *Franklin*. One plane was shot down close enough that it hit the flight deck, leaving behind a trail of soot and splintered wood as it careened off the deck edge. The ship suffered only cosmetic damage.[11]

Adm. John McCain's Task Group 38.1 had it the worst. A raid of a dozen or more planes flew at wavetop height, using the rough seas to hide their approach from shipboard radar. They were not spotted until they were well within visual range. *Hornet* scrambled fighters before ringing up emergency speed and beginning evasive maneuvers. Batteries on neighboring *Wasp* fired on the closing planes with urgency, blasting one, two, three out of the sky. One plane went down just thirty feet from *Wasp*'s starboard bow. Japanese gunners inside the aircraft continued firing as their bomber crashed just shy of the carrier.

Another Japanese pilot desperately tried to succeed where his predecessors failed. He began his torpedo run just as shipboard gunners got a bearing on his plane. The pilot pulled hard to port to avoid the guns and made a clean drop, but his evasive maneuver caused him to miss the mark. His torpedo churned through the water wide of the carriers—straight toward heavy cruiser USS *Canberra*—where it struck below the ship's armor belt and exploded. Towering columns of flame leapt up from the ship. Engine and fire rooms were completely disabled, leaving *Canberra* dead in the water. The damage was so severe that the cruiser needed to be either scuttled or quickly towed away.[12]

Intrepid's Task Group 38.2, which had borne the brunt of the attack the previous evening, lucked out, even though it was Friday the thirteenth. The afternoon faded into a rainy, cloudy evening without event. Snoopers appeared on the screen one moment and disappeared the next, refusing to close on the juicy targets—the cruisers, battleships, and carriers—at the center of the group. One bomber came within thirty miles of the screen before it was spotted by Air Group 18's snooper anti-submarine patrol (SNASP). These defensive operations used fighter and bomber pilots in tandem to intercept threats on the surface and in the air. Planes were paired up to cover pie chart–like sectors fanning out from the center of the task group. In this case, four fighter pilots, each with a dive bomber companion, spread out to cover ninety-degree sectors.

Bud Burnett was assigned to one of these boxes of airspace extending out from the carrier. He was alert and watchful and, frankly, bored. CAP and SNASP missions could drag on for hours. He had been flying the same pattern in the same area over and over again almost to the edge of sundown. His Hellcat carried a depth charge just in case he spotted an enemy submarine, but the odds of an encounter seemed miniscule at best and diminished with each passing minute. He buzzed along five hundred feet above the surface of the water, watching and waiting as the rain continued to fall.

While Burnett droned along, a D4Y Judy dive bomber flew unerringly on its course toward the carrier group at just three hundred feet, using the same strategy as the bombers that had attacked Task Group 38.1 Though low-altitude flight could foil air search equipment aboard ship, it was no match for the watchful eye of a fighter pilot. The unlucky Judy flew right under Burnett. He spotted the plane and immediately went into a diving turn to get on its tail. It looked like he would see some action after all. As soon as the enemy pilot spotted Burnett's Hellcat, he jettisoned his payload into the sea, giving his plane much-needed speed for the coming chase. The Judy's rear gunner released his 7.92-mm machine gun, following the pursuing Hellcat as it drew closer.

Wanting to make his shots count, Burnett waited until the last second before opening fire—but he almost waited a second too long. The Judy's gunner found his range before Burnett did, opening fire with the Hellcat firmly centered in his sights. Bullets tore into Burnett's propeller. His plane shuddered as the rounds gouged metal out of the prop assembly and ricocheted into the leading edge of the wings around it. Burnett returned fire before skidding to the left to dodge the continuing hail of bullets. The Judy began smoking. Its gunner was shooting straight astern, no longer tracking Burnett. He was likely dead or dying.

Burnett took a quick glance at his instruments. Everything looked good—no loss of oil pressure, hydraulics, or electrical systems. His propeller and wings appeared unaffected. In an instant his focus was back on the Judy. The bomber made a slight turn to the left as if to cut inside of him. Burnett gave a short burst from seven o'clock, conserving his ammunition by quickly tapping on the trigger. Rounds tore through the Judy's cockpit and engine area as it continued its leftward turn. The doomed bomber rolled over to port, going inverted before crashing into the churning swell below.[13]

Nightfall should have ended operations off Formosa, providing a brief respite for weary aviators across the fast carrier task force, but another day of operations was added at the last second to account for *Canberra*. Admiral Halsey had decided to tow the powerless cruiser out of harm's way. Covering operations were needed to neutralize enemy airfields until *Canberra* was safely outside the range of Japanese aircraft.[14]

Air Group 18 was once again sent to Shinchiku, which remained a threat despite successive days of damaging strikes. There was still a lack of detailed information concerning this important target. It took time to develop a better picture of the complex, figuratively and literally. Photographs snapped by Fighting 18 recon pilots, especially Redman Beatley, allowed intelligence officers aboard ship to assemble a large-scale map of Shinchiku. The strikes on 14 October could now be engineered in painstaking detail. During ready room briefings, fighter and dive bomber pilots were handed images of the specific targets they were assigned and shown maps of their location within the wider airfield.

Unlike most strike packages, there were no VT-18 planes on this mission. Though they could carry the most ordnance, Avengers were slower and forced fighters to focus more on escort duty. Instead, the strike composition was twenty Hellcats—even more than were committed during the first fighter sweep against Formosa—and twelve Helldivers. The results were excellent. Whereas damage assessment after earlier strikes had been complicated by poor weather, robust anti-aircraft defenses, and difficulty identifying exact targets, the first strike of the day on 14 October left an oxygen plant, railroad roundhouse, fuel storage, transformer station, and various buildings seriously damaged or destroyed. The action report noted with satisfaction that "it is probable that more substantial damage was done by this strike than had been inflicted by all the other operations against this target."[15]

Only a few Japanese planes were airborne over Shinchiku during the strike, including a Judy shot down by Woody Woodward and Flaps O'Maley, and a Frances downed by Rudy Van Dyke and William Bland. All that was visible on the ground were decoys and trainer aircraft. Had the previous day's raid finished off the last of the T Air Attack Force?

While Air Group 18 continued working over northern Formosa on 14 October, Japanese snooper aircraft fanned out along the coast to test the fleet's defenses and report its position. Given *Intrepid*'s investment of fighters on the morning strike, other carriers were covering CAP for the first half of the day. Planes from *Bunker Hill* and *Essex* splashed inbound attackers around noon.[16] Activity picked up considerably after that. Snooping gave way to raids by larger groups of bombers just in time for Fighting 18 pilots to have the CAP duty. They had been stellar on offense so far. It was time to see how they performed during their first real test defending their ship.

Effective CAP missions relied on fighter direction, a relatively new discipline made possible by rapid advances in radar technology. The Royal Navy started using radar for shipboard aircraft control in 1940. The U.S. Navy only started seriously distributing and testing this technology in the months leading up to Pearl Harbor. Three of the eight battleships present that day were equipped with CXAM radar sets. Carriers like USS *Yorktown* likewise had this equipment available, but the men operating it were still developing best practices with extremely limited resources. They did not have adequate staff or shipboard space allocated for their mission. That would soon change; the Navy's newest carrier, USS *Hornet*, was slated to enter service in October 1941 and was being designed as the first American carrier with a dedicated radar plot.[17]

Over the course of the next three years, the technology required to effectively detect and track targets in the air—and the training needed to turn this information into coordinated action—advanced by leaps and bounds. Fighter direction schools were established in San Diego, CA, and Norfolk, VA, in the fall of 1941. Identification friend or foe systems were widely available by the end of 1942, enhancing the ability of shipboard personnel to distinguish between attacking and defending aircraft. Plan position indicator screens had increasingly higher resolution, making it easier for radar operators to interpret developing raids.[18]

The fighter direction school in San Diego trained the officers taking center stage in this drama. Though its inaugural class was composed of just twenty-five men, in 1942 the school was moved to Camp Catlin, Hawaii, where it expanded to include instruction in air plotting, tactical radar control, and other combat information center (CIC) duties. Demand for these positions boomed. By September 1944 nearly two thousand officers and enlisted men received instruction at Camp Catlin each month.[19] In less than three years the Navy had gone from having no specific accommodations for fighter direction aboard its fleet carriers—with equipment incapable of telling friend from foe or altitude of incoming aircraft—to having an entire suite expressly for this purpose, filled with state-of-the-art equipment manned by over two dozen highly trained specialists.[20]

Lt. Robert W. "Jeep" Daniels was at the center of the CAP mission on 14 October. As *Intrepid*'s intercept officer and fighter director officer (FDO) in training, he was the principal voice guiding Fighting 18 pilots toward incoming bombers. The ship's dimly lit CIC was bustling that afternoon. Around him, radar officers, enlisted plotters, and board keepers constantly updated information on the whereabouts of Japanese planes, playing connect-the-dots with grease pencils on large plexiglass grids. Daniels could see the attack developing in real time on his plan position indicator screen, which showed a sizable blob of light where the "bandits," or identified enemy planes, were making their way toward the task group. He had to communicate all the information coming to him as quickly and clearly as possible to ensure that CAP pilots stayed between the incoming raid and the ship. Fortunately, he knew exactly what they needed to hear and how to tell them.[21]

Daniels graduated from the New Mexico Military Institute in 1941, where he earned the nickname "Jeep" for his toughness on the gridiron and in the boxing ring. He went straight into the Navy's aviation cadet program afterward. He exhibited the sort of confidence and drive the Navy looked for in its fighters. "Just call me ace," he wrote home in July 1941 while still undergoing training. Sure enough, after getting his wings in 1942, Jeep found himself in the cockpit of an F4F Wildcat participating in Operation Torch and later the Solomon Islands campaign. Before Fighting 18's deployment aboard *Intrepid*, he had as much combat experience as any of the squadron's pilots, with the possible exception of Cecil Harris. It took the allure of cutting-edge technology, the curiosity to learn new trades, and the desire to assist the war effort in a greater capacity to pull Jeep out of the cockpit and into intercept training in 1943. His combat credentials made him an instant brother-in-arms and a voice of authority among *Intrepid*'s fighters.[22]

Daniels' voice crackled through the radio. "Vector zero six zero, angels one, buster. . . . Close up, Spider."[23] He could see Lt. Bud Burnett's four-plane division heading out on his scope. Spider Foltz flew wing on Burnett but wasn't keeping station as near as Daniels wanted. "Angels one" meant a mere one thousand feet—close to the water—and "buster" meant that pilots should be flying at their maximum sustainable speed to quickly reach the target. Between the drop in altitude, change in airspeed, and excitement of the hunt, Burnett's division had shaken loose. Foltz gave a "Wilco" of acknowledgment and slid back into position, getting as close as he dared to his section leader's Hellcat. The crackling of the radio made him think the order actually came from Bud Burnett. Spider Foltz was determined to stick to his wing like glue for the rest of the chase.

"Close up, Spider!" Jeep Daniels repeated emphatically. Spider Foltz still thought it was Bud Burnett chastising him over the radio. He was getting angry. Couldn't his leader see that he'd already made the adjustment? Their planes were practically touching. They'd been flying together for hours through bad weather without issue, and now he was being heaped with abuse for one little mistake. That was the last straw. Foltz hollered back over the radio, "I CAN'T get any closer, Bud!" Daniels and Burnett thought this case of mistaken identity was hilarious. It became a big inside joke for the men who'd heard the back-and-forth. But the chase was still afoot. From that point on, they had to keep the radio circuit clear in case there were any new vectors or one of the divisions "Tallyhoed" the raid.

Jeep Daniels gave his CAP pilots a few small course corrections toward an imposing rain squall. They were at the edge of the task group now, approaching one of the picket ships forming the group's defensive perimeter. Burnett scanned up and down, from the whitecaps below to the dark gray clouds a few hundred feet above. He was used to being vectored in at higher altitude. He didn't see any sign of the approaching bombers but had faith in Jeep and the radar team aboard ship. His patience paid off. A second later, a line of twelve Japanese planes—mostly D4Y Judy dive bombers—punched out of the clouds overhead, flying almost perpendicular to his division. This was it! As the bombers flew by, Burnett reported the composition of the enemy force and brought his division into a tight turn. They needed to destroy the enemy planes as far from the center of the task group as possible, both to prevent them from succeeding in their mission and to remain clear of friendly anti-aircraft fire.

Burnett's division caught up to the bombers in mere seconds. Enemy planes broke ranks and jettisoned ordnance as soon as the Hellcats struck, jinking from side to side to throw off their aim. Rear gunners tried to return fire but found themselves shooting at open air each time their pilots changed direction. Burnett took down three of the bombers. He started from below, climbing over top of his prey with each successive pass until, on his last run, he attacked with the altitude advantage. Though one gunner managed to score hits on his plane, Burnett's sturdy Hellcat absorbed the damage without issue. He'd now scored on back-to-back days during patrol missions; twice had his Hellcat been hit by enemy fire, and twice had he been able to pull through without incident. He was a bona fide ace.[24]

Near the center of the task group, other divisions were being vectored to newly spotted raids. Men in CIC had their hands full trying to track all the planes encroaching on the carriers. Their once-transparent plot boards were now crisscrossed in grease pencil tendrils snaking through the gridlines encircling the group. Status boards on the bulkheads, looking very much like chalkboards in a classroom, were constantly updated with weather reports from the ship's aerologists and details on fuel endurance and ammunition expenditure from airborne pilots.

At 1508 a large group of low-flying bombers appeared on radar fifty miles from *Intrepid*. They closed the distance so fast that general quarters alarms rang out just five minutes later. Gun batteries were released to take care of any bombers that made it through the CAP. Topside, Lt. (jg) Lockwood Barr, *Intrepid*'s visual FDO, monitored the position of recently launched planes through a pair of binoculars. If the upcoming fight strayed into the path of the ship's anti-aircraft guns, Barr needed to distinguish friend from foe while providing rapid updates on the position of planes overhead. He was CIC's last, best hope for interception, akin to a relief pitcher stepping in during the ninth inning with the bases loaded.[25]

Lt. Cecil Harris had just taken off on SNASP duty at 1515 when he received a vector from Jeep Daniels. It was another low-flying raid, except these Judy bombers were spotted miles away in clear skies. Harris could see them coming in and knew exactly how to handle the threat. He fired a deflection shot from ninety degrees, spooking the bomber pilot into breaking off his run in a hard turn to starboard. Harris anticipated the move and had already positioned himself to take advantage. Three quick bursts of gunfire caused the Judy to explode mid-air.

Harris returned to the heading the Judy was initially following. A second bomber was there winging its way toward the fleet. He rapidly caught up to the plane, firing two bursts almost exactly where he had hit the previous aircraft. Bullets climbed along the backside of the Judy's starboard wing root into the cockpit, where they most likely hit the pilot. Harris pulled off as the plane slowly nosed over and dove smoking into the water.

By this time Harris' speed had carried him from the edge of the carrier group back to the center, where friendly anti-aircraft fire was heaviest. It was dangerous to loiter there too long. Harris pulled back to the destroyer screen instead. Scanning the horizon, he could see a Hellcat chasing a Judy, diving and circling back around for additional passes like a crow harassing a hawk.

How was the Judy still airworthy? One or two passes should have brought it down.

Lt. Frank Hearrell, the pilot of that Hellcat, had lined up his shots perfectly. His guns were barking, but the Judy didn't stagger or smoke; it just kept evading. Harris knew that something was wrong. He closed to two hundred yards before opening fire. The Judy burst into flames. At only one hundred feet altitude, it didn't take long for the plane to crash into the sea. It was later determined that Hearrell's Hellcat had not been properly inspected before he received it, and that its guns were improperly sighted. If this had been a strike mission over enemy territory or if Japanese fighters had accompanied the bomber, this could have been Lt. Hearrell's final mission.[26]

Although CAP and SNASP pilots splashed more than a dozen enemy planes at the edge of the carrier group, some had broken through the defensive perimeter. Ens. George "Laffy" Naff was one of the aviators braving friendly fire from his own ship to drive off the attackers. He shot down a Judy from three o'clock, stitching gunfire over its nose. His diving attack gave him enough speed for a quick climb above another bomber, which he blasted out of the sky. But a third Judy was flying low over the water, apparently unseen by the ships' gunners. Naff watched it pull up off the ocean's surface in a near-vertical climb over the carriers. Anti-aircraft fire blossomed all around as it drew closer to the apex of its climb. Naff yanked back on the stick in a desperate attempt to catch the plane before it could dive. He closed rapidly with friendly fire all around him. Just when he got within range for his guns to find their mark, the bomber nosed over and began to pick up speed.

Both pilots raced downward. They pushed through a barrage of 40-mm shells and streams of tracer fire from 20-mm guns. Naff's Hellcat was much faster than the Judy, though. He let himself reach extreme close range despite the danger, waiting until the last second before opening fire. The Judy's wing erupted in flames and practically ripped off the fuselage where Naff hit it. The plane spun out of control before crashing harmlessly into the water. Naff had prevented its pilot from completing his mission. With friendly fire still bursting all around him, Naff hit the deck and got out of there as fast as he could. His prop wash whipped the wavetops as he zigzagged over the ocean's surface to throw off the gunners' aim. By the time he cleared the anti-aircraft fire, he was drenched in sweat.[27]

At a cost of over two dozen attack aircraft and crews, the Japanese scored near misses and a glancing blow that bounced off one of *Hancock*'s 20-mm gun tubs, detonating in the water alongside the ship. It was a paltry showing for the vaunted T Air Attack Force. In their first real test on CAP duty, on the other hand, Fighting 18 had passed with flying colors. Admiral Bogan's own FDO, Lt. Cdr. Francis Winston, said it was the best interception work he had ever seen.[28]

Given the difficulties involved with towing *Canberra* and the need for additional covering ships, USS *Houston* bid goodbye to *Intrepid*'s Task Group 38.2 on the afternoon of 14 October and headed south to provide additional support to Task Group 38.1. But that unit's hard luck continued. *Houston* had no more than reached its new station when nighttime raids developed. Even with fighters downing nineteen enemy planes and shipboard gunners claiming ten, a single Frances bomber from the T Air Attack Force's 762nd Air Group slipped through the cracks, scoring a torpedo hit on *Houston*. Now Task Group 38.1 had two disabled ships to deal with.[29]

Admiral Halsey again made the decision to tow rather than scuttle the vessels. He planned to use the slow-moving ships as bait for Japanese surface forces. Halsey detached *Houston* and *Canberra* from Task Group 38.1 along with a small number of escorts, dangling them out on a line for the enemy. That decision invited more attacks by determined Japanese air forces, which scored a second torpedo hit on *Houston* on 16 October. Thanks to Herculean efforts by damage control teams, however, *Houston* remained afloat.

Japanese aviators returning from these nighttime attacks off the coast of Formosa reported the country's biggest victory since Pearl Harbor. Their estimates included eleven carriers and two battleships sunk, and dozens of other vessels damaged.[30] These wild claims in no way reflected the reality of the situation—two cruisers were seriously damaged and no ships were sunk—but they were shared with the Japanese public anyway through newspaper articles with headlines such as "Desperately Fleeing Enemy Warships Completely Destroyed."[31] The news triggered celebrations in Japan and even an imperial rescript from the emperor marking this "unprecedented victory."[32]

To be fair to the Japanese pilots participating in these attacks, identifying targets in the dark and avoiding duplication of claims were difficult even for experienced aviators. Exaggerated claims occurred on the Allied side as well. Over the course of the Formosa air battle, Halsey's pilots reported 655 enemy aircraft destroyed on the ground and in the air. Post war researchers using Japanese sources peg a more accurate loss estimate at 492 aircraft, which would mean claims by Task Force 38 pilots were inflated by as much as 25 percent.[33]

This should not be attributed to intentional distortion when a simpler explanation exists. In the ferocious air combat of 12 October, for example, how could any pilot traveling hundreds of miles per hour with dozens of planes around him be expected to perfectly account for the difference between damaging and destroying an enemy, or to disentangle his own victory from another pilot hitting the same target? Regardless of the final figures, the most important result of the Formosa air battle was that Japan suffered huge losses of trained aviators and aircraft. There was no way to replace said losses, especially not the carrier pilots who had been diverted to the defense of Formosa. In contrast, Halsey's fleet was left almost fully intact. His carriers lost fewer than one hundred aircraft out of over one thousand.[34]

Returning to 16 October, Japanese combined fleet planners believed *Houston* and *Canberra* were part of the fleeing remnants of Halsey's "defeated" carrier force. In response, Admiral Kiyohide Shima's surface forces, including a few cruisers and a destroyer division, were sent down from Japan's Inland Sea to take advantage of the situation.[35] As tired as Fighting 18's aviators were after successive days of intense operations, the prospect of engaging the Japanese fleet greatly excited some of them.

Punchy Mallory flew CAP on the afternoon of 16 October after being held in readiness all morning. He got his hopes up when a sighting report came in from *Bunker Hill*, but they were quickly dashed. The search aircraft had been spotted, and Admiral Shima made the prudent decision to retire from the area realizing that Halsey's carriers were still a threat. Mallory landed back aboard *Intrepid*, dejected. The next day he scribbled in his diary, "All of us are rather disappointed that the Japs didn't come on out and attack but we still have hopes. This is the most confident bunch of fighters I've ever seen. Just itching for a scrap."[36]

With the Formosa air battle behind them, Halsey's carrier groups were ordered to shift their focus back to the Philippines in anticipation of Operation King II, Gen. Douglas MacArthur's long-awaited return to the Philippines. Half of the carrier task groups were assigned to strike central Luzon around Manila, while *Intrepid*'s Task Group 38.2 went to northern Luzon.

Pilots' experiences at Manila and northern Luzon could not have been more different. Whereas the two carrier groups covering Manila Bay on 18 October ran into serious airborne opposition, leading to the destruction of dozens of enemy aircraft,[37] *Intrepid*'s group saw no Japanese planes in the air during their morning sweep to the north. In fact, only one plane was encountered in northern Luzon airspace during the whole day. On the plus side, there were still aircraft on the ground and shipping vessels in the waterways.[38]

Strike 2A took off from *Intrepid* at 0815 led by CAG Ellis, who once again served as overall target coordinator. It was a short hop to the northeastern coast of Luzon where the verdant Sierra Madre Mountains—the longest mountain chain in the Philippines—stretched over the horizon to the south. To the west, flat farmland flanked the Cagayan River, the longest river in the Philippines. After weeks of strikes on tiny islands in the Palaus, Ryukyus, and Visayas, the landscape sprawling out below them must have seemed truly epic.

Planes from *Bunker Hill* were sent farther west to Laoag, where more parked aircraft were reported, while *Intrepid*'s air group took on shipping at Aparri, situated at the mouth of the Cagayan River. A fighter sweep launched earlier that morning had reported good hunting at the Aparri port. When the groups arrived at their respective targets, however, it appeared to be a bust. "Little of interest" was found. Conflicting feelings likely swirled in cockpits: sighs of relief for a milk run after the meat grinder of Formosa and grumbles of disappointment at lost opportunities to run up scores or bomb targets of value.[39]

Lt. Fred Tracy, one of the senior men in Fighting 18, flew with Commander Ellis at the head of the group, keeping a lookout for something worth dropping his five-hundred-pound bomb on. As he continued following Ellis, Tracy saw a sudden flash of silver in the direction of Cape Engaño, a horn-shaped spit of land jutting out from the northeastern corner of Luzon. It was just a momentary glimpse, but it amounted to more than he had seen all day. Tracy radioed his intent to investigate and received permission to break off from the group. His descent revealed the glinting objects to be Japanese float-planes bobbing in a little bay between Luzon and nearby Palaui Island. One plane, a single-engine Jake fighter, barely made it off the water before Tracy's Hellcat screamed down from above. Its pilot didn't stand a chance. A second Jake was still tied to a nearby buoy. Tracy raked it with his guns, sinking it easily. He continued over to a nearby boat, firing on the hapless vessel until he forced it to beach itself on a nearby island.

Tracy had a good haul given the paucity of action at Aparri and Laoag, but as he pulled up from his run, he spotted an even juicier target. His dive had taken him north of the strike to within visual range of the Babuyan Islands. Four large transports were nestled in a bay on the west coast of the closest island. They were still at anchor, blissfully unaware that enemy planes were right around the corner. Tracy radioed Ellis with the news, and the CAG immediately shifted the bulk of the strike to destroy the transports.[40]

Bunker Hill fighters and dive bombers took on the largest of the vessels while *Intrepid* aviators were assigned to the remaining targets. This opportunity was too good to pass up: target practice on real enemy ships with virtually no danger posed to the pilots involved. Ellis instructed his men to take their time. Dive bomber pilots made repeated dives, judging their angle of attack and practicing high-speed pullouts. They blew through more than three thousand rounds of 20-mm ammunition.

"It was a fruitful morning's work," the aircraft action report concluded before moving on to photo documentation of the strike. Silhouettes of passenger-cargo ships converted for military use were visible along the shoreline, each one trailing long streamers of smoke. One photo captured close-up details of a ship, including the pennants running between its superstructures. The next image was of a massive smoke cloud completely obscuring the ship, which sank.[41]

The invasion of Leyte began a few days later. The flagship of Task Force 77 under Vice Adm. Thomas Kinkaid arrived at the approaches to Leyte Gulf on A-day, the morning of 20 October 1944, to help usher in a massive landing force consisting of 202,500 men. The weather was perfect, and after naval bombardment and airstrikes by Kinkaid's planes, ground forces advanced rapidly without encountering much resistance. It was an auspicious start to one of the biggest logistical undertakings in the Pacific.[42]

One day later, Air Group 18 knocked out enemy airfields in the vicinity of Leyte. These were expected to be milk runs compared with previous missions, but after Formosa, the men remained on guard. Morning fighter sweeps and strikes always seemed to encounter the stiffest resistance. War correspondent Ray Coll Jr. could feel the tension among the pilots in the fighter ready room waiting for their afternoon assignments. There was little of the chatter that indicated light spirits and easy minds. In lieu of conversation, someone put Bing Crosby's "San Fernando Valley" on the phonograph. The song's lyrics talked about settling down and forgetting the past after a long, lonely journey. It was aspirational, if a bit saccharine. The waiting fighters kept on smoking, drinking coffee, playing acey-deucy, and waiting to hear the news as Crosby crooned in the background.[43]

The fighter sweep was assigned the islands of Masbate and Panay, to the west of Leyte. Strafing fighters destroyed twenty parked aircraft at San Jose airfield on Panay. The only plane encountered in the air was a Sally, a Japanese heavy bomber of 1930s vintage that stood no chance against a pack of hungry Hellcats. Its pilot tried to sneak away at low altitude. Cecil Harris quickly spotted the plane and dove with his wingman, Franklin Burley, in tow. Harris hit the Sally first, causing it to trail a streamer of smoke. Burley struck next. The plane caught fire, unable to withstand the abuse it took from a combined twelve .50-caliber machine guns. It was heading for the ground when Harris came back around for a second pass. The lumbering bomber exploded midair.[44]

When the morning strike and sweep returned without incident, the mood in the ready room changed. Conversation started back up. Men milled around to hear the latest news. It would have been easier for the squadron's intelligence officer, Lt. Harry Cropper, if they all stayed put. He was busy interviewing the new arrivals about their experiences. In the report he drew up later that day, credit for destroying the Sally went to Burley, making him an ace. There was no official Navy guideline for determining who to credit when two or more pilots downed a single enemy. Instead, it was up to individual air combat intelligence officers like Cropper to decide how to divvy up credit.[45] Harris and Burley may have flipped a coin, like they had on 12 October, or Cropper may have thought, based on the pilots' debriefs, that this decision made sense. Harris also could have advocated for his wingman to ensure he became an ace. Regardless of the reason or outcome, both Harris and Burley knew that at the end of the day, what mattered was teamwork, not bragging rights.

The full strikes turned out to be as uneventful as the sweep: A couple of cargo ships were attacked, some flimsy structures around airbases were flattened, and two more airborne enemies—a Helen bomber and a Zeke fighter—were encountered. Snuffy Mayer destroyed the Helen on the first strike, strike 2A, but Punchy Mallory could only claim a probable on strike 2B after chasing the Zekes away.[46] His photographic mission took priority over tangling with enemy fighters. Mallory was annoyed with how close he'd come to scoring and quietly scolded himself for the missed opportunity. He was determined that next time, he'd formulate a plan of attack before springing into action.[47]

The air group had now been in combat for almost two straight weeks. This pace was unsustainable, but with boots freshly landed on Leyte, the odds of receiving a break were slim to none. This was doubly true since Task Groups 38.1 and 38.4 were scheduled to head to Ulithi for replenishment. *Hancock* was detached from *Intrepid*'s Task Group 38.2 to serve as escort for its war-weary siblings, leaving Task Group 38.3 as the only full-strength carrier group off the Philippines.[48]

Maintaining morale at this halfway point of the squadron's deployment was vital. Jam sessions in the torpedo ready room were a popular diversion. The air group war history recalls the aviators as talented musicians but poor singers and dancers. The basketball team led by Pop Thune usually won its games against the ship's company, boosting spirits.[49] And Ed Ritter put a lighthearted touch on their shared experiences with a series of watercolors focused on the misadventures of Snipo Blankenship. Snipo stresses over pre-launch routine, endures friendly fire, kisses the flight deck after surviving his first mission, and finally returns home as a featured guest at war bond drives. Ritter's art left an impression on visiting press photographers as well. They snapped pictures of Ritter and all twenty-six watercolors he produced aboard ship.[50]

If the men in Fighting 18 were tired after Formosa, those in *Bunker Hill's* Fighting 8 were completely exhausted. They had been at sea since March 1944 on a tour of duty that never seemed to end. On 20 October the air group's flight surgeon grounded twenty of the fighters—roughly half of the squadron—due to combat fatigue. The next day, Admiral Bogan suggested the whole air group be sent home. *Bunker Hill* was subsequently detached from Task Group 38.2 to drop Air Group 8 off at Manus and pick up a replacement group.[51] *Intrepid* was the last fleet carrier left in its depleted task group.

VF-18 group photo taken in Hawaii in May 1944. Seated on ground (*left to right*): Charles Gillaspie, Louis Michaud, Irby Johnson, Lonnie Passmore. *First row* (*left to right*): Robert O'Maley, Roy Burnett, Robert Morris, Franklin Burley, I. Wesley Keels, Ralph DuPont, Anthony Denman, Rudy Van Dyke, John Valentine, Edward Murphy, Clarence Blouin, Frank Hearrell, Harold Thune, Harry Cropper, Art Haig, Richard Cevoli, Leonard Woodward, Donald Watts, George Griffith, William Murray. *Middle row* (*left to right*): James Newsome, Harvey Picken, Robert Hurst, Robert Davis, Frederick Wolff, W. Henry Sartwelle, Winton Horn, William Bland, C. Paul Amerman, Arthur Mollenhauer, Redman Beatley, Edward Ritter, William Ziemer, Egidio DiBatista, George Eckel, Robert Simpson, J. Larry Donoghue. *Back row* (*left to right*): John Herlihy, Robert Gowling, Charles Mallory, Thomas Rennemo, Robert Brownell, John Mayer, James Neighbours, Noel Thompson, Cecil Harris, Bryant Walworth, William Mufich, Frank Foltz, Edgar Blankenship. *Collection of the Intrepid Museum, gift of Fred DuPont*

One of the operational training units where Fighting 18 pilots first formed friendships. This group included John Herlihy (*kneeling, front left*), Bill Ziemer (*kneeling, third from left*), and James Newsome (*standing, third from left*). Courtesy of John Herlihy

Another operational training unit with future members of VF-18. This group, referred to in Bryant Walworth's diary as Flight 65, included future VF-18 pilots Walworth (*kneeling, far right*), Franklin Burley (*standing, second from left*), and C. Paul Amerman (*standing, third from left*). Thomas Sorensen (*kneeling, far left*), Walworth's roommate, was killed during training with this unit. *Collection of the Intrepid Museum, gift of the family of Charles Paul Amerman*

Division training in Hawaii (*left to right*): John Herlihy, James Newsome, Clarence Blouin, and Edgar Blankenship *Collection of the Intrepid Museum, gift of the family of Lt. E. G. Blankenship*

Division training in Hawaii (*left to right*): Harvey Picken, Harold Thune, George Griffith, and Bill Murray Courtesy of Jackie Case

Division training in Hawaii (*left to right*): Bill Mufich, Robert Davis, George Eckel, and Tony Denman *Courtesy of Robert L. Lawson Collection, Emil Buehler Naval Aviation Library, National Naval Aviation Museum*

Division training in Hawaii (*left to right*): Robert Gowling, I. Wesley Keels, Ralph DuPont, and Frank Hearrell *Collection of the Intrepid Museum, gift of Fred DuPont*

Edgar Blankenship, John Mayer, and Noel Thompson sometime between late 1943 and mid-1944 *Collection of the Intrepid Museum, gift of the family of Lt. E. G. Blankenship*

Robert O'Maley and Robert Morris pose for the camera during training. *Collection of the Intrepid Museum, gift of Larry Donoghue*

Squadron members cool off somewhere in Hawaii. The man jumping into the water at right appears to be Charles Mallory. *Larry Donoghue collection, courtesy of Patti Cashman*

Spearfishing and hunting game were popular pursuits on days off in Hawaii. These men returned empty-handed but in good spirits. *Left to right*: Robert Gowling, C. Paul Amerman, Charles Mallory, Donald Watts, and Robert Hurst. *Collection of the Intrepid Museum, gift of the family of Charles Paul Amerman*

Skipper Edward Murphy, standing at right, poses for a press photo with (*left to right*) Charles Mallory, Frederick Wolff, and John Mayer. *Courtesy of the Murphy family*

This aerial view of USS *Intrepid* was captured during Air Group 18's time aboard ship. Aircraft visible on the flight deck have an equal-armed cross painted on their tails, which was used as a recognition symbol specific to the group. *Collection of the Intrepid Museum*

Men position a VF-18 Hellcat fighter plane onto *Intrepid*'s number-two deck edge elevator to get it topside for the next strike, 29 October 1944. *Collection of the Intrepid Museum*

Looking aft on *Intrepid*'s flight deck, the spotting order is evidenced by the sleek F6F-5 Hellcats on the left side in the shadow of the tower; the vertical folding wings of SB2C Helldivers unfurling in preparation for takeoff; and barely visible behind them, TBM-1c Avengers with wings folded back along the fuselage. The foremost Helldiver on the right is receiving a checkered flag for takeoff. *Collection of the Intrepid Museum*

Men watch from the gun tubs and catwalks on *Intrepid*'s port side as Hellcats prepare for launch. *Collection of the Intrepid Museum*

A view of flight operations from *Intrepid*'s bridge. An F6F-5 Hellcat of Fighting 18 is catapulted off the starboard side of the flight deck. An SB2C Helldiver is visible to port. This picture was taken some time after *Intrepid* suffered its first kamikaze attack on 29 October 1944. Collection of the Intrepid Museum

Lt. Richard Moot, *Intrepid*'s landing signal officer, used his paddles to help bring aviators safely back aboard ship or to wave them off for another pass if their approach was poor or the deck was fouled. Charles Mallory and Bryant Walworth both attested to Moot's skill, crediting him with bringing their damaged Hellcats in for successful arrested landings.

Collection of the Intrepid Museum, gift of Albert Brody

Lt. Kenneth Crusoe, a replacement pilot added to VF-18 on 27 October 1944, participated in one of the squadron's biggest air battles on 29 October over Clark Field. His Hellcat sustained serious damage, leading to a crash-landing aboard *Intrepid*. Crusoe had to be helped out of the cockpit and onto a stretcher for transportation to the carrier's sick bay. *Collection of the Intrepid Museum*

VF-18 photo unit members (*left to right*) Lt. (jg) Charles Mallory, Lt. Harvey Picken, and Lt. (jg) Redman Beatley, flank their peer, Lt. (jg) Edward Ritter, as he works on one of his shipboard watercolors during their deployment aboard USS *Intrepid*. The man at far right is identified as Chief Pharmacist's Mate Don Fray. *Collection of the Intrepid Museum, gift of Mike Fink*

Edward Ritter's finished watercolor as seen in the press photo. The image is captioned, "Home Sweet Home! The carrier deck, to the Zoomie on his first return from a mission, looks good enough to kiss. The Hellcat too looks as though it could use a little 'shut-eye.' "

Collection of the Intrepid Museum, gift of Edward Arthur Ritter and Valerie Junge

Edward Ritter depicts himself sketching goings-on from the back of the Fighting 18 ready room. In the aisle between chairs, Edgar Blankenship is exchanging words with John Mayer. In the front left corner of the room, two men—likely including skipper Ed Murphy—play a game of acey-deucey. *Collection of the Intrepid Museum, gift of Edward Arthur Ritter and Valerie Junge*

Lt. Cecil Harris (*left*) and Ens. Arthur Mollenhauer are shown aboard their carrier on 13 October 1944 after they shot down nine Japanese planes between them during the first day of the attack on Formosa. Lieutenant Harris accounted for four of the Japanese would-be defenders, and Ensign Mollenhauer is credited with five. *Photo by Bettmann Archive/Getty Images*

Wingman Lt. (jg) C. Paul Amerman (*left*) and his section leader, Lt. Donald Watts. Together with VB-18's Lt. (jg) R. Max Adams and his rear-seater, Aviation Radioman Third Class Cornelius Clark, they helped locate and report the composition of Admiral Kurita's battleship force on 24 October 1944 during the Battle of Leyte Gulf. *Collection of the Intrepid Museum, gift of the family of Charles Paul Amerman*

Men fight fires topside as smoke pours out of *Intrepid* after back-to-back kamikaze attacks on 25 November 1944. In total, sixty-nine officers and men were killed, making this the deadliest attack on *Intrepid* in the ship's history. *Collection of the Intrepid Museum*

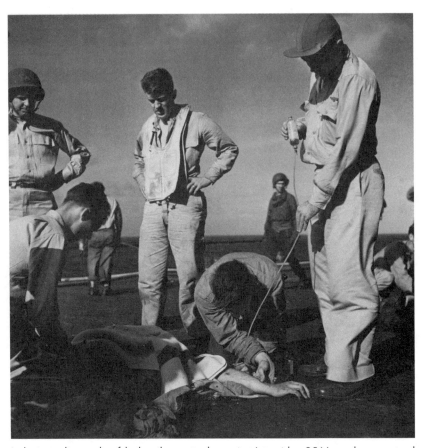

In the immediate wake of the kamikaze attacks against *Intrepid* on 25 November, men tend to the wounded and dead. Lt. R. W. Daniels, *Intrepid*'s intercept officer (*standing center*), and other men attempted to resuscitate Lt. Cdr. John Fish, the air group's flight surgeon, to no avail. Fish was killed while providing aid to men injured in the first attack. *Barrett L. Gallagher photographs and film, Division of Rare and Manuscript Collections, Cornell University Library*

A party for the fighters. When Dive and Torpedo 18 learned they would be home for Christmas 1944 but their counterparts in Fighting 18 were being retained in the Pacific, they celebrated their friendship and showed their appreciation with a huge party in the torpedo ready room. From left to right in the front row are VF-18's Rudy Van Dyke, Freddy Wolff, John Mayer, Thomas Rennemo, and VT-18's Kenny Barden. In the second row, VF-18's Edgar Blankenship is second from the left, smiling, with his arm around VT-18's Bud Williams. Second from left in the back row, behind Williams, is VF-18's Frank Hearrell. To the right of the liquor bottle in the back row are Noel Thompson and VT-18's Bernard St. John (*both shirtless*) and VF-18's Charles Mallory, with an unidentified man at far right. *Collection of the Intrepid Museum, gift of the family of Lt. E. G. Blankenship*

After breaking his leg bailing out of his damaged plane during the Formosa air battle, Egidio DiBatista was sent home to convalesce. Sometime in early 1945 he was visited by squadron mates John Herlihy (*left*) and James Newsome. *Courtesy of Kent Newsome*

This group photo appears to date from early 1945. Seated at the bar (*left to right*) are Franklin Burley, Noel Thompson, and Thomas Rennemo. Standing (*left to right*) are Rudy Van Dyke, John Mayer, Frederick Wolff, Clarence Blouin, Edgar Blankenship, Frederick Tracy, and Harvey Picken. *Courtesy of Jackie Case*

Lt. Cecil Harris (*left*) of VF-18 and Cdr. David McCampbell (*right*) of Air Group 15 sign autographs at a publicity shoot celebrating the Navy's top two aces of World War II. Their combined score of fifty-eight enemy planes destroyed in aerial combat is displayed behind the group. *Collection of the Intrepid Museum, gift of Mike Fink*

CHAPTER 8

LEYTE GULF
In the Sibuyan Sea

ORGANIZING INVASION FORCES, managing resupply logistics, coordinating air support, and all the other individual elements of large-scale campaigns required painstaking scientific management. This was doubly true of the war in the Pacific, whose supply chain stretched across thousands of miles of ocean. Bringing these component parts together at a particular place and time was even more complicated due to all the knock-on effects produced by changes to any one part of the larger plan. The decision to move the invasion of Leyte from December to October 1944, for example, promised to keep the initiative firmly in Allied hands, but also meant there was no hope for land-based air support when troops first made landfall on 20 October.[1] The new plan required carriers in the Third and Seventh Fleets to conduct all of the strike, close air support, and fleet patrol missions before, during, and immediately after this critical initial phase of operations.

Admiral Halsey knew his carrier task groups were reaching their breaking point because of this heightened tempo. His aviators were flying constantly; shipboard crews were laboring day and night to load, arm, and spot aircraft. Task Force 38 desperately needed to rest before Operation Hotfoot. This next move on the naval chessboard called for carrier strikes against the islands of Kyushu and Honshu—the very heart of Japan.[2] Steaming that far into enemy waters required Admiral Halsey's carriers to be at full strength. On 21 October, only a day after Army forces swarmed over the beaches at Dulag and Tacloban on Leyte, Halsey asked General MacArthur for permission to withdraw from the area.

Halsey was rebuffed by both his own boss, Admiral Nimitz, and by MacArthur. The plan they had agreed to relied on the support of the Third Fleet. If Halsey's carriers withdrew, it would leave the network of support vessels in Leyte Gulf at the mercy of enemy aircraft. Halsey decided that if he could not fully replenish his forces, he would have to rotate individual task groups piecemeal, hoping that he could maintain a watchful eye on the Philippines while slowly reconstituting his striking power.[3]

There did seem to be a silver lining. Allied Army and Navy planners believed that the Imperial Japanese Navy would conserve its surface forces for a fight closer to home. Instead of committing warships to contest control of Leyte Gulf, they would send convoys through the Philippines to support their ground forces.[4] Convoys of Japanese troops and supplies, nicknamed the "Tokyo Express," were undoubtedly a problem, but they did not pose an existential threat to the Third Fleet or the ships of the Seventh Fleet under its protection. Neither Admiral Halsey nor Admiral Kinkaid, his counterpart in command of the Seventh Fleet, believed a major surface battle was brewing. In fact, even after Admiral Kinkaid received sighting reports on 22 October indicating the possible presence of Japanese battleships off the western Philippines, he messaged Halsey and the commanders of the Army's Fifth and Thirteenth Air Forces that he regarded "the approach of enemy combatant ships and tankers . . . as the first phase of the build up of magnified Tokyo Express runs against Leyte."[5]

Halsey and Kinkaid received a rude awakening the following day, when submarines *Darter* and *Dace* shadowed and attacked this "magnified Tokyo Express." The enemy force reportedly consisted of approximately a dozen ships—all surface combatants—which *Darter* suspected to be the Imperial Japanese Navy's "first team."[6] This wasn't a resupply mission: the enemy had unleashed its largest, most heavily armed warships to stop the invasion at its source.

If the Japanese fleet was finally coming out to fight, it only had a few ways to reach Leyte Gulf. Admiral Halsey divided responsibility for covering these approaches between his carrier task group commanders based on their location along the eastern flank of the Philippines. Task Group 38.3 covered the extreme northern approach in case of an end run around Luzon; Task Group

38.2, *Intrepid*'s group, covered the middle area leading to the San Bernardino Strait, just above Samar and Leyte; and Task Group 38.4 covered the southern flank in case the Japanese fleet transited the Surigao Strait, which separated the southern tip of Leyte from Mindanao.

Aboard *Intrepid*, Adm. Gerald Bogan and his staff began drafting their search plan. He needed over two dozen planes to cover the assigned search area of 230 to 290 degrees true. Admiral Bogan's final plan called for six teams assigned to contiguous ten-degree sectors of airspace. Each team comprised a Helldiver and two Hellcats. They were numbered clockwise so that team one flew southwest to the edge of Palawan; team three flew due west over the southern end of Mindoro Island; and team six flew northwest to Manila. Separately, a special search of four Hellcats was assigned to reconnoiter Palawan's Imuruan Bay in case the enemy fleet stopped there after its run-in with *Darter* and *Dace* the previous day.[7]

These were huge distances to cover. Search pilots had to fly upward of six hundred miles round trip while scanning the sea surface for long, white wakes indicating nearby ships. Even if they located the enemy, transmitting sighting reports would be difficult from so far away. To ensure clear, speedy receipt of communications from search pilots, two radio relay fighters were stationed between *Intrepid* and the searchers to rapidly retransmit any urgent reports. Lt. Bill Millar and Ens. Bill Herpich, two of the former night fighters, were chosen for this role.

Excitement rippled through *Intrepid* just after midnight as rumors of advancing enemy forces finally reached the crew. In room 115, Punchy Mallory was reading and killing time before bed. He didn't have morning flight duty, so he could afford to stay up, unlike his bunkmate Boot Amerman, who needed to be up in less than four hours.

Mallory had been in a reflective mood lately. He had recently decided to do something every day to improve himself, starting with cursing less and writing more letters home. Shortly after charting this course, he attended a shipboard religious service that ended with a sermon on the destiny of life. It left a serious impression. It was in this frame of mind that Mallory first heard about Japanese battleships in Philippine waters.[8]

Mallory's mind likely wandered from his small room on the forward starboard edge of the hangar deck up to the forecastle and the junior officers' bunkroom. Three of its seventeen beds were vacant after Bill Ziemer, Harry Webster, and Ralph DuPont were shot down over Formosa. That was only a fraction of the air group's losses since coming aboard. What did destiny have in store for the remaining pilots? Would there be more empty beds in "boys' town" tomorrow night? Amerman was fast asleep, blissfully unaware of the news. He was scheduled for the morning sector search. What fate awaited him?

Fighting 18's ready room was electric the next morning. Men in Mae West life preservers with their goggles pulled up over the tops of their flight helmets excitedly traded scuttlebutt and made bets about the day's outcome. Amerman sat down next to his section leader, Lt. Donald Watts, as the last of the pilots filed into the room. When all those assigned were present, Lieutenant Commander Murphy pointed to a large map at the head of the room and cleared his throat. All eyes suddenly converged where the skipper was pointing—on a long, slender stretch of land that looked like it was drifting westward away from the Philippine archipelago. It was Palawan, where enemy battleships had been sighted the previous day. The room went quiet.

Murphy quickly began handing down assignments for the morning search. There was a lot of information to get through in a short amount of time. Harris would lead the special search southwest to Palawan. Murphy then paired men off into sectors sweeping clockwise up from Palawan. Sectors one and two would head into the northern end of the Sulu Sea, where a sort of cul-de-sac was formed by Coron to the west, Mindoro to the north, and Panay to the east.

Murphy continued to sector three, Watts' and Amerman's assignment. The skipper indicated a ten-degree-wide wedge stretching straight out from *Intrepid* across the southern end of Mindoro Island. Their three-hundred-mile outbound leg would take Watts and Amerman over dozens of islands and the numerous passes, gulfs, and seas dividing them. Even with the extensive search efforts being organized, the Japanese fleet was a needle in the haystack of thousands of square miles of ocean. The one saving grace was the Helldiver coming along for the ride. Lt. (jg) Max Adams would follow on Watts' and Amerman's heels while his rear seater, Aviation Radioman Third

Class Cornelius Clark, kept close watch on radar. If the enemy force was as big as they were predicting, it should appear clear as day on Clark's scope, even if the ships were beyond visual range.

The skipper continued. Sectors four and five were assigned southern Luzon from the Sibuyan Sea to Tayabas Bay. Sector six would fly as far north as Manila. While Murphy finished wrapping up his briefing, *Intrepid* steamed steadily into position under the cover of night, cutting a serpentine path toward the predawn launch point above Samar. This overnight run was followed by a turn east to get wind over the deck for rapid-fire flight operations starting just after 0600. Condensed launch times gave the planes maximum endurance for the long trip west, quickly cleared the deck of armed and fueled aircraft, and allowed *Intrepid* to get out of range of land-based bombers before the Japanese could respond.

Watts and Amerman followed the procession of search pilots as they made their way through the gallery deck. They lugged parachute packs, plot boards—all manner of gear that weighed them down and caught the wind as they stepped out onto the catwalk. They were now in the darkness swaddling the ship, groping their way aft to the ladder leading to the flight deck. When they finally made it topside, amorphous shadows loomed out of the predawn twilight where their aircraft stood ready and waiting. They trotted over to their Hellcats for a final check with their plane captains before strapping in to wait their turn for launch. Watts and Amerman felt *Intrepid* slowly turning east. Sunrise falling on the planes in front of them coalesced their silhouettes into tangible figures, limning the dark blue aircraft in pale gold light. Once Harris and the first two search sectors were airborne, Watts, Amerman, and Adams took off for southern Mindoro.

Watts led the trio of aircraft in sector three west over Masbate and through the Sibuyan Sea. The skies were clear, offering unlimited visibility of the beautiful scene below. Masbate's heavily forested eastern coast was a verdant emerald green. The lush vegetation tapered off toward the jagged western promontory forming Asid Gulf. All the islands, especially the smaller ones, seemed to be ringed in turquoise where shoal waters extended off the coast. After an hour and a half flying through this serene landscape, Clark began to pick up a radar return. Something big was out there, only about twenty-five miles away. Adams immediately relayed the news to Watts and Amerman. Together, the three let down from nine thousand feet and changed course to follow the mystery contact.

At 0746 they saw six long, white lines extending across the ocean's surface beyond the horizon. Wakes of this size indicated large ships moving quickly through the water. There was no doubt: sector three had just located a major element of the Japanese fleet. Watts immediately transmitted an emergency contact report. Bill Millar, one of the two pilots assigned to expedite communications between the searchers and the carrier group, quickly received, acknowledged, and relayed the report. Now they just had to get a proper accounting of the force so Admiral Halsey knew what he was up against.

Watts, Amerman, and Adams continued their descent until they could clearly see the enemy force. There were far more than six ships down there. In fact, there were two groups arranged in concentric circles about four miles apart, each containing more than a dozen ships. The spectacle was simultaneously breathtaking and terrifying. Getting an accurate assessment of the exact number of ships and their types required buzzing over both formations, within anti-aircraft range, for extended periods of time.

This force was deceptively named the "1st Diversion Attack Force." It would be substantially more than a diversion if it reached Leyte. Its lead group contained both of Japan's *Yamato*-class battleships, *Yamato* and *Musashi*, which each displaced over 71,000 tons fully loaded. They were the heaviest battleships ever built. Their main batteries consisted of three turrets, each sporting three 18.1-inch guns, which were the largest guns ever mounted on a warship. After the Battle of the Philippine Sea in June 1944, they were equipped with radar consoles and covered from bow to stern with additional anti-aircraft guns to account for the Allies' air superiority. Admiral Takeo Kurita, commanding the force from *Yamato*, had already ordered his ships from cruising to battle formation in anticipation of aerial attack.[9]

Watts went down first to take notes. Incredibly, despite being spotted and reported by sailors aboard *Yamato* at 0812,[10] the ships did not open fire. Watts flew as close as three miles off their starboard beam while he tallied the enemy force. Amerman and Adams supported the effort, keeping tabs on the ships' heading and confirming their sector leader's count. Watts finally delivered the news: "The force consists of 4 BB, 8 CA, 13 DD . . . no train or transports."[11] Watts, Amerman, and Adams shadowed the enemy ships for an hour and a half in total, keeping tabs on their heading and speed as they steamed intently toward Leyte Gulf.[12] Bill Millar retransmitted Watts' detailed report without missing a beat. He continued sending out amplifying transmissions as additional details came in fast and hot from the searchers in sector three.[13] Pilots in sectors four and five, like Flaps O'Maley and Chuck deMoss, got a chance to see these ships on their return to *Intrepid*. deMoss was thunderstruck. He flew as close as he dared to see the massive force for himself before continuing his journey back to the carriers.[14]

Admiral Halsey didn't need an hour of updated reports to spring into action. The first detailed report told him all he needed to know: there were no transports. Five minutes after receiving the message, he ordered his task

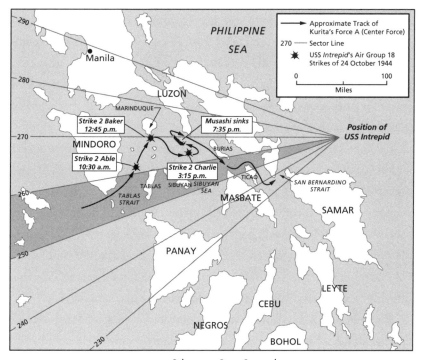

MAP 3. Sibuyan Sea Searches

group commanders in 38.3 and 38.4 to converge toward *Intrepid*'s middle position off San Bernardino Strait.[15] If the enemy force was as big as reported, he'd need all available carriers and battleships for the coming showdown. Admiral Bogan was similarly decisive. His two daytime flattops were locked and loaded with forty-five aircraft ready to launch at a moment's notice. He radioed Halsey the composition of his air forces, effectively asking permission to let his warbirds loose. He had a reply in just two minutes: "Strike repeat strike. Good luck."[16]

While all this was going on, aircraft in sectors one, two, and six encountered separate groups of ships more than fifty miles to the north and south of sector three. Lt. (jg) Ed Ritter was in sector six with VB-18's Lt. George Searle. They spotted light cruiser *Kinu* and destroyer *Uranami* off the coast of Corregidor, at the extreme northern end of *Intrepid*'s searches.[17] Searle dove through intense anti-aircraft fire from shore batteries and enemy ships, dropping his one-thousand-pound bomb close to *Kinu*'s bow before he, Ritter, and the other Hellcat pilot in their sector thoroughly strafed the damaged vessel. To the south, overlapping with search-strike aircraft from Task Group 38.4, sectors one and two observed planes from *Franklin* attacking a small group of destroyers with bombs and rockets.[18] Aircraft from *Enterprise* attacked a group of battleships even farther south. Though this last force was larger than any of the ones spotted in sectors one, two, and six, it was still much smaller than the one in sector three.[19]

Off Luzon to the north, Task Group 38.3 faced attacks by Japanese aircraft within minutes of receiving Admiral Halsey's orders to join *Intrepid*. Masterful work by *Essex*'s CAP pilots kept most of the enemies at bay. During the engagement, Cdr. David McCampbell and his wingman, Ens. Roy Rushing, shot down fifteen Japanese fighters and bombers. The enemy's attacks proved ineffective with one exception. A single plane managed to slip through the CAP's strong defenses, scoring a direct bomb hit on light carrier *Princeton*. The ship was grievously damaged and had to be scuttled later that day.[20]

Between the many groups of surface combatants being reported one after another and this fresh attack from enemy aircraft, Admiral Halsey's picture of the developing battle was confused at best. Even if it was clear that the strongest surface force was located directly in *Intrepid*'s path, the question remained: Where were the Japanese aircraft carriers? The lack of information about their whereabouts was especially troubling in the wake of the strong attack against Task Group 38.3. Ironically, while Halsey puzzled over the location of the enemy's flattops, Japanese carrier commander Vice Admiral Jisaburo Ozawa was actively trying to be found.[21]

Although the original Japanese plan of attack envisioned an active role for the once mighty *Kido Butai*, or "mobile force," Admiral Ozawa's carriers did not have enough competent aviators left to function effectively after the Formosa air battle. Even Japan's shore-based air forces were spread thin. This lack of airpower was evident where Fighting 18's searchers operated. Lieutenant Watts shot down a twin-engine Frances bomber over Samar on his return trip, and Lieutenant Harris encountered two Petes, single-engine recon seaplanes, coming back from Palawan.[22] The skies were otherwise clear. Unlike the Navy's Third Fleet, which at that moment had dozens of planes on CAP duty and scores more on attack missions, Japanese commanders had to choose between protecting their fleet and offensive operations.[23]

Due to these shortages, on 17 October Admiral Ozawa proposed to use his ships as a decoy.[24] He would sacrifice his toothless flattops to lure Admiral Halsey away from Leyte Gulf. It would be worth it to lose the carriers if the big battleships could reach the gulf unopposed. Despite his best efforts, however, Admiral Ozawa was not spotted all morning.[25] Surface forces would have to survive the coming storm without the benefit of air support or misdirection.

Commander Ellis led Air Group 18's first strike against Admiral Kurita's battleships in the Sibuyan Sea. He took off at 0850 with a combined nineteen fighters, twelve dive bombers, and thirteen torpedo planes from *Intrepid* and *Cabot*.[26] Neighboring carrier groups were still too far away to augment Task Group 38.2's meager strength. The limited number of aircraft available to Ellis for this opening salvo meant less ordnance to expend against the world's most heavily armored warships. It also meant Japanese gunners had fewer targets to focus on, allowing them to concentrate their firepower. The strike group was in for a bumpy ride.

The dive bombers were up first. Large, fluffy clouds above seven thousand feet obscured the otherwise clear sky, leaving Helldiver pilots and rear gunners in suspense until the last second. VB-18 pilot Lt. (jg) John Forsyth could feel his heart thumping in his chest from the anticipation. When his division finally emerged into the clear, it was as if someone had flipped a switch. The soft white clouds were suddenly replaced by angry puffs of orange, purple, and black smoke left behind by artillery shells. The different colors helped shipboard spotters determine which ship fired which shells so that gunners could quickly correct their aim. Forsyth and the men around him had no choice but to push through this technicolor blanket of death to complete their mission.

The two *Yamato*-class battleships fascinated Forsyth. All the ships maneuvering around them looked like toys in comparison. Almost in a trance, he navigated the buffeting blasts of anti-aircraft fire through muscle memory and instinct. He snapped out his reverie just in time to evade a cluster of shells detonating all around him. Forsyth's wingmen had already pulled clear of the danger. He watched his skipper, Lt. Cdr. George Ghesquiere, wing over hard into a nearly vertical dive on the nearest of the two massive battleships, the *Musashi*. Forsyth was next. Once he began his dive, there was no going back.[27]

VT-18's Avengers descended through the clouds after the Helldivers began their attack. The well-established order of operations had dive bombers come in first, followed by strafing fighters, torpedo attack, and then fighter cover while the lumbering Avengers did their best to get out of gun range. For their part, the torpedo pilots and crews wished the clouds would have come down a bit. Low ceilings were a nightmare prospect for dive bombers, as they had been over Kiirun Harbor, but served as a safe haven for the slow Avengers, obscuring their approach and therefore minimizing their exposure to anti-aircraft fire.

Ensign Willard "Will" Fletcher was one of six VT-18 pilots preparing for a "hammer-and-anvil" attack on *Musashi*. By splitting up into two divisions of three planes each, the Avengers could approach the target from both sides simultaneously. No matter which direction the 862-foot-long *Musashi* turned, its broadside would be exposed to torpedoes churning through the water. Fletcher's division approached the hulking battleship at 310 knots, more than 5 nautical miles per minute. Even though the dive bombers had focused on *Musashi* and Fletcher could plainly see the flashing blue specks of VF-18's Hellcats harassing the ship, anti-aircraft fire still blossomed all around him.[28]

Fletcher nosed down until he was three hundred feet above the water, hoping the drop in altitude would minimize his exposure to the dozens of guns winking in his direction. He continued slaloming his aircraft side to side to throw off their aim. Fletcher looked to his left to check on his squadron mate, Lt. (jg) Ray Skelly. The second he laid eyes on Skelly's plane, a booming thump reverberated through the air around them. Skelly's Avenger was momentarily obscured by a ball of fire. It emerged from the smoke and flame missing a wing, barreling out of control into the sea below. The gunners had found their range. Fletcher pulled his stick hard to starboard to get clear of the bursts, but the incessant sound of metal clanging off his plane told him that the gunfire was still too close for comfort.

Only moments later, Fletcher ceased his evasive maneuvers. He needed to hold his Avenger steady during the final phase of his bombing run, no matter how many guns were pointed at him. His plane could only carry a single torpedo, meaning he had just one shot to hit the battleship. Fletcher's radioman, Robert Westmoreland, called out the range: "Two thousand yards." Fletcher held his Avenger perfectly still, thought of his family and the likelihood of his imminent death, and squeezed the button on his control stick.[29]

Fletcher's Avenger surged upward as the two-thousand-pound torpedo fell away. He tried to eke out as much power as he could from his plane's engine, dipping a wing to cut away from the enemy force. He could finally start juking and jinking again to throw off the gunners' aim. Westmoreland radioed Fletcher to confirm a clean drop, but his transmission was suddenly and violently interrupted. A phosphorous shell blasted through the Avenger's port wing. It left behind a blinding white trail of flames and a three-foot hole. Fletcher's canopy was now open to the air. His leg bled where shrapnel pierced his thigh. No response came through the intercom when he tried to reach his crewmen. After crash-landing at sea, Fletcher found his turret gunner, George Christman Jr., dead inside the turret, decapitated by flak. Westmoreland, the radioman stationed inside the Avenger, did not respond. The plane was so sieved by shrapnel that it seemed like a foregone conclusion that he had been killed, too.[30]

Meanwhile, Fighting 18's Hellcats continued zooming over the wildly maneuvering Japanese ships, strafing and drawing anti-aircraft fire as the bombers made their escape. A hail of bullets from the swarming fighters pinged noisily off the ships' sides and gun mounts. Splinters flew where bullets chewed through wooden decks. Casualties among the topside crews mounted rapidly. Even experienced Japanese sailors were shaken by the ferocity of the attack. The officer in charge of *Musashi*'s flak batteries pleaded with the ship's captain, Admiral Inoguchi, to load the 18.1-inch guns with special "beehive" anti-aircraft shells. The rounds weighed nearly three thousand pounds each and contained massive amounts of shrapnel and incendiary. Inoguchi was reluctant to load his biggest guns for anti-aircraft use, especially since the beehive shells could damage their bores. Despite his initial reluctance, however, the relentless air attack caused Admiral Inoguchi to change his mind.[31]

At the end of the mission, the cost to Air Group 18 was two Helldivers in need of serious repair and two Avengers missing in action.[32] Given the size of the strike and volume of anti-aircraft fire, these numbers boded poorly for the Japanese. This pattern continued through the afternoon. Admiral Ugaki, commander of *Yamato*'s Battleship Division 1, jotted down in his diary, "The small number of enemy planes shot down is regrettable."[33] In exchange, strike 2A alone produced several hits and near misses, including Ens. Will Fletcher's torpedo and Lieutenant Forsyth's one-thousand-pound armor-piercing bomb, both of which damaged the mighty *Musashi*.[34] The heavily armored ship continued steaming ahead as damage control crews counter-flooded compartments, minimizing the list caused by torpedo damage.[35]

Heading back to the carriers after strike 2A, Lt. Frank Hearrell heard reports urging friendly aircraft to steer clear of the task force until enemy attacks subsided. A Japanese dive bomber had dropped a bomb about three hundred feet off USS *Cabot*'s port quarter, causing nearby ships to release their anti-aircraft batteries. Any plane flying within range, whether friend or foe, could come under fire. Hearrell knew the attacking plane had completed its mission and would be flying on an opposite heading to return to the Philippines. He kept his eyes open as he continued cruising east. Sure enough, a Jill dive bomber appeared about one thousand feet below him. He charged his guns, adjusted his gunsight for the coming engagement, and dipped a wing down to begin his pursuit.[36]

Destroying the Jill would prevent its pilot from returning to base with information about the task group's location and composition. Hearrell had more than enough experience to ensure that would not come to pass. He was a born and bred Texan who grew up on a farm hunting game. He'd been leading fast-moving targets well before he entered Navy flight training in September 1941. Hearrell bent the curve of his approach, pointing the nose of his Hellcat ahead of the Jill. He dialed thirty millimeters of lead into his gunsight to account for the distance and speed relative to his target, and when he had the enemy lined up in the crosshair, he pressed the gun button. A quick tap on the trigger made his plane shudder as its machine guns barked to life. Hearrell's aim was spot-on. The stream of bullets disappeared into the bomber, which exploded a moment later. What was left of the plane rained down in tiny pieces, leaving an oil slick on the ocean below.[37]

Things started to calm down around Intrepid, so Hearrell continued back to base. He descended through a cloudy patch until he broke out into the clear. Another plane was low over the water in front of him. It was a Yokosuka P1Y Frances bomber, a newer, land-based twin-engine type whose pilot was scouting the position of the fleet. Hearrell followed closely behind as the Frances ducked into a cloud. He knew roughly how fast the bomber was travelling, where it was heading, and where the cloud cover ended, so he lined himself up where he expected to see the Frances emerge.

It arrived right on schedule. Hearrell fired; the Frances' port engine smoked. He pressed his gun button again a fraction of a second later; tracers smashed through the cockpit and over top of the fuselage. A third tap lit up the starboard engine. The plane finally nosed down in a shallow, uncontrolled dive before crashing into the water. When Hearrell finally made it back to Intrepid, his wingman was impressed by how he bore down on the bomber despite return fire from the Frances' rear-gunner. Hearrell was surprised; in the heat of the moment, he had not even registered that the enemy was shooting at him.[38]

Strike 2B, the second strike against Kurita's forces, launched from *Intrepid* at 1030 with a similar number of aircraft and composition as strike 2A. However, two of the Hellcats sent out were F6F-5(P) photo planes operated by lead photographic officer Lt. Harvey Picken and Lt. (jg) Redman "Beetle" Beatley. Rather than strafing, they loitered at high altitude, taking as many photographs as possible. They could only hope that the ensuing engagement distracted enemy guns long enough for them to get the job done. Like Adams, Watts, and Amerman before them, they would have to hold steady in the face of enemy fire to ensure the success of their mission.

Despite damage to power systems controlling some of *Musashi*'s guns, casualties among gun crews, and other problems caused by strike 2A, Admiral Kurita's forces continued to send up a tremendous barrage of anti-aircraft fire. Incoming planes were greeted by a "large black mattress" of smoke at five thousand feet, with blinding phosphorous flashes and multicolored explosions at higher altitudes.[39] Flak remained so severe that it seemed "capable of being walked upon."[40] From their positions high above the action, Picken and Beatley marveled at Kurita's warships. They were titans, forces of nature scarring an otherwise placid blue sea with serpentine ribbons of white. It had been less than two hours since strike 2A attacked. In that time, the enemy force had traveled over thirty miles; the first strike had barely slowed them down. Picken and Beatley's onboard cameras snapped and clicked incessantly to document the scene as their compatriots closed in for the attack.

As the bombers headed in, crewmen in VB-18 and VT-18 dumped window to foil radar-tracking guns. The strips of metal poured out behind their planes and hung in the air overhead, spinning and glinting in the wind like slow-falling rain.[41] As usual, VB-18 dove first. The Helldivers scored multiple hits on *Musashi*, though the behemoth battleship seemed to shrug the damage off as a mere annoyance. Two of the dive bombers went down in the face of murderous flak. Fighting 18 entered the fray as soon as the survivors pulled out of their dives.

Pop Thune charged his guns for strafing. He had six .50-caliber machine guns arrayed against the largest artillery pieces ever put to sea, not to mention over a hundred 25-mm guns sweeping bullets all around him. The disparity in firepower seemed absurd. He would be fully exposed from the moment he approached, through multiple strafing runs, and then finally for hundreds of yards as he attempted to make his escape. The odds did not matter, though: He had a job to do.[42]

Lt. Richard "Dick" Cevoli was also strafing, but he had even more reason to gripe than Thune: it was his twenty-fifth birthday.[43] If he could bomb an enemy ship to mark the occasion, that might have cheered him up, but the squadron's Hellcats were just there to strafe and draw fire. Given the assignment, his odds of surviving to see twenty-six felt like a coin flip. Cevoli and Thune charged forward anyway. They knew their peers in VB-18 and VT-18 were counting on them. Gunfire from the two Hellcats added to the carnage aboard *Musashi*. The bodies of those unlucky enough to be caught in the open piled up along the length of the ship, leaving streams of blood running over its wooden decks.[44]

Window, dive bombing, and diversionary strafing by the fighters set VT-18 up for successful hammer-and-anvil attacks against *Musashi*, which remained the focal point throughout strike 2B. Admiral Kurita's ships maneuvered wildly around each other as the Avenger pilots made their drops. The ships' wakes overlapped in chevron ripples that looked beautiful from Picken's and Beatley's perspective at ten thousand feet. Other, smaller wakes streaked toward the ships, indicating the presence of torpedoes churning through the water at over thirty-three knots.

Three torpedoes slammed into *Musashi*'s port side in succession, causing the ship to list to port as its damage control capabilities were finally overwhelmed. A propeller shaft had to be locked, slowing *Musashi* down. Tons of seawater sloshed in flooded compartments belowdecks, reducing the ship's maneuverability.[45] The situation was rapidly deteriorating for Admiral Kurita and his men. *Musashi* fell behind as the rest of the force steamed ahead, determined to achieve their objective no matter the cost.

Without protection from the bulk of Kurita's forces, and without speed and maneuverability on its side, wave after wave of planes pummeled the hapless *Musashi*. Afternoon strikes were even fiercer than the morning's thanks to the long-awaited arrival of Task Groups 38.3 and 38.4. The sixth and final attack on Kurita's ships included planes from *Intrepid, Cabot, Essex, Lexington,* and *Franklin*. Over the course of this last strike, *Musashi* was hit by no fewer than ten bombs and eleven torpedoes, providing the coup de grace.[46]

Altogether, 259 sorties were flown against Kurita's forces on 24 October.[47] Air Group 18 could boast that it had contributed to the first and final blows against *Musashi*. The cost had been high, especially for the "torpeckers" of VT-18. They had lost nine men and ended the day with only seven Avengers in serviceable condition. The results, however, seemed to justify their sacrifice. At 1640 Commander Ellis reported that the enemy fleet was retreating west at eighteen knots, moving briskly away from San Bernardino Strait and the approach to Leyte Gulf.[48]

The last strike of the day had convinced Admiral Kurita that forging ahead would simply doom his men. Appeals for air cover sent earlier in the afternoon had gone unanswered. It was clear he was on his own. To explain his actions to his superiors in the combined fleet, Kurita sent a message shortly after turning around, assuring them this was a temporary measure: "The best course open to us was to temporarily retire beyond the range of enemy planes and reform our plans."[49] As his ships headed west, they passed within a few miles of *Musashi*. It was obvious for all to see that the once-proud battleship would not survive the evening. Water swept over its weather deck; the bow was similarly awash, dunking the ship's gold-painted chrysanthemum crest—the imperial seal of Japan—into the water, as if mimicking the setting sun.[50]

CHAPTER 9

LEYTE GULF
Anticlimax

THOUGH THE LOSS OF *MUSASHI* was discouraging in the extreme, Admiral Kurita was determined to regroup and complete his mission. He waited until 1714, when the carrier and scout planes harassing his forces departed, then ordered his ships to turn back east toward their objective.[1] He could not have known at the time due to poor communication between Japanese forces, but events to the north had given him a reprieve for the evening. Even better, it had bought him safe passage through San Bernardino Strait and into Leyte Gulf.

While *Intrepid*'s second strike was in the thick of it over *Musashi* earlier that afternoon, Task Group 38.3, the northernmost of the carrier groups, was attacked yet again by waves of Japanese aircraft. Light carrier USS *Langley* detected them around 1245. The ship scrambled CAP pilots to intercept and began firing, heeling over hard as enemy bombers closed in. Though the Japanese pilots failed to score during these attacks, they successfully completed Admiral Ozawa's diversionary mission. Reports indicated that these aircraft approached from seaward and sported tailhooks.[2] Their appearance spurred Rear Adm. Frederick C. Sherman, in command of Task Group 38.3, to launch searches as soon as the attacks abated. At 1640 search aircraft finally spotted Ozawa's ships to the north. Halsey received the report from Vice Adm. Pete Mitscher, his overall carrier commander, at 1730.[3] He now knew there was an enemy carrier force nearby.

The picture seemed to be coming into focus. Kurita's warships were retreating to the west after reportedly suffering serious losses; the smaller battleship force to the south was being addressed by Admiral Kinkaid; and now Japanese aircraft carriers, the biggest threat to Halsey's ships, were only a night's swift transit to the north. Halsey's orders from his direct superior, Adm. Chester Nimitz, gave him explicit permission to seek out and destroy a major portion of the enemy fleet if the opportunity arose.[4] This seemed to fit the bill. The only question that remained for Halsey was how to split his two overarching duties: protecting the invasion forces, and destroying the enemy fleet.

Halsey's nickname, "Bull," suited his personality. He was aggressive, decisive, even single-minded. But as the commander of a large seagoing force, he also had to account for contingencies. What if Admiral Kurita turned around to enter San Bernardino Strait? At 1512, well before Kurita's retreat or the appearance of Japanese carriers, Halsey issued a notice to his superiors that he intended to strip his surface combatants into a separate force. He stated that his battleships and a number of cruisers and destroyers "will be formed as Task Force 34" to "engage decisively at long ranges" while his carriers remained "clear of surface fighting."[5] In other words, if Kurita forged ahead, Halsey would detach his battleships to duke it out with the enemy in the strait, leaving his carriers free to respond to any incursion by separate elements of the Japanese fleet.

This message reached ears it was not meant for, including Admiral Kinkaid to the south, who reasonably interpreted the phrase "will be formed" as a fait accompli. San Bernardino Strait was as good as guarded. Even Halsey's superiors interpreted the message this way, including Admiral Nimitz in Hawaii. In actuality, after receiving reports that Kurita was retreating, Halsey broadcast a short-range message to his local carrier commanders at 1710 that Task Force 34 would only be formed "if the enemy sorties" or turns back around, and only "when directed by me." Due to the method of transmission, this message reached neither Nimitz nor Kinkaid. They remained confident Task Force 34 would be guarding San Bernardino Strait.[6]

Halsey received word there were Japanese carriers to the north just twenty minutes later. He did not yet know that Kurita had turned his battleships around. The information available to him and his predisposition for bold, aggressive action told Halsey there was no reason to leave his surface forces behind. Instead, he would take his flagship, USS *New Jersey*, north with the carriers and form his battle line during the chase. Besides adhering to the doctrine of concentration of force, this decision would allow him to personally witness the long-awaited final showdown between the main battle fleets of the U.S. and Imperial Japanese navies. Halsey had been absent during the great carrier battles up to this point at the Coral Sea, Midway, and the Philippine Sea. He was not about to miss his last chance at glory.[7]

As 24 October drew to a close, Admiral Halsey turned in to get some much-needed rest. *New Jersey* rang up a brisk twenty-five knots to keep pace with the rest of Task Group 38.2 during the all-night run up the coast of Luzon.[8] Nearby, aboard *Intrepid*, the men of Fighting 18 prepared themselves for the morning. They had gotten off largely scot-free the previous day, especially compared with the bombers. Day two of the battle was shaping up to be different. Word came down that they would be carrying five-hundred-pound bombs against the enemy carrier force. They would have to face tremendous volumes of anti-aircraft fire with the same steel nerves as their brothers in VB-18 and VT-18.

Flight officer Lt. Cecil Harris worked late into the evening assigning VF-18 pilots to search, communication relay, CAP, and strike duty. Because they had to provide CAP for both the carrier task group and the nearby battleship force, only seven fighters could be allocated to the day's first strike.[9] When Harris finished the roster, he posted it on the bulletin board in the squadron ready room. The usual chorus of pleased murmurs, complaints, and quiet contemplation likely greeted its arrival.

Harris selected some of the squadron's senior aviators for search and strike duty. George Griffith and Freddy Wolff were each paired with one of VB-18's Helldivers to find Admiral Ozawa's flattops.[10] The strike, which would be launched just fifteen minutes later, included Fred Tracy, Donald Watts, and Watts' wingman, Boot Amerman.[11] They had already proved themselves as some of Fighting 18's most successful pilots operating against targets on the water, having sunk or seriously damaged everything from small motor launches to one-thousand-ton vessels.[12]

Watts and Amerman also likely received strike duty to keep things fair: rotating pilots through CAP, searches, sweeps, and strikes ensured a more equitable distribution of opportunity to score in the air or damage targets at sea or on the ground. This rotation was not always possible or practicable, though. At least one pilot assigned to the morning strike had been on strikes the previous day as well: Lt. Dick Cevoli. The recent birthday boy was getting a proper present on 25 October. Fighting 18 had missed the Battle of the Philippine Sea in June 1944. Being assigned strike duty again gave Cevoli a chance to personally attack an enemy carrier—a naval aviator's dream scenario.

Sunrise on 25 October revealed perfectly clear, blue skies for the searchers, with sixteen-knot winds to help get their planes aloft.[13] Just like the previous day, search pilots were assigned ten-degree sectors of airspace, only this time there were just three wedges to patrol, stretching directly north and fanning only slightly out to the northwest. Freddy Wolff, the stout, curly-haired New Yorker, accompanied VB-18's Donald Wilson on the westernmost patrol leg. Less than an hour after taking off, the men sighted Japanese destroyers off Santa Ana, a little horn-like protrusion sticking up from the northeast corner of Luzon. As soon as the destroyers spotted the duo of carrier planes, they desperately opened fire.[14] They had good reason to worry. Lieutenant Wilson had scored a confirmed hit on a battleship the previous day and wanted to keep his streak going.[15]

Wilson pulled up to higher altitude, circled over one of the destroyers, then nosed steeply down from six thousand feet. The ship seemed to grow larger and larger as he raced toward it. He waited as long as he dared to release his one-thousand-pound bomb. Just as he hit the release button, his Helldiver shuddered from the force of a medium-caliber anti-aircraft round. Shrapnel chewed through his plane's bomb bay and starboard wing. If he had been hit any earlier, the bomb could have detonated inside the plane. Instead, it tumbled down into the water just behind the destroyer. The ship's gunners had succeeded in throwing off his aim. Wilson barely recovered from his dive. His plane was so badly damaged that upon return to *Intrepid*, it was deemed irreparable and pushed over the side of the ship.[16]

Wolff had to face the same accurate anti-aircraft fire to drop his bomb, but unlike Wilson, he did not have dive brakes or an internal bomb bay to work with. He pushed down as low as he dared before making his drop, then eagerly advanced his Hellcat's throttle to get out of anti-aircraft range. His five-hundred-pound bomb threw up another geyser, a near miss, abeam one of the nimble destroyers.[17]

Despite the excitement, these ships were not part of Admiral Ozawa's carrier force. *Intrepid*'s search sectors were too far west to detect it. Searchers from *Essex* located Ozawa's ships in their area instead, broadcasting their sighting report at 0710.[18] *Intrepid*'s first strike of the day, 2A, was already orbiting in a holding pattern just outside its task group, waiting to receive the enemy's coordinates. Thanks to rapid transmission of the report, the strike reached Ozawa's ships only an hour later.[19] Given the diversionary mission of his carrier force, it was fitting that the ensuing battle took place off of Cape Engaño—in English, Cape Deception.[20]

Strike groups from multiple *Essex*-class carriers arrived over the Japanese fleet in two back-to-back waves. The first wave was led by Cdr. David McCampbell of *Essex*'s Air Group 15. The second wave, consisting of about eighty aircraft—including those from *Intrepid*—was led by Cdr. Theodore "Hugh" Winters of *Lexington*'s Air Group 19.[21] More planes meant more ordnance, but such large gatherings also required McCampbell and Winters to take leading roles as target coordinators.

A good target coordinator was like a conductor bringing the disparate parts of the orchestra into harmony. Winters conferred with the leaders of the air groups under him, including Commander Ellis of Air Group 18, to divvy up responsibilities. The enemy carriers were the most high-value targets. Fleet carrier *Zuikaku* and light carrier *Zuiho* were at the top of the list, followed by the converted carriers *Chitose* and *Chiyoda* and the hybrid battleship-carriers *Ise* and *Hyuga*. There were plenty of targets to go around.

When the radio chatter died down and everyone finally knew their role in the larger strike, Winters gave the order to check all switches. It was time to commence high-speed bombing runs. Down below, anti-aircraft fire from hundreds of guns formed a deadly dome of shrapnel around the Japanese carriers. Watts and Amerman must have felt extremely vulnerable. Their role over Admiral Kurita's forces a day earlier permitted them to maintain station at a relatively safe distance from the enemy force. They reported its position rather than charging through flak. Now they had to follow on the heels of the dive bombers as shells exploded closer and closer, jostling them in their cockpits.

Dick Cevoli, who had strafed Kurita's ships the previous day, was going through it all over again with the carriers, except this time his Hellcat was encumbered by a five-hundred-pound bomb attached to its belly. Along with Watts and Amerman, his target was a light carrier flanked by cruisers and destroyers doing their best to fill the air with flak. The battleship-carriers, *Hyuga* and *Ise*, were also nearby. They carried beehive shells like the ones on *Musashi*, and their captains had no compunction about using them. They fired at long range. Puffballs from shell detonations hung in the air all around the fighters; pinks and greens and oranges interspersed with flashing white light from phosphorous made the sky look like a heavily decorated Christmas tree.[22] A small number of enemy aircraft were also present but only provided token protection for their ships. Cevoli scored hits on a Zeke fighter on the way in, but the enemy never pressed the attack. It wasn't worth chasing after such distractions when the principal objective was down below.

Cevoli, Watts, and Amerman began their dives soon after, hurtling down through the colorful barrage of anti-aircraft fire. Seventy-degree dives sent the blood rushing to their heads as they descended hundreds of feet per second. They had front-row seats to the initial hammer blows dealt to the light carrier by VB-18. John Forsyth pulled out of his run just ahead of them. His Helldiver lurched and bounced awkwardly through the air to throw off the enemy's aim, but that was not what drew the fighters' attention. Towering columns of water and smoke erupted along the port side of the ship where Forsyth planted his bomb. There was one, then another, then another as the rest of the bombers completed their runs.

The three fighters added to the ship's misery. Watts, Amerman, and Cevoli all either hit or narrowly missed it, and a string of torpedoes from VT-18 struck the beleaguered carrier. Based on these descriptions and VT-18's identification of the ship as either *Zuiho* or *Chitose*, it would appear the carrier in question was *Chitose*, which bore the brunt of attacks from *Essex*, *Lexington*, and *Intrepid* aircraft.[23] The burning, wrecked remains of the carrier sat dead in the water as the strike departed. It sank shortly thereafter.[24]

With the light carriers soaking up most of the punishment, Lt. Fred Tracy went after bigger game. Admiral Ozawa's flagship, *Zuikaku*, led the force with a cadre of destroyers and cruisers milling about on all sides. The fleet carrier was more than one hundred feet longer than either of the light carriers steaming in its wake.[25] Avengers, Helldivers, and Hellcats closed in to make sure the ship did not escape unscathed. As Tracy and bombers from other squadrons entered their dives, *Zuikaku* maneuvered radically to starboard, entering a nearly 180-degree turn to throw off the attackers' point of aim.[26]

It was no use. Three bombs hit *Zuikaku*, including Tracy's. They started fires in the ships' hangar spaces. The follow-up by VT-18 sent three torpedoes lancing out against the ship's freshly exposed port side. Waterspouts erupted where their torpedoes struck home. Generator and engine rooms flooded in the wake of the savage blow, slowing the ship and causing it to list rapidly to port. Damage control crews aboard *Zuikaku* raced to save their ship. Though it rolled almost thirty degrees before their efforts began to show, they quickly reduced the list to a mere six degrees.[27] *Zuikaku* was not out of the fight just yet. If it was going to be sacrificed as a distraction, it would remain afloat as long as possible to keep Halsey's forces tied up off the cape.

The fighters on this mission strafed after dropping their bombs. They focused primarily on the hybrid battleship-carriers and cruisers to draw fire away from the torpedo bombers making their slow, steady runs. Lieutenant Watts selected a light cruiser for strafing—one he identified as *Natori* but that was more likely *Tama*, a ship with a strikingly similar profile. Watts aimed at the base of its stacks as he zoomed down from five thousand feet to a mere five hundred feet, sweeping machine gun fire amidships. He rapidly leveled off after his run, skidding and rolling his plane evasively until he was a mile away from the target. Only then did he bank a wing down to turn and witness the ship's fate.[28] The cruiser was smoking heavily. At almost the same time Watts turned to look, it was hit by a torpedo from a Task Group 38.4 Avenger. A massive explosion obscured *Tama*. Though the cruiser was able to limp away from this blow, it was sunk later the same day by submarine USS *Jallao*.[29]

This pattern repeated itself throughout the day as strikes rained down over the unprotected carrier force. Lt. George Griffith of VF-18 and Lt. (jg) Temple Prahar of VB-18 were in the northern search sector initially launched at 0613. They did not encounter Admiral Ozawa's force until their return trip home four hours later, at 1013. They arrived between strikes and were the only planes over the enemy force. What they saw was heartening. *Chitose* was nowhere to be seen. Two other light carriers were dead in the water, and one of them was smoking badly.

Even though they didn't have dozens of friendly planes to draw anti-aircraft fire, like their peers had on the morning strike, Griffith and Prahar got into position to attack *Zuikaku* at the center of the formation. Then all the ships below them began opening fire. They had to quickly divert to secondary targets. Prahar dropped his one-thousand-pound armor-piercing bomb on a cruiser but narrowly missed. Griffith missed the battleship-carrier he went after.[30] The fact that they attacked at all given the concentration of anti-aircraft fire speaks volumes about their courage.

Between 527 sorties by carrier aviators,[31] gunfire from Halsey's surface forces, and torpedoes fired by submarines lurking in nearby waters, Admiral Ozawa lost four carriers, a cruiser, and two destroyers on 25 October.[32] These were not unexpected losses. In fact, Ozawa had performed his role admirably. Halsey had chased him all night and all morning as Kurita brought his still-formidable surface force through San Bernardino Strait completely unopposed. Even farther south, at Surigao Strait, Admiral Nishimura and his old battleships had also sacrificed themselves for Kurita's sake during the night of 24–25 October. By engaging Rear Adm. Jesse Oldendorf's surface forces at Surigao, Nishimura ensured that the only protection available for the support ships in Leyte Gulf on 25 October was the vulnerable escort carrier groups of Task Force 77.[33]

At 0822 that morning, as his aviators began their deadly dives on Ozawa's carriers, Admiral Halsey received the first report from Seventh Fleet's Admiral Kinkaid that his escort carriers were under attack by Japanese battleships.

Eight minutes later Kinkaid amplified this message, "URGENTLY NEED FAST BATTLESHIPS LEYTE GULF AT ONCE."[34] A whole slew of messages arrived, but the point seemed moot. Halsey's forces were well out of range to assist. He felt compelled to focus on events within his power: finishing off the carriers. As the situation to the south became more and more desperate, Halsey finally received a message from his immediate superior officer, Adm. Chester Nimitz, at 0944. In short, the message read, "WHERE IS REPEAT WHERE IS TASK FORCE 34. RR. THE WORLD WONDERS."[35]

The last sentence was just padding. It originated as a regular component of encryption and should have been deleted by signals staff aboard *New Jersey* before it reached Admiral Halsey. Instead, it was accidentally included in the decoded message, causing it to read like a stinging rebuke from Admiral Nimitz. Halsey erupted in anger when he first read the query from his boss. After calming down and sorting things out with his staff officers, at 1115 Halsey ordered most of his surface combatants south with Task Group 38.2 as cover.[36] While the air groups in Task Groups 38.3 and 38.4 continued to hammer Ozawa's forces throughout the afternoon, Air Group 18 and *Intrepid* headed back down to San Bernardino Strait. The ship's crew and air group personnel were crestfallen at being pulled away before they could deliver the final blow to *Zuikaku*.[37] *Intrepid*'s band belted out a rendition of "There'll Be a Hot Time in the Old Town Tonight,"[38] but it likely did little to raise spirits. Many felt that Admiral Halsey and the battleship forces in particular had missed a huge opportunity. Now *Intrepid* was stuck tagging along on a wild goose chase instead of mopping up the carriers.

While Halsey's forces were taking on Ozawa's flattops on the morning of 25 October, the Navy's escort carrier groups, or "taffies," made a stand against Admiral Kurita's surface ships at the Battle off Samar despite being massively outgunned. The ferocity of their counterattack led to Kurita's sudden reversal and withdrawal through San Bernardino Strait. This David versus Goliath episode rightly serves as the Navy's foremost example of courage under fire and forms the dramatic climax of the Battle of Leyte Gulf, though it is outside the scope of this book.

Task Group 38.2 steamed overnight to get within striking distance of Kurita's fleeing warships after missing the Battle off Samar. Admiral Bogan's carriers were ready to launch aircraft by 0600 on 26 October in tandem with TG 38.1, led by Adm. John McCain.[39] Unfortunately, it took over two hours for scouts to locate Kurita's forces. By then, the Japanese battleships were northwest of Panay and heading swiftly out of range.

Twelve Hellcats, sixteen Helldivers, and seven Avengers from *Intrepid* arrived over the Kurita fleet to make his battleships pay for the previous day. Even though anti-aircraft fire was still extremely heavy, Japanese gunners waited to open fire until bombing runs started, marking a significant departure from the pilots' experience on 24 October. The ships may have been running out of artillery shells.[40] Fighting 18, on the other hand, was now equipped to do even more damage than they had in the Sibuyan Sea. Whereas their Hellcats had only been loaded with machine gun ammunition during their first meeting, they now carried five-hundred-pound bombs. That meant Fred Tracy had yet another chance after his success bombing *Zuikaku* the previous day. It meant an opportunity for Dick Cevoli to score a hat trick. This was not only his third day in a row directly participating in the largest naval battle in history—a feat few others could boast—but he was also scheduled to take part in the follow-up strike that afternoon.

Cevoli and Tracy tag-teamed an Aichi E13A Jake reconnaissance floatplane on the way to the enemy force. Just like the day before, the plane proved to be an easy kill. Fighting 18 had strength in numbers, superior aircraft, and a level of training that made such encounters one-sided. Once the skies were clear and all strike aircraft arrived over the target, Cevoli and Tracy circled at 13,000 feet while the dive bombers attacked.[41] It would be their turn in a matter of minutes.

Dive Bombing 18, nicknamed the "Sunday Punchers," focused almost exclusively on a target identified as battleship *Kongō*. They claimed four hits on the port side and another on the starboard side amidships. This latter hit was attributed to Max Adams, the Helldiver pilot who had originally helped locate Kurita's forces. All told, fifteen out of sixteen *Intrepid* dive bomber pilots made their drops on this target, completely blanketing it in one-thousand-pound semi-armor-piercing bombs and wing-mounted one-hundred-pound general-purpose bombs.[42]

As it turned out, they weren't the only pilots interested in taking down this ship. Chuck deMoss of VF-18 wanted a piece of it, too. There were cruisers and other ships nearby, but he was absolutely fixated on the battleship. It was moving slower than its escorts, probably due to preexisting damage. deMoss had an eye for this sort of thing. He had been a dive bomber pilot before coming to the squadron, but search and CAP assignments the previous two days kept him from putting his skills to use. In his excitement, deMoss started his dive too high. His Hellcat came screaming down through the flak more steeply than intended. It did not matter. He was not going to miss this opportunity. deMoss dropped his bomb and pulled out perilously close to the water. He was so low he could feel the concussion of his bomb exploding on the fantail of the enemy ship.[43] Cevoli went for the *Kongō* as well but narrowly missed. They both strafed nearby destroyers after their bombing runs, doing their best to make things easier for their colleagues in VT-18.[44]

Half of the VF-18 pilots focused on *Yamato*, but the results were disheartening. Out of six bombs dropped, only Spider Foltz scored a hit. His bomb exploded just behind one of the ship's massive 18.1-inch gun turrets. *Yamato* barely registered the damage.[45] It was clear there was no winning strategy to employ for the fighters. Five-hundred-pound bombs were not guaranteed to cause significant damage. Buck Newsome scored a hit or damaging near miss on the stern of a heavy cruiser. Like *Yamato* and *Kongō*, the ship just shrugged it off. Their bombs had the best chance of mortally wounding the smaller ships in Kurita's force, like the destroyers, but these were also the hardest targets to hit given their size, speed, and agility. The three VF-18 pilots who dropped bombs on destroyers all missed their mark.

Strike 2A had been a bust. The *Kongō*-class battleship was the only one showing significant damage when the strike departed. For this paltry outcome, Ens. Harold Meacham, a replacement pilot who had joined Fighting 18 after Formosa, was missing in action. Things got worse on the return trip to *Intrepid*. The combination of poor weather, poor coordination, time spent loitering, and distance to the target meant that some planes ran out of fuel before they could make it back aboard ship. Five ultimately landed in the water: three due to fuel consumption, and two more due to flak damage.[46]

The Battle of Leyte Gulf ended anticlimactically for Fighting 18. The last strike of the day included ten VF-18 Hellcats armed with five-hundred-pound bombs to inflict further punishment on Kurita's forces. The battered and defeated battleships made it out of range before the strike could get there. Pilots were forced to jettison their bombs since it was too dangerous to land back aboard ship with ordnance. Men watched as five thousand pounds' worth of weaponry dropped into the sea, imagining what could have been if *Intrepid* had arrived sooner.

Although the mood was muted by disappointment, the weather returning to the task group was breathtaking. Towering rectangular columns of cumulus clouds stretched into the distance like the banks of an airborne canyon. Punchy Mallory took turns admiring the soft white walls around him and the green-blue droplets of islands lining the edges of the Visayan Sea below. The only distraction from the beauty around him was a radio transmission indicating possible enemy ships in the vicinity. Mallory let down from the cloud canyon to get a better look. Though the report turned out to be negative, when he broke into the clear, a Nakajima Ki-44 Tojo fighter crossed right by him. Both pilots were probably equally surprised to see one another in the otherwise clear sky.

Mallory pulled back hard on the stick to arrest his descent, feeling gravity push him firmly into his seat. He dipped his port wing to follow the path of the enemy fighter. Even though he had to bleed speed to climb, Mallory easily overtook his opponent. He dropped back down on top of the Tojo with gunfire that drew smoke from its engine. As soon as he was hit, the Tojo pilot executed a snap roll and dive, turning inside the Hellcat in an attempt to shake Mallory off his tail. The maneuver gave the pilot a temporary reprieve from the Hellcat's guns, but in clear skies with unlimited visibility, there was nowhere to run. Mallory was back on his tail a few moments later, riding him from nine thousand feet down toward the sparkling waters of the Visayan Sea. Mallory pushed his gun button again but got nothing in response. Something was wrong with his guns. Even though he was temporarily unarmed, Mallory still firmly held the advantage. He was on the enemy's tail, had a superior aircraft and friendly planes nearby if things went south, and had already damaged the Japanese fighter. At fifty feet, the two zooming planes evened out just over the wave tops. After giving his guns a minute or so to cool off, Mallory tried them again. This time they barked to life. Tracer fire drew a clear line into the enemy's cockpit and engine area. The plane staggered and sputtered, slowly losing altitude until, ten seconds later, it slammed into the water.[47]

When *Intrepid*'s last strike arrived back aboard ship on 26 October, the men were exhausted. Mallory had logged 8.5 hours between the strike and earlier CAP assignment. Other members of the squadron had logged as many as ten hours of flight duty. Their summer flight suits were dark with sweat, and their hair was disheveled from hours in flight helmets. They were likely too tired to appreciate the important role they had just played in one of the largest naval battle in history.

Fighting 18's aviators disseminated the initial sighting reports leading to the Battle of the Sibuyan Sea. They supported Air Group 18's bombers and torpedo planes during damaging attacks on Admiral Kurita's and Admiral Ozawa's forces over the course of three days. Some of them had even scored hits with five-hundred-pound bombs. Their air group had embodied the name of their ship, *Intrepid*, by being among the first into the fray against enemy battleships and carriers, and among the last to land blows in the closing hours of the engagement. There was much to be proud of.

Still, the knowledge that more ships could have been sunk stuck in their craw. They had been yo-yoed back and forth over three days while other air groups got to polish off Japanese carriers or take breaks to refuel and rest. Fighting 18, meanwhile, accompanied strikes over extreme distances that were more likely to lead to water landings than significant damage to enemy forces. *Intrepid*'s dive and torpedo bomber squadrons were no happier about their lot.

On the Japanese side, the Battle of Leyte Gulf marked the effective end of the combined fleet. There was a sort of symbolism to the battle best captured by the sinking of *Zuikaku* off Cape Engaño and the role played by battleships like *West Virginia* at Surigao Strait. *Zuikaku* was the last surviving carrier that had participated in the attack on Pearl Harbor, an event that helped usher in the predominance of naval airpower. Now it was a sacrificial lamb sunk by a vastly superior carrier force. To the south, at Surigao Strait, *West Virginia* scored a hit on Japanese battleship *Yamashiro* as part of Adm. Jesse Oldendorf's complete rout of enemy forces. A little less than three years earlier, *West Virginia* had been sunk during the attack on Pearl Harbor. It had since been patched, pumped dry, refloated, and modernized for continued service.[48] These two examples capture the decline of Japanese naval capabilities at the same time American industrial and training systems transformed the U.S. Navy into the most powerful seagoing force the world had ever seen.

In an ideal world, *Intrepid*'s air group would have time to rest after this epic, days-long battle. As things stood, however, that was simply impossible. New planes needed to be flown aboard to replace lost Avengers and Helldivers. Fighting 18 needed to provide CAP and SNASP over the fleet. There was no time to celebrate the victory at Leyte Gulf.

On 28 October, in squally, overcast weather, Fighting 18 provided two dozen Hellcats for a series of afternoon patrols off the coast of Luzon. The first CAP was led by XO Lt. Clarence Blouin. They were quickly vectored out to two Yokosuka P1Y Dinah twin-engine bombers closing on *Intrepid*'s task group. Both Dinahs turned and ran as soon as they were spotted. The planes were so fast that Blouin had to use water injection to catch them.

After a fifteen-minute chase, he managed to make one of the Dinahs dive toward the water with a long-range burst of gunfire. The bomber pilot serpentined on the ocean surface rather than pulling up and losing precious speed. Blouin closed the rest of the distance faster now. He held his fire until he couldn't miss. At point-blank range, he finally tapped the gun button, spraying the Dinah's starboard engine with bullets. The pilot pulled up sharply, but it was already too late. His starboard engine belched flame before the plane rolled over and crashed into the water. Replacement pilots Ens. John Zink and Lt. (jg) Melvin Hayter took care of the other bomber soon after. With the threat neutralized, Blouin's men returned to the center of the task group to await a reprieve by the next CAP.[49]

Lt. George "Griff" Griffith sat in his Hellcat, finishing up his preflight checklist while Blouin's group made its way back. His work in the preceding months had earned him a promotion from section leader to division leader, and this upcoming CAP mission was going to be one of his first opportunities to lead his own four-plane unit.[50] Based on Blouin's experience, Griff's CAP promised to be a routine affair—certainly less stressful than his mission on 25 October when he flew headlong into naval artillery fire. After completing his checklist and finding no issues with his Hellcat, Griff taxied forward to his starting position. Now he just had to wait for the starter to wave the checkered flag, the signal that he could gun his engine to begin takeoff. The usual gaggle of crewmembers was watching flight ops from "vulture's row," the observation platform on *Intrepid*'s island overlooking the length of the flight deck.

The checkered flag finally twirled off Griff's starboard wing. He released his Hellcat's brakes and surged forward. The plane's tires rolled over the rain-slick deck, picking up speed as he passed the island. About one hundred feet into his run, his engine began cutting out in staccato fits. Something was wrong. His propeller slowed; his motor quit entirely. Griff slammed on the brakes, but it was already too late. Between his speed and the wet deck, there was no stopping his Hellcat's momentum. The men on vulture's row gripped the railings and leaned out over the platform as the plane passed the edge of the flight deck.[51]

Griff's Hellcat immediately sank out of view. It had not picked up enough speed to stay airborne. The plane splashed into the water a dozen or so feet in front of the ship. There was no time for *Intrepid* to avoid him and no time for Griff to get clear of the fast-moving carrier. A split-second after he crash-landed, he was gone, pushed out of sight by thousands of tons of steel.[52] After surviving Formosa, Leyte Gulf, and all the other dangers of his deployment, Lt. George Griffith was killed by a malfunctioning engine.

Lt. Donald Watts was heartbroken. Griff Griffith was one of his closest friends in the squadron. He thought long and hard throughout the night about how he was going to break the news to Karolyn, Griff's wife. The next day he sat in the ready room for over an hour and a half before he could muster the strength to write to her. He and Griff had hung out on the flight deck the previous morning. They had listened to the ship's band and gotten lunch that afternoon. It was a day like any other. The accident came down to pure bad luck. When he found out what had happened, Watts rushed into CIC to monitor search and rescue operations. There was no sign of his squadron mate despite hours of searching.

Watts heaped praise on Griff as a pilot and, more importantly, as a friend. He, Harvey Picken, and Robert Simpson packed up Griff's things to mail to Karolyn. He ended his letter by saying, "Griff loved you dearly, his whole life was built around you, that was evident by all his actions since we left the states almost a year ago and became one big family. This war has hit a lot of us and is going to effect [sic] a lot more. I hope and pray you haven't taken it too hard. I know Griff would want it otherwise—his prime aim in life was to make people happy."[53]

CHAPTER 10

KAMIKAZES
AND CLARK FIELD

THE FIRST SUCCESSFUL KAMIKAZE MISSION took place on 25 October, during the Battle off Samar. While *Intrepid* and its air group sprinted down from Cape Engaño to pursue Admiral Kurita's fleeing Center Force, kamikaze suicide pilots in Leyte Gulf began crash-diving into the small escort carriers directly supporting General MacArthur's invasion forces. USS *Santee, Suwannee, Kalinin Bay, Kitkun Bay*, and *St. Lo* received direct hits, and another handful suffered damage and casualties from near-misses.[1] Use of such desperate measures had been considered by some Japanese military officials as early as 1943 but was put off as an unthinkable last resort. Now they seemed to be Japan's last hope to sue for peace.[2] The success of these early missions and their propaganda value ensured that kamikaze attacks would become a regular occurrence. A new, even deadlier phase of the War in the Pacific had begun.

The pace of flight operations in October had been frantic, and the month was not over yet. Strikes on Formosa forced many pilots to fly eight hours a day on consecutive days, in miserable weather and against swarms of enemy aircraft. Running engagements with the Japanese fleet at Leyte Gulf were not much better. Fighting Squadron 18 lost so many men on these missions that it needed two infusions of aviators: one on 16 October consisting of seven fresh young ensigns, and another on 27 October made up of eleven experienced fighter pilots transferred from Fighting Squadron 11.[3]

The air group's shipboard crew had also reached the limit of their endurance. They were constantly refueling, rearming, moving, and repairing aircraft as part of a schedule that started before 0600 and sometimes did not end until 1900. Lt. (jg) Larry Donoghue oversaw maintenance of the squadron's Hellcats in the hangar deck. At the end of a long day of strike operations, Donoghue assessed damaged aircraft and assigned enlisted personnel to work on them. Once he was satisfied that repairs were under way, he found a tire in the hangar to use as a pillow. After a twenty-minute catnap, he was back on his feet reviewing ongoing work, assigning new repairs, and checking to make sure everything was ready for the morning.[4]

Japanese airpower in the Philippines still posed a mortal threat to support vessels in the gulf and to troops moving inland during this critical phase of operations. The danger was further exacerbated by kamikaze tactics. To eliminate this threat, carrier pilots needed to drop as much ordnance as possible on Japanese airfields, which meant equipping Fighting 18's Hellcats with bombs. Serving in the fighter-bomber role was nothing new for the men of Fighting 18. They had just bombed the Japanese fleet in the face of serious anti-aircraft fire. On 29 October, however, they were called upon to simultaneously bomb enemy airfields while escorting VB-18 and VT-18 aircraft. Splitting these roles posed a challenge. Bombing forced fighters to drop down below three thousand feet, while escort duty required defending from higher altitudes in case Japanese fighters lurked nearby. The need to work double duty like this showed just how thinly Admiral Halsey's forces were stretched after Leyte Gulf.

The day of 29 October began with a sweep of fifteen fighters armed with five-hundred-pound general-purpose bombs. There did not seem to be many targets of value at the airfields in southern Luzon, but the situation improved as the sweep headed north. Japanese cruisers under repair in Manila Bay provided attractive targets for bombing runs. Six members of the squadron, including Clarence Blouin, attacked a cruiser anchored north of Cavite. Though stationary, the ship bristled with anti-aircraft guns, making bombing runs extremely dangerous. Blouin and one of the replacement pilots scored near misses with their bombs.[5]

A second cruiser a mile north was bombed by another division. Lt. William Thompson and Ens. Donald Matheson missed just shy to starboard, but they came back around to make strafing passes.[6] These ships were further worked over by strikes from *Hancock's* air group, which reported phosphorous and lavender-colored anti-aircraft fire previously seen during the Battle of Leyte Gulf. These cruisers were probably *Nachi*, which had survived the Battle of Surigao Strait, and *Kumano*, which had been present during Air Group 18's shellacking of the main battleship force in the Sibuyan Sea.[7]

While the main element of the sweep continued harassing fleet elements over Manila Bay, a handful of pilots attacked nearby airfields. Bombs dropped at Nielson Field destroyed single- and twin-engine aircraft, though strafing proved just as effective. Some enemy fighters were already airborne. Pilots thought they saw a handful of J2M Jacks, but it is possible these were N1K1 Georges instead.[8] Whatever their identity, these fighter types were unmistakably different from the ones they were used to seeing.

Jacks and Georges both had four-bladed propellers attached to powerful engines, making them faster than any Japanese fighters the squadron had previously encountered. Their cockpits were positioned much farther back than the iconic Zeke. Jacks and Georges also packed four 20-mm cannons, giving them more firepower than the average enemy fighter.[9]

The sweep encountered two of these new aircraft. Their pilots were seriously outnumbered and in no mood to fight. The pilot of the first plane, engaged by Lt. Fred Tracy over Clark Field, tried to outrun the Hellcat. Tracy had to use full throttle to catch him, but in the end his Pratt & Whitney engine proved more capable than its Japanese counterpart. Tracy waited until the enemy plane filled his gunsight and then let loose. His guns hammered the Japanese aircraft until flames leapt up from the base of its port wing. Its pilot bailed out rather than press his luck.

Dick Cevoli's introduction to the new enemy fighter type was likewise anticlimactic. After destroying a Tony fighter under attack by another Hellcat, Cevoli spotted a Jack or George well below the group. He dove on his target and, like Tracy, used full throttle to catch the fleeing plane. He destroyed it with little difficulty. The only danger any of the men over Clark and Nielson fields faced was from anti-aircraft fire, which damaged three planes.[10]

Intrepid's first full strike of the day, strike 2A, followed on the heels of the sweep. Twelve dive bombers, eight torpedo bombers, and twelve fighters—a total of thirty-two planes—grouped up at the same rendezvous point used by the sweep as they headed to Clark Field. VF-18 Hellcats were once again armed with five-hundred-pound bombs. VB-18's Helldivers carried one-thousand-pound bombs internally and one-hundred-pound bombs under each wing, more than doubling the fighters' payload. VT-18's Avengers carried fragmentation and incendiary bombs.

Pilots peeled off one after another starting with the Helldivers. They entered their bombing runs at ten thousand feet with their canopies locked open, their bomb bay doors open, and their split diving flaps popped to keep their speed within a safe range. Altimeters unwound as they pointed the noses of their aircraft almost straight down into an onrush of anti-aircraft fire. After almost two miles plunging toward the earth, their planes reached terminal velocity at about three hundred knots. They released their payloads at 2,500 feet and suddenly felt their planes lighten. Their runs inflicted serious damage on hangars and a nearby cluster of aircraft.[11] The Avengers came in next, executing much shallower glides over the target, leaving them within range of anti-aircraft fire for an extended period. After dropping their bombs over a concentration of hangars and barracks at the end of a runway, the Avenger pilots likewise pulled up, following on the heels of the dive bombers as they attempted to gather back up at a safer altitude.

Fighters covered the bombers throughout their dives and pull-outs. Once the Helldivers and Avengers were done, it was Fighting 18's turn. One four-plane division focused on the dive bombers' target; one division followed the "torpeckers" in; and one division, led by skipper Edward Murphy, stayed at 13,000 feet to serve as cover. He was accompanied by his wingman, the Formosa ace Ens. Moe Mollenhauer, and Ens. Daniel Naughton, one of the fresh young replacement pilots brought in after Formosa. They served as the last line of defense in case of enemy ambush.

They were needed almost immediately. A group of six Imperial Japanese Army Air Force Oscar fighters sprang on VB-18's Helldivers when they pulled out of their runs. Incredibly, pilots and gunners from the "Sunday Punchers" managed to down four Oscars without suffering a single loss. Skill played a role, but the bomber crews rightfully considered it "a matter of luck" that they made it through the initial attack unscathed.[12]

Another force of fifteen to twenty enemy fighters was biding its time above the clouds at the opposite end of Clark Field. They sprang as soon as they saw VF-18's fighter-bombers enter their dives. Lieutenant Commander Murphy "tallyhoed" the enemies, calling out their number and heading, but it was clear his escort division was outnumbered at least three to one. The attackers swarmed over VF-18's fighter-bombers at low altitude. Only one pilot accurately dropped his bomb in the face of this onslaught. The rest jettisoned their payloads and began fighting for their lives.

Months of combat operations had improved the squadron's discipline and teamwork. Wingmen learned how their leaders reacted to different situations. Sometimes they could even anticipate their movements, allowing them to stick closely to the lead plane even as it maneuvered radically through the air. As a result, most two-plane sections stayed together throughout the fight. This proved critical over Clark Field. Not only were the *Intrepid* fighters outnumbered, but their opponents also appeared to have combat experience. Japanese fighters stuck together in loose groups of three, probing and prodding Fighting 18's Hellcats to find an opening.[13]

Mollenhauer and Murphy weaved back and forth defensively, paying attention to the targets in front of them even as bullets zipped by from the rear. Murphy riddled one Tojo fighter through its wing and drop tank. As the plane went down in flames, another suddenly took its place, filling the reticle in Murphy's gun sight. A Zeke got on Mollenhauer's tail while Murphy was preoccupied. By the time Murphy was able to weave back in and force the determined enemy off Mollenhauer, the young pilot's plane had been gravely damaged. The two of them finished off the Zeke before the melee separated them. The last time the skipper saw his wingman, Mollenhauer was "in a shallow gliding turn at 2,000 feet."[14]

Murphy's other section was also in trouble. Ensign Naughton was weaving with his leader when he felt heavy anti-aircraft fire wallop his Hellcat. After recovering from the initial shock, he found himself flying alone. Naughton climbed for altitude to get away from artillery fire before taking a quick survey of the damage. Wind was whipping into his shattered canopy. His head was bleeding profusely down his face and neck. His starboard wing sported a large hole. Most worryingly, his engine was running ragged. It did not seem like his Hellcat would make it very far.[15]

Naughton radioed for help. In short order, three Hellcats appeared to escort him east. Naughton constantly lost altitude as his engine began to fail, but each time it seemed like he might not make it over the next ridgeline, he somehow found a pass between the mountains. Naughton leaned his fuel mixture for maximum economy. He put his propeller in low pitch to eke out every second of life from his engine. When he finally made it over the water, he knew there was no time left to spare. He did not want to risk a deadstick landing—descending with no power whatsoever—if his engine quit. With limited control of his damaged Hellcat, Naughton made a perfect water landing six miles off the coast of Luzon and clambered into his life raft to await rescue.[16]

Meanwhile, in the ongoing battle over Clark Field, Frog Hurst and his wingman, George Eckel, constantly brushed enemy planes off each other's tails. Hurst knocked down three Zekes, including two approaching from nearly head-on. Despite this success, he and Eckel were still outnumbered. A determined pilot in one of the new fighter types got on Hurst's tail to avenge his fallen comrades. Eckel saw the danger and quickly slotted into position. He lined up dead center behind the enemy fighter, holding steady before letting out a quick burst from his guns. His aim was true. Rounds struck in and around the cockpit until the enemy plane tumbled toward the ground. Hurst was safe—for the time being.

Eckel's brief moment of well-aimed fire left him exposed. Before he could resume weaving with Hurst, his plane lurched from multiple hits. Fire from enemy planes and anti-aircraft guns on the ground found its mark almost simultaneously. His engine cowling was damaged, but the engine continued to run true. His port wing had a hole blown through it and a 20-mm round almost took out his starboard flaps, but his controls continued to respond. A shell tore a ten-inch hole out of the fuselage near the cockpit. Any closer and it would have killed him outright. Incredibly, Eckel's luck held. His Hellcat somehow made it all the way back to *Intrepid*.

The air battle above Clark Field finally started to taper off. The last stragglers were Flaps O'Maley and Chuck deMoss, who were having trouble shaking three determined Japanese fighters from their tails. O'Maley and deMoss were among the most senior men in Fighting 18. deMoss had over one thousand hours of flight time, and O'Maley had double that. It was clear from their plane-handling and persistence that their opponents had experience as well. They flew newer fighters capable of keeping pace with the Hellcats and took advantage of their numerical superiority.[17]

When tracers began to flash past O'Maley and deMoss, they finally decided they'd had enough. They radioed each other a single word: "Water."[18] Water injection, or "war emergency power," was a new feature of the F6F-5 model Hellcat, and though neither of them had much experience with it, the system was easy to initialize. deMoss reached up with his left hand to flip the water pump switch located just beyond his engine controls. With his right hand, he advanced the throttle beyond the usual stopping point to the full forward position. deMoss held his breath for a second as O'Maley activated his own water injection system. Suddenly the two Hellcats lurched forward as if they'd been shoved from behind. The Japanese planes faded into the distance. Their opponents did not even bother trying to catch up.[19]

This strike raised important questions. How were the fighters supposed to simultaneously protect the dive and torpedo bombers while conducting ground attack missions of their own? Fighting 18 destroyed eight enemy planes over Clark Field, including victories by Ens. Arthur Haig and Ens. Winton "Windy" Horn, but achieved very little with their bombs. Even worse, they were out of position when enemy fighters began attacking because of the fighter-bomber assignment. As a result, two VF-18 pilots were missing in action and a third was lucky to have made it back aboard ship. This did not seem to be a winning strategy.

While the survivors of strike 2A headed home to *Intrepid*, the second strike of the day, strike 2B, was just getting airborne. It revisited Clark Field to continue where the previous strike left off. The importance of suppressing airfields in the northern Philippines, especially the massive complex at Clark, was not lost on these pilots. In fact, just before strike 2B took off, CAP fighters from the nearby carrier *Hancock* downed three Japanese planes only twenty-five miles from the fleet. The question was not *if* the enemy would launch a counterattack, but *when*.[20]

Frog Hurst landed aboard *Intrepid* just before noon. He knew he only had about two hours of downtime before he was scheduled to fly again. He hustled out of his Hellcat, down the ladder to the gallery deck, and made a beeline for refreshments. Hot chocolate was calling his name. After securing a piping-hot cup, Hurst finally reached the squadron ready room and its cushy leather chairs. It was time for some rest and relaxation: bull sessions with fellow flyers, a catnap, maybe a game of acey-deucy.

The GQ alarm rang out as soon as Hurst hit his seat. Despite the urgency of the klaxons and the hustle of shipboard personnel, Hurst stayed put. The air group did not have separate battle stations the way *Intrepid*'s crew did. They were supposed to report to their ready rooms, and Hurst was already in his. He listened for the sound of the ship's anti-aircraft guns to tell him when danger was imminent. He probably sighed and took a sip of his hot chocolate while he waited for things to calm down.[21]

Topside, the GQ alarms sent men sprinting to their battle stations. A few determined Japanese bombers had made it past the CAP pilots. They were closing fast. Four minutes after the ship went to general quarters, *Intrepid*'s gunners opened fire on an Aichi D3A2 Val dive bomber. The enemy plane approached from behind the ship on its starboard side. It was headed right for *Intrepid*'s superstructure, or island, where Capt. Joseph Bolger commanded the carrier and where Adm. Gerald Bogan was busy coordinating the actions of the dozens of ships in *Intrepid*'s task group.[22]

Gunners manning 20-mm cannons on *Intrepid*'s port side swung their guns to face the aft end of the flight deck as the plane drew nearer, opening up with a hail of chattering fire that added to the deafening boom-boom of the twin 40-mm guns trying to find the enemy's range. One of these positions was at the deck edge just aft of the number two aircraft elevator, not far from Air Group 18's ready rooms. The tub contained six 20-mm cannons in separate mounts positioned side by side. When its gunners started firing, Hurst heard them loud and clear. He knew the enemy was almost over the carriers if the ship's smallest guns were firing.[23]

This was gun tub ten, the position manned principally by Black Sailors who had been credited with shooting down a plane off Formosa. These were the men who did the air group officers' laundry, made their beds, and set their tables. Segregation prevented them from obtaining combat ratings, but here they were again serving as *Intrepid*'s last line of defense.[24] Eugene Smith Jr., one of the steward's mates in gun tub ten, joined the Navy because of Doris "Dorie" Miller, the Black Sailor whose heroism at Pearl Harbor earned him widespread fame. Now Smith found himself facing down enemy aircraft just like the man who inspired him to enlist. He was strapped into one of the 20-mm guns with men working on either side of him.[25] A loader fed sixty-round magazines into his weapon to keep it firing while a spotter relayed information from Alfonso Chavarrias, the gun captain. Smith corrected his aim accordingly, swiveling this way and that as the other five 20-mm crews around him all worked together to bring down the target.[26]

The enemy dive bomber pushed through the anti-aircraft fire with unwavering determination. The gun crews stood their ground, too, remaining at their posts even as the bomber hurtled directly toward them. It was a standoff. At the last second, the gunners finally found their mark. A stream of cannon fire clipped off the Val's starboard wing and tail.[27] It veered out of control, grazing the port edge of the ship. Arcing sheets of flaming gasoline washed over gun tub ten where the plane touched down, but the Val and its payload tumbled harmlessly into the ocean. It had barely missed the flight deck and the tower, where it would have done unimaginable damage. Instead, *Intrepid* came through almost unscathed thanks to the dedication of its gunners.[28]

Damage control teams immediately sprang into action to extinguish the flames in gun tub ten. The crew pitched magazines overboard to prevent rounds from detonating in the intense heat and dragged wounded men away from the smoke and flames.[29] Despite these efforts, it was already too late for many of the brave men in gun tub ten. Virtually all of them suffered burns

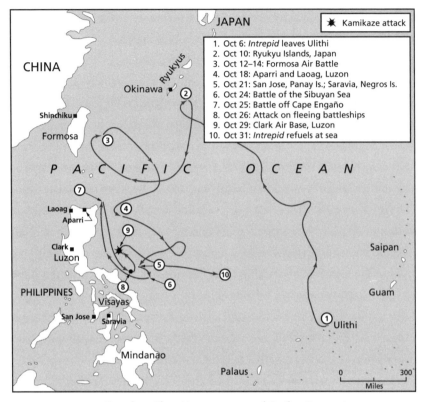

JAPAN

| ☀ Kamikaze attack |

1. Oct 6: *Intrepid* leaves Ulithi
2. Oct 10: Ryukyu Islands, Japan
3. Oct 12–14: Formosa Air Battle
4. Oct 18: Aparri and Laoag, Luzon
5. Oct 21: San Jose, Panay Is.; Saravia, Negros Is.
6. Oct 24: Battle of the Sibuyan Sea
7. Oct 25: Battle off Cape Engaño
8. Oct 26: Attack on fleeing battleships
9. Oct 29: Clark Air Base, Luzon
10. Oct 31: *Intrepid* refuels at sea

CHINA

Okinawa

Ryukyus

Shinchiku

Formosa

P A C I F I C   O C E A N

Laoag
Aparri

Clark
Luzon

Saipan

PHILIPPINES
Visayas

San Jose
Saravia

Guam

Ulithi

Mindanao

Palaus

0   300
Miles

MAP 4. October Ship Movements and Strike Operations

from the flames, flash burns from the explosions, and shrapnel wounds from the splintered aircraft. Half the men was either dead at their stations or would succumb to their wounds later in the day.[30] A somber service and burial at sea had to wait, however; *Intrepid* was in the middle of strike operations and still in danger.[31]

As the ship's crew moved the dead and wounded from gun tub ten and prepared the next strike for launch, the nineteen Hellcats, nine Helldivers, and seven Avengers of strike 2B arrived over Luzon. As with strike 2A, there was no initial opposition to the carrier planes. Torpedo bombers destroyed hangars and repair shops. They also damaged a large collection of twin-engine aircraft parked on the north side of the field. Dive bombers targeted a warehouse and dropped bombs around the runway itself, wrecking parked aircraft. That left the fighters to drop their five-hundred-pound general-purpose bombs before everyone regrouped to head home.

Strike 2B used the same rendezvous point as the sweep and morning strike. That may have made mission briefings easier, but it also simplified the job of Japanese interceptors lurking at high altitude. As the strike 2B Hellcats peeled off to bomb Clark Field, ten Japanese fighters immediately pounced on the bombers wrapping up their attack. Once again, VB-18 pilots and their gunners put up a strong fight. Three enemy fighters were brought down by a combination of wing-mounted 20-mm cannons and rear-facing twin .30-caliber machine guns. But something had to give; their luck couldn't hold through two successive attacks. VB-18's Lt. Elmer Namoski and his gunner, Aviation Radioman First Class Sterling Graham, were shot down before the fighters could come to their aid.

The torpedo bombers did not fare any better. As soon as they pulled out of their runs, four enemy fighters tore into them. Ball turret gunners rotated left and right, tracking sleek brown and silver fighters through the air in a desperate attempt to drive them off. They scored hits on two enemy planes, but not before Japanese fighters shot down Ens. Nicholas Roccaforte and seriously damaged Lt. (jg) Joseph Rubin's Avenger, forcing the latter to land in the water outside the task group.[32]

Punchy Mallory and Beetle Beatley of VF-18 were circling above Clark Field as photo recon and high cover. From their lofty position, they could see the sprawling air complex with its outlying runways stretching off into the distance. They could also see the glinting forms of Japanese aircraft rising to meet them. In addition to the dozen or so enemies they needed to peel off the bombers, Mallory, Beatley, and the rest of the fighters now had to deal with another fifteen to twenty planes coming in hot.

The two photo-fighters joined up with a nearby division. Together, the six Hellcats raced after the first Japanese aircraft that crossed their path. Mallory was attacked from behind during the chase. He pulled back on the stick and nosed his plane upward until he was inverted. He snap-rolled out of the loop, spinning his plane 180 degrees so he was now right side up and flying away from his squadron mates, directly toward the enemy that had been chasing him. The maneuver, called an Immelmann, worked, but Mallory had not anticipated bleeding off so much airspeed during his climb. His plane fell off slightly, preventing him from getting a bead on his opponent as they passed by one another. By the time he picked up enough speed to recover, he was five thousand feet below the other Hellcats and out of position.[33]

Mallory knew he was a sitting duck on his own. Now that he was back in control, he turned and began climbing for altitude to find Beatley. He could see a division just above and ahead of him. When he was close to joining up, a Zeke suddenly flew in front of him. It was practically handed to Mallory on a silver platter. He shot the enemy fighter down and continued with the division, happy to be reunited with friendly forces.

The main priority now was to get back to the rendezvous point to escort the Avenger and Helldiver crews home. That proved to be easier said than done. The remaining Japanese fighters were unrelenting. Lt. Kenneth Crusoe, one of the VF-11 replacement pilots who had only been flying with Fighting 18 for a couple of days, suddenly radioed for help. He had downed two enemy planes and damaged a third but was now alone at low altitude with four angry fighters on his tail. Mallory told Crusoe to break out over the water. He was going to try to bail him out.

Mallory unleashed a stream of machine gun fire between Crusoe and his pursuers, forcing them to break off. That was all Crusoe needed to shake them. Mallory nosed up to rejoin the flight but felt his plane suddenly shudder under the impact of enemy gunfire. One of the fighters had snuck up on him while he was focused on Crusoe. Mallory's Hellcat started handling like a truck. It sounded like he was dragging something through the air, and it felt like he was braking somehow, especially on the port side. He couldn't seem to get his airspeed above 180 knots. Mallory looked over to the right side of his cockpit. The plane's hydraulic pressure gauge was dropping. He quickly put two and two together: his left landing gear must be dangling in the breeze.

The enemy on his tail was now gaining ground. Mallory had to think fast. He remembered reading that Japanese pilots tended to "split-S" out of danger. To perform the maneuver, a pilot rolled his plane inverted, then dove down through a half-loop. The result was a kind of vertical 180-degree turn where the pilot lost altitude but was quickly able to change direction. Mallory began to roll his plane, hoping the enemy on his tail would anticipate this move. He wrestled against the weird feeling of his wheel dragging through the air as he went inverted. As expected, the Japanese pilot suddenly dove to cut inside the arc of Mallory's loop. He would be able to hit the Hellcat before its hapless pilot leveled out. There was only one problem: Mallory didn't nose down. He remained inverted, flying upside-down into a cloud as the enemy fighter found himself alone at low altitude. Mallory rolled back over and climbed, getting out of there as quickly as he could in his damaged plane.[34]

As the strike returned to *Intrepid* at 1540, plane after war-weary plane banged down onto the flight deck, giving onlookers some insight into the wild fights that were playing out over Clark Field. Nine Hellcats were damaged, five of them seriously so. One would need a whole new engine. Ens. John T. Williss, another of the VF-11 transplants, shot down two enemy fighters but came back with two gaping holes in his Hellcat's tail. Three men had shrapnel wounds, including Beetle Beatley, who had cuts all over his face from his shattered canopy. And there were still two planes having trouble landing: Crusoe's and Mallory's.[35]

Landing signal officer Lt. Richard Moot gave Mallory a wave-off on his first pass. His flaps were not responding, and he was having difficulty keeping his plane steady. Moot could tell the second pass wouldn't be much better. This Hellcat was obviously damaged; maybe its pilot was injured. Moot had to adjust his usual approach to get this plane down safely. When Mallory circled back, Moot had him come in high and fast. He gave him the cut early. Mallory throttled back, brought his plane down hard on the deck, and somehow caught a wire. Moot had given him a perfect cut, just like he did for Wally Walworth back in September. Mallory's Hellcat lurched to a stop. When he finally got out of his damaged plane, Mallory took a second to look it over. It was pockmarked with dozens of holes—sixty-seven, to be precise—from 7.7- and 20-mm projectiles.[36]

Things were not much better for Crusoe. Like Mallory, he probably got a high and fast cut to bring him down safely despite damage to his tail and flaps. Crusoe's Hellcat thumped down and caught a wire, but it didn't stop: its tailhook ripped out without slowing its momentum. In fact, the whole tail assembly broke off on impact. The plane continued forward until it smashed into the crash barrier and nosed down hard. Its propeller gouged into *Intrepid*'s wooden flight deck. Though the barrier succeeded in stopping Crusoe's plane, the crash caused the pilot to smash face first into the dashboard. As soon as the plane skidded to a halt, deck crews swarmed over the aircraft. Corpsmen helped the injured pilot out of the cockpit; ordnancemen stripped out available ammunition; machinist's mates popped access panels to the engine compartment; and tractor crews began figuring out how they were going to unfoul the deck so *Intrepid* could get back to air operations. Crusoe survived, but he had a nasty cut on his head and an injured back, requiring the corpsmen to take him down to sick bay on a stretcher.[37]

By now it seemed prudent to adjust the strike composition. Enemy fighter opposition was just too stiff. On paper, bombers participating in a full strike could inflict more damage to the target than an all-fighter sweep, but the situation over Clark Field blunted the bombers' efficacy and put them at unnecessary risk. Sending out a second fighter sweep instead of a third strike could solve this problem. However, that required de-gassing, disarming, and moving a dozen bombers while fueling, arming, and spotting additional fighters. Despite continued complaints from squadron leaders, air intelligence officers, and others within the air group, it was not feasible to make this last-second change. *Intrepid* launched strike 2C at around 1400, sending aloft fifteen Hellcats, six Helldivers, and six Avengers.[38]

On the bright side, Fighting 18 pilots on strike 2C did not take off with bombs. They were only responsible for escort duty. En route to the target, however, two Hellcats exhibited mechanical problems, requiring them to return to base. The fighters were starting shorthanded. As the strike roared over Luzon, VF-18 divisions separated to patrol at varying altitudes. A four-plane division, led by Rudy Van Dyke, orbited low; Cecil Harris' shorthanded three-plane division waited at intermediate cover; and six Hellcats, including a division led by Clarence Blouin, waited at 16,000 feet to ward off attack from above.

A gathering of low-hanging cumulus clouds over the field made it difficult for the bombers to do their work and even harder for them to gauge their success. A hangar and workshop were listed as seriously damaged, but the report was vague. Van Dyke and the low cover fighters followed the dive bombers as they began climbing away from the target, providing close protection on the way to the rendezvous site. While the bombers climbed, Blouin's high cover fighters dropped down like a hammer to strafe aircraft parked around the field. Even though the previous strikes had claimed upward of thirty enemy aircraft destroyed in combat and many more damaged or destroyed on the ground, the Clark Field area was still teeming with hundreds of planes.

While Blouin's division strafed and Van Dyke's shepherded the bombers, only Harris' shorthanded division was available to maintain watch. As he scanned the airspace over Clark, Harris suddenly caught sight of three small, glinting figures more than a mile below. They were Nakajima Ki-44 Tojos— Imperial Japanese Army fighters built specifically for interception duty—and they were making a beeline for the bombers.[39]

The three Tojo pilots were completely absorbed in their chase. They had no idea Harris was hot on their tails until his machine guns raked one of the planes from tail to nose. It was destroyed by the hail of bullets. The two remaining fighters ducked into a nearby cloudbank rather than continue their pursuit. Harris and his division mates began climbing now that the threat was neutralized, but they did not make it far before they spotted three more Tojos to the north at six thousand feet. Harris tore into them as well, setting one aflame and again forcing the others to scatter.

As *Intrepid*'s bombers reached the eastern edge of Clark Field, a massive group of twenty to forty Japanese fighters appeared more than a mile overhead. Surprisingly, these enemies ignored them entirely. They were instead focused on the *Intrepid* fighters, and they had the element of surprise, strength in numbers, and superior altitude on their side.

The Japanese fighters descended in one big, horizontal ring for mutual protection. This tactic, a World War I–era formation called a Lufbery circle, allowed Japanese pilots to protect each other's tails while they attempted to draw Fighting 18's Hellcats into an engagement. Groups of two to three Tojos,

Oscars, and Zekes broke off to attack the Hellcats. If Harris and his squadron mates gave chase, another group would jump out from the circle, hitting them from behind with machine gun fire.[40]

Experienced leaders like Blouin, Harris, and Van Dyke knew better than to fight on the enemy's terms. Time and again, when Japanese fighters dove down on VF-18's Hellcats, the men faced them head-on rather than turning onto their tails. Japanese fighters foolish enough to dive away from this game of chicken were left far from the protection of the circle overhead and vulnerable to counterattack by *Intrepid*'s fighters. Isolated and outnumbered at lower altitude, the Japanese fighters desperately opened fire from outside gun range. It was no use. For minor damage to two Hellcats during this engagement, the squadron claimed twelve enemy fighters destroyed in aerial combat.

It was a banner day for the fighters of strike 2C. Most importantly, they managed to bring all the bombers home safely. As a bonus, nearly half of the men added to their scores. Harris shot down two more planes by the end of the engagement, bringing his daily total to four. It was his third time almost making ace in a day. Frog Hurst and Rudy Van Dyke cemented their status as aces, and Bill Mufich, Buck Newsome, and W. E. Stephens also contributed to the overwhelming success over Clark.[41]

The strike finally headed back to *Intrepid*. As the men flew east, the rapidly setting sun reflected off the ocean below. Minutes ticked by, marked by a dazzling procession of color. Wave crests splashed with flaming yellow-orange faded to bright pink, then to more subdued purples, as the sea swallowed up the sun. The beauty of the scene was tempered by the stark reminder that the purple luster would soon give way to twilight blue and the perils of night carrier operations. Specialized night fighter pilots may have been used to operating purely on instruments, but most of the squadron—even senior officers—had extremely limited experience trying to land aboard ship in the dark.

Combat air patrol pilots at the edge of the fleet were equally worried about nightfall. Four fighters from *Intrepid*, including Dave Davis, had originally been launched at 1500 for snooper anti-submarine patrol duty and were armed with depth charges. As soon as they cleared the deck, however, Jeep

Daniels, *Intrepid's* intercept officer, caught a bogey that needed immediate attention.

"Dave, I've got one for you."[42] Davis perked up when he heard Jeep's voice on the radio. Hellcats from *Hancock* and *Independence* were busy chasing down Japanese bombers that had just appeared over the fleet. These pilots and their fighter director were too busy to handle the plane Jeep was worried about. He gave Davis the bogey's heading, and in the next instant the *Intrepid* fighters jettisoned their depth charges, becoming de facto CAP pilots.

Davis and his section leader, Squawkie Rennemo, led their wingmen south toward the contact. Jeep was in Davis' ear all the while, providing changes in heading based on the unknown aircraft's movement: "He's right there." Davis and his division mates looked around for the bogey but could only see clouds above and below. "You're right over him," Jeep repeated. The enemy plane, a Val dive bomber, was below the clouds, making its way steadily toward the task group. Davis finally spotted it.

The Val pilot seemed blissfully unaware of the danger, continuing along his course without changing speed. Davis let down steadily with his division in tow, gradually losing altitude to prevent himself from overshooting the target. As soon as he was level with the Val, he increased speed to make a gunnery run from the port side, crossing over the top of the bomber with all six guns blazing. It took multiple passes to bring the stubborn plane down, but after hits by Davis and Rennemo, the Val finally caught fire and crashed into the water below.[43]

Strike 2C was now within sight of the fleet. Fading daylight clung to the contours of the ships, casting them in a soft silvery light that stood out clearly against the dark blue sky. As Harris and company came in for their final approach, the ships at the head of the formation suddenly winked out of view behind a wall of dark gray clouds. The sea, the sky, and everything in between was blotted out by a squall of epic proportions. Visibility was suddenly zero.

Radio channels flooded with chatter: What were the ships' headings? Were the decks clear? The chaos enveloped strike and patrol pilots alike. Lt. John Williams held strike 2C's Avengers at the edge of the downpour. Trying to land a group of planes, all low on fuel, safely aboard ship at night in the middle of a storm was too risky. Radio channels crowded by anxious pilots made it difficult to determine the situation on the surface. The best Williams could do was keep the Avengers together, report his position, and try to make a group water landing, hoping they would be picked up sooner rather than later.[44]

All hands tried their best to guide the aircraft safely back to base. Jeep Daniels periodically provided *Intrepid*'s heading to Davis, hoping the CAP pilot could grope his way home using his plane's compass and estimated distance from the ship. Night fighters from *Independence* served as guides for planes from *Hancock*, *Cabot*, and *Intrepid*. Admiral Bogan even lit up the task group. Glow lights, truck lights, flight deck landing lights, and searchlights were brought to bear against the storm, providing beacons for pilots who could get close enough to see them through the dense cloud cover.[45]

Harris and Blouin were among the first to brave the weather over the task group. Blouin flew in and out of the storm to provide the carriers with coordinates where they could recover aircraft in the clear, but each time he broke out of the rain, he found that the storm had expanded, further enveloping the ships below. There was no way it could be avoided. Blouin coordinated with Lieutenant Williams of VT-18 since it seemed like his fighters would also have to land in the water.[46]

Meanwhile, Harris flew deeper and deeper into the storm. He cast a quick glance from the uniform dark gray view in his windshield to the altimeter and artificial horizon on his dashboard. Even throttled back, his Hellcat was covering more than a hundred feet per second. At this rate *Intrepid* would sneak up on him quickly. Harris mulled over the instrument readings with his eyes locked forward, straining to see through the darkness. He flew level at just about one hundred feet over the water. Staying low gave him the best chance of spotting his ship, but it also meant he only had a few seconds to pull up if he suddenly stumbled upon *Intrepid*.

Harris forged ahead undaunted. Suddenly, a muted column of light swept through the murky sky, then another. In a moment he could see a long, sleek shape glowing on the ocean's surface: a battleship! That meant the carriers would be close by. Harris gave his instruments another glance. The dials on his fuel gauge were below 20 percent. If he overshot his target now, he might not get another chance. He finally broke radio silence to call the ship for a heading and permission to attempt an approach—just in time for *Intrepid* to loom out of the rainy haze directly in front of him.

Harris stomped on his rudder pedal as he pulled his Hellcat's control stick to the side and angled away from the incoming carrier. He narrowly avoided catastrophe. The carrier group quickly turned into the wind to receive him. Harris made a successful landing despite poor visibility and strong winds across the deck. He was among the first to make it back. In short order, Blouin, Davis, and most of the remaining fighters were aboard ship.[47]

Davis started heading for the ready room as soon as he got out of his Hellcat, but before he made it there, a voice rang out through the gallery deck passageway. "I'm sure glad we got you back safe!" It was Jeep Daniels, the intercept officer who had helped him get home in one piece. Davis grinned and waved him off. "Oh, it was nothing." Jeep laughed. "Sure, Dave," he replied sarcastically. They both knew how rough things had been.[48]

The situation was dire for those still trapped in the storm. Landing became increasingly difficult as the wind picked up and the darkness deepened. One fighter from USS *Cabot* crashed catastrophically into the carrier's deck. The plane burst into flames, causing the rest of *Cabot*'s fighters to divert to *Intrepid* instead.[49]

Aircraft from *Hancock* were also forced to land aboard the increasingly busy *Intrepid*—with mixed results. One Helldiver pilot touched down so far to starboard that he almost missed the deck. The impact tore the bottom of his plane open and flipped it upside down. It slid along the aft end of *Intrepid* until it hit an antenna mast, bringing the Helldiver to a stop with its nose in a catwalk and its tail hanging precariously over the water. The plane's gunner crawled safely out onto the deck, but the pilot fell into the ocean. He was later rescued.[50]

Intrepid's damage control teams worked to extinguish fires caused by the crash, but the need to temporarily suspend flight operations caused further delays for pilots desperately trying to get aboard ship. Lt. William Thompson, who had been with *Intrepid*'s night fighting detachment before they were rolled into VF-18 and had made *Intrepid*'s one-thousandth carrier landing a month earlier, ran out of gas along with Ens. James Hedrick, one of the post-Formosa replacement pilots. The two landed in the water. Unlike the *Hancock* pilot, they were never found.[51]

29 October was one of the costliest days in Fighting 18's nearly two-month deployment. Four men were missing, and a fifth was seriously injured. They fought some of their most competent adversaries in some of Japan's best fighter aircraft and bore witness to suicidal attacks at the very beginning of the kamikaze campaign. Cdr. Dick Kauffman, *Intrepid*'s executive officer, wrote in the ship's plan of the day on 31 October 1944, "It would be unjust not to mention the superb courage and stamina shown by the personnel of our Air Group. For almost two months, they have operated continuously against the enemy. The flying alone has been tough—against strong enemy opposition, it has been magnificent."[52]

Flying provided the adrenaline and focus needed to stay on track in the face of this daily regimen of danger. Back aboard ship, however, the difficulty of sustaining these kinds of operations began to set in. Punchy Mallory recorded his feelings in his diary—perhaps to exorcise them. A day after these events, he was still "a bit jumpy." Mallory remained hyper-alert thinking about his close shave and the lingering specter of kamikazes. Finally, on 1 November, enough emotional and temporal space elapsed for Mallory to wind down during his off-hours. Fatigue took the place of anxiety: "Not until today did I realize just how tired I am.... It's a deadening tiredness.... Maybe a few days rest will fix us up."[53]

CHAPTER 11

STRAFING AND SURVIVING

NOVEMBER BROUGHT A NUMBER OF CHANGES to fleet personnel and operations. Legendary carrier commander Admiral Mitscher hauled down his flag aboard *Lexington* for some well-deserved rest. Adm. John McCain took his place as commander, Task Force 38.[1] Admiral McCain and his staff had to quickly develop countermeasures against the growing threat posed by kamikazes. Fortunately, McCain's air operations officer, Cdr. Jimmy Thach, was a preeminent fighter pilot with a history of implementing extremely effective tactics.[2] Thach and company went to work developing a series of training exercises, changes to strike procedures, and reinforced air patrol regimens to protect the fleet while it operated off the Philippine coast.[3]

Aboard *Intrepid*, the much-beloved William Ellis, commander of Air Group 18, was poached by the ship's company to serve as *Intrepid*'s new air officer.[4] It was a bittersweet departure. The air group was losing its leader: the man who had overseen their training, helped adapt them to shipboard service, and fought by their side in massive aerial and naval engagements. Ellis had whipped them into a fighting force. Now he was forced to leave them before the end of their deployment. It didn't seem fair.

It was an emotional moment for Commander Ellis as well. In a memorandum to "All Hands" in the air group, he stated plainly, "Although it breaks my heart to leave you, necessity dictates otherwise. I am intensely proud of this air group. . . . There have been times when I ordered attacks, knowing full well some of you would not return. Some of you did not. This was difficult for me—but none of you failed me, and more important, none of you failed yourselves. I can only believe that those who are gone must watch your performance with pride."[5]

On the bright side, El Gropo wasn't going far. As air officer, he managed launch and recovery, aviation fueling, aircraft handling on the hangar and flight decks, and rescue in case of aviation accidents. His firsthand knowledge of flight operations meant that the air group was in good hands aboard ship. Within a week of taking charge, squadron personnel felt like he had things running "slick as a whistle."[6]

The timing of Ellis' reassignment proved fortuitous. Just days later, the first of the changes instituted by Admiral McCain's brain trust made their way to task group commanders, including Admiral Bogan aboard *Intrepid*. Night interceptors and night hecklers were now assigned to cover the busiest Japanese airbases; end-of-day strike aircraft had their bombs removed and were de-gassed for damage control purposes due to the kamikaze threat. And most importantly for the fighters, new flight schedules were being drawn up.[7] While it seemed like the big air and sea battles of October were in the rear-view mirror, pilots expected to fly just as many hours in November to keep the kamikazes at bay.

Fighting 18 flew its first four-plane Jack patrol on 7 November. These defensive operations put fighters low over the water within visual range of screening destroyers. Unlike combat air patrol missions, Jack pilots were separated to cover quadrants of airspace corresponding to the cardinal points on a compass. They had to rigidly adhere to their assigned stations. Jack patrols were not flown in lieu of higher altitude CAP missions. Rather, they provided an extra set of eyes where they were needed most.[8]

Ten days later, Task Group 38.2 undertook its first "moosetrap" exercise. Two picket destroyers were stationed to the east of the force while CAP and Jack fighters orbited overhead. *Intrepid* launched seven bombers at 1000 to act as faux kamikazes. Jeep Daniels and the other men in CIC waited with bated breath as VB-18's Helldivers headed away from the center of their radar scopes. The "kamikazes" flew out beyond the picket destroyers with their identification, friend or foe beacons on. Moments later, the bombers turned around and switched their beacons off. They would only turn the systems back on if they were successfully attacked by patrolling fighters. It was like a high-stakes game of tag.[9]

Moosetrap was meant to test the efficacy of new air defense procedures like Jack patrols and their implementation as part of a wider defensive strategy. How quickly and effectively could officers in CIC disseminate information leading to the successful destruction of incoming threats? How smoothly could they coordinate communication between shipboard and airborne forces? Effective interception was difficult. A success rate of 80 to 90 percent was considered excellent in October. The new reality in November was that anything less than a 100-percent intercept rate imperiled the carriers, jeopardizing thousands of lives and some of the Navy's most valuable ships.[10]

The results were underwhelming. The weather was poor and the bombers came in at varying altitudes, compounding the difficulty for the men coordinating interception. Both the *Intrepid* and *Hancock* war diaries note that virtually all the bombers made it through VF-18's patrols. It was obvious that more practice was needed to iron out the wrinkles. Unfortunately, the kamikazes weren't going to wait for fleet defenses to improve.[11]

McCain and Thach had one more major anti-kamikaze measure to implement: the "blanket." Strike schedules previously left gaps of time between missions where no carrier planes were present over Japanese airfields. This gave the enemy a brief period of clear skies to launch a counterpunch. Thach's new strategy was to quite literally blanket target sites by leaving fighters on station over enemy airspace while the next strike came in and did their work. Once the second strike completed its attack, *their* fighters took up patrol stations while the first group headed back to the ship. The third strike launched while the first was inbound, and the second strike's fighters remained on station while the third strike arrived and attacked, ensuring there were always carrier planes over enemy fields.[12]

While Jack patrols and moosetrap exercises could be implemented in November, the blanket strike rotation took more time to develop. It required a complete retooling of carrier air group composition, which was not feasible in the middle of a deployment. As a result, Fighting 18 had to push through

November the old way: flying constantly, oftentimes pulling double duty, to provide added offensive and defensive firepower against kamikazes.

STRAFING

While Helldivers and Avengers could carry larger loads of ordnance over a target—making them ideal for ground attack missions against reinforced structures—they were not as effective when the mission called for destroying aircraft on the ground. Attackers had to get low to find their whereabouts and needed to be able to safely make multiple passes to get the job done. Japanese planes were often hidden or parked in revetments that shielded them from even the biggest general-purpose bombs. Fighters were best equipped to do this kind of work and were needed in large numbers, even though more Hellcats were simultaneously being committed to patrol duty.[13]

On 5 November a large sweep of twenty fighters left *Intrepid* to hit a cluster of fields on southern Luzon. These kamikaze-hunting missions had the aspect of cat-and-mouse games. Intelligence reports indicated that Bulan and Legaspi airfields were bustling. Fighters arrived to find absolutely no planes on Bulan and only a handful at Legaspi. They had to weather intense anti-aircraft fire at these fields just to strafe a few aircraft. The danger seemed to far outweigh the benefits.[14]

Strike 2A closed quickly on the sweep's heels. Lt. Robert Brownell, one of the fighter division leaders, got down low and lit up a grounded Frances bomber, sending smoke and flames into the air where it burned. His squadron mates followed this burning beacon, making additional strafing runs until all nearby aircraft were pockmarked with bullet holes. Dive bombers damaged barracks around the strip, and the "torpeckers" of VT-18 dropped fragmentation bombs and incendiaries in the woods around the field where more planes may have been hidden. As the attackers pulled up from their runs, one fighter found that his belly tank was on fire. A piece of shrapnel from an exploding shell must have punched through it. He jettisoned the tank, hoping there wasn't any other damage to his Hellcat.[15]

Lieutenant Brownell was getting his division together at the edge of the field when another of his men, Lt. Chuck deMoss, radioed that he was hit.

Brownell looked over to see deMoss' plane hemorrhaging oil. The two men had gone to junior college together in California and had somehow wound up in the same Navy fighting squadron years later, halfway around the globe. Now it looked like one of them might not make it home.

All eyes were on Chuck deMoss as his division headed out over water. After less than ten minutes, his Hellcat's oil pressure reached zero.[16] It was clear that he was not getting back to the fleet. Looking around, deMoss realized that the ten to fifteen minutes spent cruising toward *Intrepid* had put him dozens of miles offshore. He radioed that he was going to land in the water as soon as possible.

DeMoss undid his chute and made sure his canopy was locked back. He didn't want it slamming shut if his landing was less than graceful. His propeller started running away, spinning at high revolutions per minute due to lack of oil pressure. Now was as good a time as any to splash down. He braced for impact. The belly of deMoss' Hellcat skipped across the water, jostling him in his seat before settling on the glittering sea surface. The hard part was over. Free of his heavy parachute and assured of easy egress, deMoss stepped out onto the wing of his rapidly sinking plane and inflated his life vest. He pulled out his briefcase-sized raft pack next. DeMoss unfolded the flat raft on the wing before turning the valve to inflate it.

Nothing happened: no hissing sound, no sudden swell—just flat yellow rubber sitting on an increasingly water-washed wing. There wasn't much time left. DeMoss' Hellcat was about to slip under the waves. He shrugged off his pack so he wouldn't sink along with his plane. If he made it ashore, he would now be without fresh water, food, or survival equipment. He dog-paddled and assessed his situation. It was hard to keep a clear head while the freezing cold water soaked through his thin summer flight suit. It didn't seem like there was much to do except pray that rescue was nearby.

Brownell watched this all play out with increasing concern. DeMoss didn't stand a chance without a raft. Brownell radioed their coordinates, but there was no way of knowing how long it would take for rescue to arrive on the scene. He already knew what he had to do, even if it put his own life in danger. Brownell flew low over the water to drop deMoss his raft.

Brownie Brownell's aim was so good he almost beaned his friend in the head. Chuck deMoss did not mind; the raft was a godsend. He clung to the pack, unfolded it to the best of his ability, and turned the valve. It immediately puffed up, and deMoss scrambled in. He was shivering head to toe but happy to be afloat. After making sure deMoss was alright, Brownell looked at his fuel reserves. He was getting low. He took one last reading of deMoss' coordinates, dropped some dye marker near his raft to mark his position, and headed back to the carrier with the rest of his men.[17]

The last strike of the day went to Clark Field. There either wasn't enough game at the satellite fields, or the planes there were too well hidden to seek and destroy without photo reconnaissance. Clark, on the other hand, was bustling. Dive bombers went in with one-thousand-pound bombs, and the "torpeckers" once again carried frags and incendiaries. By the end of their runs, planes spread throughout the field were burning fiercely, sending towering black columns of smoke hundreds of feet into the air. Given the way the planes were obscured, however, it was difficult to determine whether they had destroyed five of them or fifty.

Japanese fighters serving as air defense over Clark made only a token effort to intercept the strike. The one Zeke pilot bold enough to attack was intercepted by Spider Foltz, who missed on his first overhead run due to a tight turn by the enemy pilot. Foltz wasn't going to make that mistake twice. When he saw the Zeke swing back in the opposite direction, he led his target a bit more, sending out a few bursts that chewed through the plane's engine and cockpit area. Spider was so dedicated to the escort mission that he didn't follow the Zeke down to confirm its destruction. He went right back to shepherding the bombers in case a new threat emerged. Fortunately, another member of the strike saw the plane crash. It was Spider's fifth victory, adding yet another ace to the squadron's roster.[18]

The following day provided another opportunity to hit kamikaze bases. The pattern of strikes remained the same: planes were routed to outlying fields in the morning and to Clark later in the day. Anti-aircraft fire was meager at the first target, Lipa, and air defense was almost nonexistent. The field initially looked empty. Though its runways and taxiways were mostly abandoned, it was clear upon closer inspection that planes had been widely dispersed in the wooded area around the base. They weren't just hiding nearby, either: in some cases, paths stretched for miles from the ends of runways into the trees. It was a clear indication how desperate the Japanese were to protect their remaining aircraft.[19]

Camouflage and dispersal once again made damage assessment difficult, but regardless of the quantitative outcome, the pace of attack could not slacken. More carrier planes over more enemy airfields for more hours per day meant fewer kamikazes. This logic only yielded when counterattack was imminent. For example, orders were received on the morning of 6 November to change the third strike of the day into a fighter sweep. The Helldivers and Avengers earmarked for the attack were stripped of their bombs, de-gassed, and stored in the hangar in case enemy forces breached air patrols. That meant *Intrepid* had just one more opportunity to send a full ordnance load over enemy targets.[20]

The last full strike of the day on 6 November, composed of eight Hellcats, seven Helldivers, and four Avengers, headed out just before noon to hit Clark and its associated fields, including Mabalacat. Though pilots may not have known its significance at the time, Mabalacat was the birthplace of the kamikaze. On 19 October Admiral Takajiro Ohnishi arrived at the field to create the first official "special attack" unit. He told the men of the local 201st Air Group, "The salvation of our country is now beyond the power of the ministers of state, the General Staff, and lowly commanders like myself. It can come only from spirited young men such as you. . . . You are already Gods." Pilots from the 201st Air Group were subsequently responsible for the opening salvo of suicide dives that mauled escort carriers off Samar on 25 October.[21]

Lt. Cecil Harris led *Intrepid*'s fighters down toward the target. As his two divisions of Hellcats scouted the field, they noticed rows of planes flanking a gulley about a mile southwest of Mabalacat. The planes were partially obscured by brush, but it seemed as if there were at least a dozen. With limited anti-aircraft fire rising to meet them and no airborne enemies visible, the strike broke into separate groups to hit as many targets as possible.

Helldivers roared down over the gully as they dropped their one-thousand-pound bombs one after the other. Branches flew off from the concussive blasts. The parked planes burst into flames. Fighters followed right behind them to strafe; the combined effort left behind smoldering, hole-filled wrecks. The torpeckers dropped their usual mixture of frag and incendiary bombs on a dispersal area near "Clark North." Some of the twenty to thirty planes spotted there had already been worked over by previous groups, but they burned fiercely nonetheless. If they were still fueled up, they remained a threat.

Results were visibly better than they had been on the previous day's visit to Clark, but Lieutenant Harris was not done yet. After both fighter divisions finished strafing, he radioed the strike leader to ask if they could make another pass. There was more game to the north, and they had ammunition to spare. Permission was granted. Harris brought his men around for a pass over the adjacent field, descending in slaloming arcs to avoid anti-aircraft fire until they were buzzing right over the target. He and his wingman, Franklin Burley, lit up planes parked along the field, destroying three and damaging another fourteen. It was a banner afternoon for the men on strike 2B.[22]

The final sweep of the day consisted of two dozen Hellcats from *Intrepid* and *Hancock*. As they neared the complex at Clark, pilots dove through light cloud cover into perfectly clear skies. Parked Japanese aircraft were indistinct little shapes in their illuminated gunsights at the beginning of their dives. When pilots reached three thousand feet, they pulled back slightly on the stick and opened fire. Enemy planes began to fill their reticles as they pressed their strafing runs as low as fifty feet, ensuring they scored hits. Flying three hundred miles per hour this close to the ground was extremely dangerous, but it got results.[23]

The sweep succeeded in destroying enemy aircraft and providing additional photographic intelligence regarding Clark. Men on the sweep estimated there were still nearly two hundred operational aircraft present. These estimates were probably accurate. Japanese air commanders had been steadily feeding available planes into the Philippines. Over the course of

November alone, around eight hundred enemy aircraft made their way to the various bases flanking the landing forces at Leyte. It was going take many more sweeps and strikes to neutralize this threat.[24]

Despite the pressing need to continue pummeling these bases, the four carrier task groups could not sustain such operations indefinitely. Instead, a rotational schedule had been developed to leave some groups on station while others steamed back to Ulithi for refueling, replenishment, and rest. After a month of continuous combat operations, it was finally Task Group 38.2's turn for a break. *Intrepid* refueled on 7 November but continued its streak of bad luck by running through a typhoon en route to Ulithi. The ship had weathered storms before, but the ferocity of the wind and waves on 8 November was like nothing *Intrepid*'s crew and air group had experienced.[25]

Ed Ritter was berthed in the forward portside area of the ship. He bounced around in his bunk like a jumping bean as *Intrepid* rose and fell. There was no point in trying to sleep through the sound of twisting metal and the thump of the ship plowing through whitecaps. He went down to the wardroom for some coffee.[26] Punchy Mallory was berthed on the starboard side of the ship. The wave action was much worse there for some reason. He was unceremoniously hurled out of bed multiple times. The way *Intrepid* was fitfully rocking reminded him of a dog shaking off water.[27] Three rooms had their portholes blown in by waves and received minor flooding, including room 105, where Dick Cevoli and Fred Tracy slept.[28]

The pilots could at least rest when things cleared up on 9 November, unlike *Intrepid*'s enlisted men. Damage control teams began working on repairs despite their sleepless night. When the ship arrived at Ulithi later that day, rearming and reprovisioning started almost immediately and continued nonstop for four days. On 10 November alone, 190,000 rounds of .50-caliber ammunition, 72 incendiaries, 9 one-ton general-purpose bombs, 27 five-hundred-pound bombs, and over a dozen two-thousand-pound torpedoes were loaded aboard ship. Nine new Hellcats were craned aboard from lighters, bringing the ship's complement back up to fifty-four fighters—no doubt a godsend for Larry Donoghue and his aviation mechanics. Sailors worked at a superhuman pace to keep the group on schedule. More than ten days' worth of provisions were loaded in four days' time. It was a testament to the morale and efficiency of *Intrepid*'s crew.[29]

Air Group 18's new commanding officer, Cdr. Wilson M. Coleman, came aboard ship on 11 November. He was just in time to witness his aviators reveling at the officers' club on Mog Mog Island, a tiny island earmarked for recreation and refreshment. The men were in rare form after back-to-back days swilling beer under the hot Pacific sun. Rudy Van Dyke rode a landing craft back to *Intrepid*, standing on its bow to hurl insults at passing battleships. The next day, Captain Bolger, *Intrepid*'s skipper, was persuaded to visit Mog Mog. Mouthy pilots let the captain know half in jest how to run his ship and generally gave him a playful berating, wagging fingers at him while clumsily spilling beer down his pant leg. Captain Bolger took it all in stride and even seemed to like the banter. His willingness to play along added to his popularity among members of the air group. Commander Coleman must have wondered what he was getting himself into with this wild bunch.

One thing was certain: *Intrepid* was now truly Air Group 18's ship. Back in August 1944, the men had to be reminded not to crack any jokes about *Intrepid*'s reputation for bad luck.[30] In September they still felt like visitors as they learned how to work with the ship's company and adjusted to life at sea. In October *Intrepid* and its air group weathered some of the biggest air and sea battles in the Pacific. They had proved their mettle together and had become a singular fighting force. By November the air group would not abide any slander on *Intrepid*'s name.

Aboard one of the ships ferrying pilots back from Mog Mog, Vernon "Duke" Delaney of VT-18 overheard a pilot from another air group boasting about his squadron's role at Leyte Gulf. He could have ignored the bragging, but the pilot added in disparaging remarks about the "Queen of the Drydocks" (*Intrepid*) and her "green air group" (Air Group 18). Duke moved closer to the man to see if he was finished. When he opened his mouth again to continue the stream of insults, Duke walloped him so hard that he tumbled off the bow onto the deck below. Duke followed the man down, jumping on top of him before looking up at the surprised crowd. "Anyone else from his group here?" Duke asked. There apparently wasn't.[31]

On 14 November the twenty-seven ships of *Intrepid*'s task group sortied out of Ulithi to participate in a one-day hit-and-run mission against targets on Luzon scheduled for 19 November.[32] The repetition of area of operation, the predictable schedule of joint strike operations, and standardized launch times made it possible for Japanese base commanders to anticipate the arrival of the fleet. But that didn't mean they could capitalize on the opportunity. Bogeys were encountered after midnight on 19 November, apparently following the task group's high-speed run toward the Philippines. They tested the Navy's defenses throughout the day. Out of seven separate raids, only one reached visual range of the carriers. The bombers were stopped at the edge of the destroyer screen, miles away from their intended targets. Fighting 18 pilots flew a total of forty CAP and eighteen Jack patrol sorties throughout the day in addition to assigned strike and sweep duty.[33]

Air Group 18's targets for the day were air bases around Manila, including Nielson and Nichols Fields. They were also assigned to destroy shipping in Manila Bay. Any attempt by the Japanese to reinforce garrisons around Leyte needed to be stopped as soon as possible for the insurgent U.S. Army forces to maintain their advantage in personnel and materiel.

The first strike headed north until pilots ran into foul weather, forcing them to divert to Clark Field instead of assessing enemy strength at Nichols and Nielson. On the way to the backup target, VT-18's Avengers were shadowed by Japanese fighters. The enemy kept their distance but were still in plain view of strike aircraft. It was strange. Rather than pressing the attack, the Zeke pilots performed aerobatics as if showing off their plane-handling prowess. Their sleek planes rolled and looped tightly behind the much clumsier, slower Avengers. Maybe they were biding their time.

When the strike arrived at Clark, there were many attractive targets including administration buildings at the former Camp Stotsenburg—a cavalry garrison established in 1902 by order of President Theodore Roosevelt—as well as hangars, planes, and anti-aircraft positions. The torpeckers picked out the largest buildings at the site for their bombing runs. They came down in formation instead of splitting up in case the show-boating Zeke pilots decided to spring on them at the last second. The enemies didn't bother.

Bomber crews believed their aim was true and that a good deal of damage was inflicted on the target, but it was hard to assess the outcome since they dropped their bombs almost simultaneously.

Fighting 18 had two divisions assigned to the strike for a total of eight Hellcats: one photo division including Punchy Mallory and Brownie Brownell, and one escort division led by Cecil Harris. Mallory spotted a group of four Zekes just ahead of them at 19,000 feet. He and Brownell led the attack, each quickly shooting down an enemy plane. After Mallory damaged a third Zeke, the remaining fighter decided he'd had enough and ran for it.[34] Escort and photo duty trumped chasing the plane, so the lucky Japanese pilot lived to fight another day. Mallory rated these fighters as "not to [sic] sharp." It was obvious that the Japanese were scraping the bottom of the barrel.[35]

Separately, Cecil Harris spotted one lone Zeke at higher altitude. Harris opened up on the fighter from long range. In what became his most anticlimactic victory of the war, the enemy pilot bailed out before his plane showed any sign of damage. Harris and his division followed the empty plane out of curiosity. The pilotless Zeke continued to fly straight and true for nearly five minutes before it began to lose altitude. Harris's division practiced their deflection shots on the plane as it hurtled to earth before turning back around to finish their mission.[36]

The weather improved enough for the next strike to hit the primary target, Nichols Field. This was Commander Coleman's first opportunity to lead his men in combat. During the mission briefings in his respective squadrons' ready rooms, he made sure photographs of Nichols Field were handed out by air combat intelligence officers. Each man was given a specific building or area to attack to ensure they spread the damage around. It was also Air Group 18's first opportunity to impress Commander Coleman. After the extremely warm reception they gave him on Mog Mog Island, they wanted to make sure he knew they could fly as well as they could party.

Anti-aircraft fire over Nichols was heavy in volume but light in caliber. As bombers and fighters dove down over the field, bullets pinged off their planes, doing only minor damage to their tough warbirds. It wasn't nearly enough to throw off their aim. Dive bombers obliterated a hangar at the northeast end of the strip. There must have been a fuel dump or oil storage nearby; Coleman noted with satisfaction that the hangar area was obscured by a tremendous fire and billowing black smoke. The torpeckers hit a set of hangars near the center of the field. These buildings went up in similarly spectacular fashion. Nichols was taking a serious beating.

Fighting 18 hit the target last. Pilots strafed twin-engine aircraft dispersed at the southern end of the field. It was clear they were lighting the planes up, but with none of them catching fire, it was hard to say if they were operational, dummies, or wrecks. Pulling out of his strafing run, Fred Tracy's Hellcat caught a 20-mm shell in the nose. His engine was seriously damaged. Like Dan Naughton and Chuck deMoss before him, he knew he would not make it back to the fleet.

Commander Coleman and fellow Fighting 18 pilot Ens. William Murray escorted Tracy out over the water toward Polillo Island, just off the east coast of Luzon. After making a successful water landing, Tracy hunkered down in his raft, watching gratefully as Coleman and Murray circled overhead. While the rest of the strike continued home, they remained above Tracy for several hours, waiting until relief planes arrived to take custody of the downed avia-tor.[37] Later that evening, once they were back aboard ship, Coleman received word that Tracy had been picked up in good condition by the destroyer USS *Cooper*.[38] Commander Coleman breathed a sigh of relief. His strike had inflicted serious damage without suffering any losses. He was full of praise for the excellent bombing at Nichols, and he no doubt earned the respect of his aviators through his stubborn determination to leave no man behind.

One fighter sweep was all that remained after *Intrepid*'s long morning off Luzon. Sixteen Hellcats armed with five-hundred-pound bombs launched one after the other starting at 1235. The bulk of the sweep went to Manila Bay to attack shipping, while Punchy Mallory's division headed back to Nichols Field for photo recon. As it turned out, anti-aircraft fire over the bay was more intense and better aimed than at the airfields. Armed cargo vessels and shore-line batteries filled the sky with flak to discourage strafing pilots from getting too close. The men of Fighting 18 pushed through it anyway. They selected targets at around ten thousand feet, diving shortly thereafter and only pulling out a few thousand feet over the bay. Their bombs hurtled down at steep angles on top of the ships. The results were disappointing, not because their bombs fell wide of the targets, but because upon closer inspection, the ships were already seriously damaged.

The only target marked destroyed on the mission was a high-voltage transmission tower attacked by Donald Watts and Boot Amerman. It was frustrating to get such meager results after weathering serious anti-aircraft fire. One Hellcat had a huge hole in its wing from a 40-mm shell. The pilot made it back aboard *Intrepid*, but the wing was beyond repair.[39]

Over Nichols with the recon group, Punchy Mallory tried to hold steady in the face of intense anti-aircraft fire. The internal cameras in his F6F-5P clicked away as he watched tracers and shells whizz by him. Focused as he was, he didn't see the four Zekes creeping up on his division. Ensign William Eccles, one of the replacement pilots who joined the squadron in late October, suddenly called out, "Bogies!" Mallory whipped his plane around just in time for 20-mm cannon fire to come blasting past him from above. The enemy fighters were only a few hundred feet away.

Mallory shoved his stick forward and kicked hard on one of his rudder pedals, bringing his plane into a skidding dive as the enemies overshot him. When he reversed the maneuver and pulled up, he was on their tails. The closest Zeke pilot made the mistake of pulling up in a vain attempt to escape. Mallory's Hellcat overtook it easily. His guns raked across the exposed topside of the fighter. Its desperate pilot tried to maneuver away, nosing his plane down and rolling over to reverse direction, but it was no use. Mallory fired again. This time, parts of the enemy's cockpit broke off.

The Japanese pilot lucked out. His seriously damaged plane plummeted into a nearby cloud, allowing him to run away from the action. Mallory couldn't go off chasing just one plane when there were more above him swarming his division. He pulled back up to help his squadron mates.[40] Pop Thune fired a burst on a Zeke chasing Eccles. The enemy quickly broke off. Eccles meanwhile took one of the enemy fighters head-on, scoring hits that set the plane on fire. It dove straight down like a comet, illuminating the thin cloud layer below as it passed out of sight. At this point the fight was petering out and the adrenaline was wearing off. Mallory noticed his starboard wing had picked up two big holes in the fight. Now two Hellcats needed new wings.[41]

Buck Newsome and Chesty Herlihy were busy strafing Nichols while the photo division tangled with the Zekes overhead. Their work proved just as dangerous. At 1330 Newsome felt his plane jolt from the impact of a 40-mm shell. His Hellcat was still responsive, but something was wrong with its powerplant. Newsome radioed Herlihy that he'd been hit. Together, the two headed east toward the fleet. Newsome's Hellcat could not maintain altitude, and its oil pressure was dropping rapidly. To complicate matters, his compass was out, so he was actually heading southeast instead of directly toward friendly forces. The two fighters flew low over Laguna de Bay, the large body of water reaching up between Manila and the eastern shore of Luzon like three big fingers, but even making it over the hills to the south of the bay proved challenging. Newsome carefully navigated through the valleys. He was determined to get "feet wet" over open water rather than taking his chances on the ground.[42]

At about 1400, after eking out every spare second of flight from his wounded Hellcat, Newsome knew his time was up. His oil reserve was depleted, and he was losing control of the plane. He radioed Herlihy that he was heading down. Incredibly, his voice was calm. He even cracked jokes: "I wish I had a screwdriver with me . . . I'd take the clock out of this plane before I have to leave it."[43]

Newsome landed in the water south of Marinduque Island, one of the northern borders of the Sibuyan Sea where he had previously attacked Japanese warships. He crawled into his raft while Chesty Herlihy circled overhead. Newsome flashed his buddy the "okay" signal to indicate he was unhurt. Herlihy circled as long as he could, taking careful note of Newsome's location before heading back to *Intrepid*. Once aboard ship, he dutifully gave as much information as he could to the officer coordinating rescue work.[44]

Both Herlihy and skipper Murphy wrote letters to Buck Newsome's parents. Given his role in the squadron, Lieutenant Commander Murphy's tone had to be more professional than Lieutenant Herlihy's, but his letter was still encouraging: "It is my sincere belief that Buck is alive and will return to you but because I do not know this to be a fact regulations require that I report him missing in action."[45] Chesty Herlihy, meanwhile, had the leeway to write, "Buck's chances of being picked up by friendly forces either military or otherwise are as good or better than any pilot that has gone down around here. ... [W]e are all sure we will hear from Buck in a short while." The familiar tone of Herlihy's letter resonated with Newsome's parents. A handwritten note at the bottom of the typed letter reads, "God only knows what Johnny [Herlihy] and his letter mean to us."[46]

SURVIVING

Where and when pilots were shot down dramatically impacted their experiences. Bill Ziemer survived his crash landing on Formosa on the morning of 12 October. He managed to evade enemy patrols all day and night. His survival training paid dividends. When he reached the water, however, he found that his raft would not inflate. It had been punctured by either the crash or his bushwhacking. Before he could patch it and get out to sea, he was spotted. Ziemer became the squadron's first and only prisoner of war.[47]

Dan Naughton, the replacement pilot who went missing during the wild fight over Clark Field on 29 October, landed in the water off the coast of Luzon and successfully inflated his raft. Friendly planes circled overhead where he went down, radioing coordinates and dropping dye marker to make his position more visible, but the elements worked against him. Rain and clouds obscured his position and prevented him from using his signaling mirror. Even though he put out his sea anchor to keep from drifting too far, rough seas dragged him toward a nearby island.

When night fell, Naughton paddled in to make landfall. The breakers surrounding the island proved stronger than he anticipated. His raft capsized, dunking him under the current and dragging away his parachute, poncho, and life vest. He clambered up the rocky beach under a torrential downpour, wearing his raft in lieu of the poncho that had been swept out to sea. He found a flat rock, laid down, and tried to get some rest.

After a night of cold, sleepless discomfort, Dan Naughton set off for the island's interior to avoid enemy patrols and find food. He walked all day, using his cloth survival maps and compass to navigate. When the sun began to set, he built a lean-to, only to discover his campsite was infested by leeches. He got up, pulled a leech off his eyelid, and continued on until he ran out of energy. When he found a suitable spot, he simply laid down and covered himself with palmetto leaves. He was too tired to build another shelter. Naughton ate a malted milk tablet and a piece of candy from his survival kit, then went to bed.

The next day, he ran into a Filipino boy who appeared to be about sixteen years old. Though he didn't speak any English, the boy urged Naughton to follow him, and they soon met up with some English-speaking locals. Naughton was taken in, had his wounds washed and dressed, and was well fed. He went to sleep feeling much better about his situation. They moved to a larger encampment the following morning, where he was told a rescue submarine was on its way. He was picked up just days later, on 2 November. Going down in the Philippines as opposed to Formosa had made all the difference.[48]

Chuck deMoss, who went down 5 November 1944, had a much closer call. Though Brownell was able to lend deMoss his raft, rescue never came. A combination of bad weather and bad luck prevented friendly forces from picking him up. So he waited, adrift and alone. Freezing cold water splashing into his raft dampened any hope of rescue. DeMoss' only concern was staying warm. As day slipped into night and the weather worsened, Chuck deMoss passed out.

He awoke at dawn with bleary eyes. He bailed out his raft and surveyed his situation. Off in the distance, it looked like there might be land. It didn't seem possible at first; deMoss had been at least eight miles offshore when he went down. As the day grew brighter, he realized there really was a beach ahead of him. The storm had carried him to a tiny island off southern Luzon. DeMoss made landfall and was almost immediately met by a small Filipino fishing vessel. The men inside were conversant in English. They told him the island wasn't safe and that they were going to smuggle him to a better location.

They brought deMoss to their village. He was finally getting warm and was able to think more clearly. Though he was reluctant to part with his pistol, he eventually handed it over to his rescuers. In short order they brought it back cleaned and freshly oiled. Their hospitality, despite the risk of harboring an Allied aviator, was incredible. But deMoss' travails were just beginning. Unlike Naughton, who was reunited with friendly forces in a matter of days, deMoss spent a month shuffling between villages and various guerrilla forces.[49]

He was moved slowly south from Legaspi to Tacloban. During this time, he watched Japanese floatplane operations, received a map indicating exactly where enemy fortifications were located, and coordinated a daring three-day boat trip around Japanese patrols to get an injured Avenger crew desperately needed medical attention. Through it all, he remembered Brownie Brownell's simple act of kindness, which had made his improbable return a possibility. DeMoss wrote in his survival debrief, "Due to a faulty valve, my rubber life raft did not inflate and I owe my life to Lt. Brownell, my division leader, who threw me his."[50]

When Buck Newsome watched Chesty Herlihy head back to *Intrepid* on 19 November, he decided that his best bet was to let his raft do the work. Pulling the poncho from his pack, Newsome stretched the material over his raft and laid down under it to avoid the elements. The current was pulling him northwest—back in the direction he'd come from—but it didn't really matter. What mattered was conserving his strength. The only effort he expended was during the first night at sea, when fish attracted to his raft kept knocking into it. Newsome emptied a container of dye marker around the raft. The thumping slowly subsided as the fish swam clear of the green film on the water. He could finally get some sleep.

After two days afloat, he sighted a small island. He was undoubtedly happy to see land. Japanese floatplane fighters kept passing overhead at dawn and dusk, clearly on patrol. The sooner he got to cover, the better. The island was Baco Chico, the smallest of three tiny islands strung between the coast of Mindoro and Luzon. It was uninhabited and heavily forested, teeming with snails, shellfish, and the ubiquitous coconut. Buck Newsome had cover and plenty of food. After he'd spent two days subsisting on the bounty of the island, a large sailboat passed nearby. He flagged down the vessel and spoke with its owner, Nicomedes Salcedo. The two talked for a while and presumably planned the best way to keep Newsome out of enemy hands. Salcedo sent his ship ahead but stayed on the island, waiting for an opportunity to hail a smaller, less noticeable vessel. Then he could serve as Newsome's translator and guardian.

A few days later the pair tried to get the attention of a passing boat, but its captain refused to stop. Perhaps he would continue to Luzon to alert the Japanese. Baco Chico was no longer safe. Since neighboring Baco Medio was a stone's throw away, Newsome swam over while Salcedo paddled behind him in the raft. Their fortunes improved on the new island. Someone had left a sailboat unattended. Hopefully its owner would forgive them for "borrowing" it.

They piloted the boat down the east coast of Mindoro but were unceremoniously dunked into the water when it capsized in a heavy wind. Fortunately, they were already within walking distance of Salcedo's hometown, Nanjan. There, they met up with guerrilla forces happy to protect the American aviator. A month later, a grateful Buck Newsome was back with friendly forces, singing the praises of the Filipino people.[51]

CHAPTER 12

THE DARKEST DAY, THE END IN SIGHT

AS NOVEMBER WORE ON, the men of Fighting 18 became accustomed to the new normal of CAP, Jack, and SNASP missions taking up the bulk of their flight time. The air and sea battles that characterized October were behind them. This change of pace caused men's minds to wander during long hours on patrol. All of them were homesick, doubly so with Thanksgiving just days away. They were hoping for a light at the end of the tunnel.

Robert "Fox" Morris of Fighting 18 was a slim, clean-cut young ensign from Long Island. The blonde-haired, blue-eyed heartthrob always kept his collar starched and his hair parted just so. He also constantly had his ear to the ground, serving as the squadron's chief source of scuttlebutt. Fox heard through the grapevine that they'd be home in time for Christmas. He repeated the rumor ad nauseam, as if saying it often enough made it true. During downtime between missions, Ed Ritter painted a watercolor portraying the scene. It shows Morris sharing the Christmas news with an incredulous, but hopeful, Snuffy Mayer. The caption reads, "Our Little Ray of Sunshine!—(Typhoon Forming)."[1]

Ritter was fond of Morris but knew he had a penchant for tall tales. Morris had previously been certain the men were getting shore leave (wrong) and had confidently stated that beautiful island women awaited them on their Pacific adventure (also wrong). His yarns had gotten so bad that any time Morris shared news in the ready room or in the officers' mess, it was dubbed a "Foxogram." But this time he had some corroboration.

George Searle of VB-18 had recently come back from a visit to USS *Hancock*, where he heard that the air group was going to be relieved on 15 December. Lest anyone think he was just blowing hot air, Searle put his money where his mouth was: he wagered fifty dollars that his information was correct. It was a sum too princely for most of the pilots, but an incredulous Doc Fish, the air group's flight surgeon, was a betting man. He wagered against Searle. Doc must have figured that if he was right, he'd have extra money for presents, and if he was wrong, well, at least he'd be home for the holidays.[2]

Intrepid's cooks were used to working around the clock to feed three thousand hungry men every day, but they outdid themselves to make sure Thanksgiving aboard ship had a touch of home. Baked Virginia ham, roast Princess Anne turkey, apple pie à la mode, and plum pudding were on the menu. The commissary even offered complimentary cigars.[3] After the feast, space was made in the hangar deck to screen the tragic Western love story, *The Woman of the Town*. Punchy Mallory greatly enjoyed it. Even though he'd already had a drink in Freddy Wolff's room before chow, parties in other officers' bunk rooms continued well into the night, giving men time to digest and unwind after a well-earned day off.

Despite the revelry and the momentary escape from the stresses of war, there was still a sense of foreboding in the air. The loss of "lanky, likeable Buck Newsome" continued to dampen spirits.[4] Mallory couldn't seem to get away from books and movies with sinister undertones. *For Whom the Bell Tolls* and *It Happened Tomorrow* hinted darkly at an unavoidable fate. On 24 November someone had the bright idea of screening *A Wing and a Prayer, the Story of Carrier X* in the ready room. It was a new release based loosely on the battles of the Coral Sea and Midway.

Watching a film portraying the loss of numerous naval aviators and their aircraft was bad enough, but the movie anachronistically used Hellcats and Helldivers in lieu of Wildcats and Dauntlesses. It gave the men an uneasy feeling. Later that night, Mallory jotted down in his diary, "It's not the picture I'd see the night before a strike. . . . It's plenty good but not quite true to life."[5]

Mallory's worry was not without merit. Since Task Groups 38.3 and 38.4 had recently participated in strikes on Yap, they needed to return to Ulithi to rearm. Instead of one group off and three on, the upcoming day of strikes on Luzon was limited to Task Groups 38.1 and 38.2.[6] In other words, there were fewer aircraft available to blanket the targets, meaning more enemies could potentially slip through the cracks.

After midnight on 25 November, Radarman Second Class Ray Stone reported to the gallery deck for his shift in CIC. Three full pots of coffee—an indispensable tool on the night shift—made sure he stayed alert during his four-hour duty period. The young, red-haired New Yorker was one of *Intrepid*'s plankowners, a crew member present during the ship's commissioning. He had been with the carrier through thick and thin, from Truk Atoll and torpedo damage to fleet battles and kamikaze attacks. While the men of Fighting 18 slept, Stone was responsible for keeping watch over the task group.

He spent half an hour on radar, monitoring the plan position indicator scope for activity, before swapping out to man the plot board for a half-hour. Making these regular adjustments kept radar operators' eyes fresh and allowed them to stay sharp through their whole shift. At 0405 CIC picked up a bogey forty-nine miles away and closing. Night fighters from *Independence* were vectored out to intercept.[7] With things heating up, Stone hopped up from his seat to fetch the flag fighter director, Commander Winston, who had stepped away from his almost constant vigil for a brief nap. Stone threaded through the narrow corridors of the gallery deck to the commander's anteroom and hurriedly entered, shaking the officer awake. Winston grumbled. He gestured to a bottle of scotch on a small round table and said, "Pour yourself a shot and make sure I'm on my feet before you leave."[8] It was going to be a long morning.

As it turned out, the bogey managed to fly within gun range of the ships before turning away. *Independence*'s night fighters made multiple contacts, even identifying the plane as a twin-engine, single-tailed aircraft, but they couldn't close the distance to bring it down. The bogey faded from radar as men aboard *Intrepid* manned torpedo defense stations. No attack developed. It soon became apparent that the plane was a snooper conducting reconnaissance of the fleet. It had returned to base, reported the location of the carriers, and was about to kick off the largest kamikaze attack since Leyte Gulf.[9]

Attempts to suppress enemy air activity began with a morning sweep over Nichols and Nielson fields, the same targets attacked on 19 November. Seven *Cabot* fighters joined *Intrepid*'s eleven Hellcats. Even though they arrived at the crack of dawn, enemy fighters were already airborne for interception.

Ens. Ed Toaspern and Ens. Bruce Throckmorton, two replacement pilots serving with VF-18, were part of a division attacking a group of planes twice their size. Strength in numbers didn't matter if the enemy pilots couldn't stick together, though. The Japanese fighters scattered as soon as Toaspern's division bore down from above. Throckmorton was able to pick off one of the fleeing planes with a quick burst of machine gun fire before slotting back onto his section leader's wing. Together they pursued two Zekes attempting to run for cover. Throckmorton hammered one of these planes so hard it lost its tail or part of its wing before it disappeared into the clouds. The two Hellcat pilots cut off their pursuit and climbed to rendezvous with the rest of the sweep. When they broke into the clear, however, the other Zeke suddenly popped into view. It was a deadly mistake. Throckmorton throttled back, nosed down, and smoothly slid behind it. Two bursts caused the plane to explode midair.[10]

Snuffy Mayer brazenly attacked a pair of Japanese fighters from head-on. His opponents were attempting to weave together as they approached, but they were doing so more vertically than horizontally. Mayer passed almost between them, firing several bursts at the plane above. Flames flared up where his bullets found their mark. The pilot bailed out, while the lower fighter raced ahead to put as much space as possible between him and the Hellcat. Mayer then chased after an even bigger group of four planes. These fighters didn't have the discipline of the earlier pair; they broke ranks almost immediately. Mayer shot down the nearest plane before heading off to regroup with his section mate.[11]

Freddy Wolff was ganged up on by a group of four Tojo fighters as soon as the sweep arrived over Nielson. Quick thinking and fast reflexes kept him and his Hellcat from picking up any bullet holes. After evading the attack, Wolff spotted a friendly pilot below him with two Tojos on his tail. A tap on his gun button caused one of the Japanese fighters to nose down and wing over in a split "S," escaping the engagement before it got out of hand, but the other enemy didn't flinch. He continued trying to take down the Hellcat. Freddy fired through the pilot's engine and wing, forcing him to bail out from the sinking, smoking wreck.[12]

The fighting over Nielson that morning once again demonstrated how far the squadron had come since its first strikes in September. It also showed unequivocally the success of Cecil Harris' Hellcat tactics. Harris and his wingman, Burley, were on this last Fighting 18 sweep. In his signature style, Harris was being pursued by three enemy fighters before he turned the tables on them. He pulled back hard on the stick, chopped the throttle, and let his pursuers pass. Then it was stick down, throttle to the stop, and pour on the coals until he was nipping at their heels. The chase continued over the edge of the field all the way out to Manila Bay. Harris flamed one Tojo fighter over the water, watching it crash into the bay as its pilot slowly parachuted down.

Harris and Burley were then attacked from overhead by a group of eight fighters. Burley turned hard in front of them at the last second, causing them to seriously overshoot their run as they dove steeply down toward the bay. Burley turned hard again, sticking his Hellcat's wingtip up as he looked out the top of his canopy across the water. The enemies were coming out of their dives. Burley leveled out, closed the distance, and fired, watching his tracers converge on and tear into his target. He had just evened things up with his section leader.

Harris also managed to dodge the wild attack. He flew past the flashing arc of machine gun fire before circling to chase a handful of fighters back toward Nielson. More aircraft were crisscrossing the field, some pursuing Hellcats, others being pursued. It seemed like enemy planes were everywhere. Harris exploded another Tojo fighter with a burst of well-aimed gunfire before he was once again attacked from above. As the plane bore down, Harris pulled up into him. He trusted his Hellcat to trade blows with any Japanese fighter and come out on top. But the enemy pilot turned away at the last second, realizing too late that he was outmatched.

Harris wasn't about to let his enemy slink away. He activated water injection and easily caught up to the running fighter. After a quick burst, the Tojo began trailing tongues of flame. It crashed into the Manila suburbs. The pilot bailed out before the plane went down, but Harris could see that his chute didn't open. It was a difficult thing to witness. Air combat was usually impersonal compared to fighting on the ground. Planes moved quickly and often engaged each other at considerable distances. Pilots did not have to see their opponents to shoot them down. In this instance, however, the human price of war was painfully obvious.[13]

The sweep returned to *Intrepid* at 0930 amid a flurry of activity. Strike 2B was launched to continue suppressing enemy airfields; CAP and Jack pilots were sent airborne to provide defensive cover over the carriers; and general quarters alarms rang out with increasing frequency as wave after wave of Japanese planes appeared on radar.[14] Within just a few hours, things would change dramatically for Fighting 18. *Intrepid* was about to experience its darkest day in service.

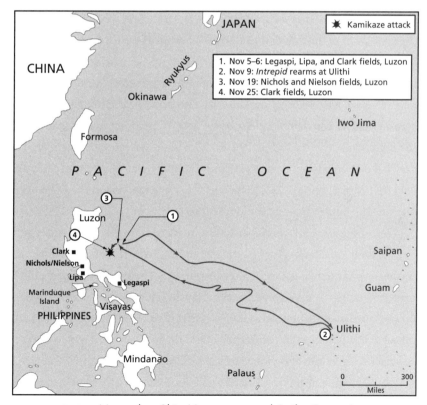

MAP 5. November Ship Movements and Strike Operations

At 1254 the first kamikaze punched directly through the flight deck, exploding under the gallery deck where radar operators were desperately trying to keep track of enemy planes. Casualties came streaming into the nearby battle dressing station, coughing and wincing in pain. Doc Fish was there with corpsmen and available air group personnel to patch up the wounded. Fires raged below them in the hangar deck, where fire marshal Don DiMarzo led his men in a valiant fight against the flames. Their dedication to their ship and crew kept them rooted in the most dangerous areas of the carrier, racing against time to restore *Intrepid* to fighting trim.

When the second kamikaze hit just minutes later, the effects were catastrophic. DiMarzo was near the number two aircraft elevator amidships, directing men to hose down flaming aircraft in the hangar. They were hurled off their feet by the blast. The hangar was immediately wreathed in impenetrable smoke. Survivors had to take turns holding hoses, rotating out at intervals to get fresh air. They didn't know it yet, but their leader had been killed by the sheer force of the detonation along with seven of the men around him.[15]

Lt. George Race, the air group ACIO, was in the middle of a huge procession moving slowly from deck to deck when the second explosion jarred *Intrepid*. Race marveled at how the crew continued evacuating in an orderly fashion despite the danger all around them. When they finally made it to the flight deck, the scene was hellish. Men were sprinting through smoke, doubled over, retching, or scattered around in the peaceful repose of death. And in the background, an inferno raged up from the hole in the flight deck marking the impact point of the kamikazes.

One of Fighting 18's shipboard personnel ran across the deck, making a beeline for Race. There were men trapped in the torpedo workshop down on second deck. If someone didn't get them out soon, they would suffocate. Race tried to requisition smoke helmets, but none were available.[16] Fortunately, it was because men had already taken the initiative. The ship's landing signal officer, Rit Moot, must have poached one early on. He went down to the gallery deck to fight fires and didn't surface for almost two hours.[17]

Jeep Daniels and Ralph Christian had done likewise, turning themselves into an impromptu rescue party. They knew time was of the essence and air was running out. When Christian arrived at the torpedo workshop, he found the inboard door billowing smoke and the outboard door blocked by bodies. He charged headlong into the compartment. In the swirling blackness, he found the men and told them to hold hands in a daisy chain. They calmed down and followed him upward to the flight deck.

Christian was running out of breath shuttling back and forth to make sure everyone reached the open air. He remained topside while Jeep finished rescuing those slowly making their way out of the conflagration. When Jeep made it back down to the workshop, he could see why some of the men were having trouble reaching the flight deck. One man had his foot almost completely severed at the ankle. He was in agony and in no shape to walk. Jeep had to carry him up from deck to deck. He left the injured man with a corpsman for medical care and a much-needed morphine injection.[18]

Jeep looked around the flight deck at the wreckage of his ship and the bodies of his shipmates. He spotted Doc Fish laid out among the dead and dying. The explosion from the second kamikaze had ripped through the battle dressing station, tearing the space's heavy steel door off its hinges. The concussion had knocked everyone in the room unconscious—or worse.

Race, Jeep, Commander Coleman, and several corpsmen all worked in shifts from 1330 to 1600 trying to urge life back into Doc Fish. Even Admiral Bogan came over to check on Fish, a remarkable gesture given how much work Bogan had to do coordinating his forces in the wake of the attack. After almost three hours trying to revive Fish, they had to face the sad truth. The man who had cheerfully stitched up countless aviators, who made sure they had a stiff drink to calm their nerves and steel their resolve, was no more.[19]

Thirty-eight Fighting 18 pilots were airborne at the time of the attack serving on CAP, Jack, and strike duty.[20] Their experience of the kamikaze was from thousands of feet above the fleet, circling the towering column of black smoke coiling up from their ship. Afterward, they landed on Leyte or nearby carriers such as *Essex* and *Ticonderoga*. They only learned about Doc's death days later, on 29 November, when they finally returned to *Intrepid*. The carrier was temporarily out of commission and headed back to Hawaii. It seemed like everything in their area of the ship's gallery deck had been obliterated. Their log books were burned. Their clothes were reduced to ash. Bulkheads were bowed in, pockmarked, and blackened with soot. The aviators had dropped countless bombs on targets. They had seen the destruction these weapons wrought, but only at a distance. Now they were standing inside a structure that had endured such an attack.

After everything Fighting 18 had been through, they were suddenly reassigned to serve additional duty aboard *Hancock*, leaving them exposed to further kamikaze attacks instead of returning home with their ship and shipmates. They had to wait nine long days for an update. Nine days of frayed nerves; nine days of wondering when it was their turn for a reprieve. Finally, just after the anniversary of Pearl Harbor, they received some good news. They had orders to return stateside.[21]

Their transport out of Ulithi was the former MS *Klipfontein*, a Dutch ocean liner that had been requisitioned by the War Shipping Administration in 1942. The men almost couldn't believe the accommodations aboard ship. Their rooms had baths and chaise lounges. The food was better than at some of the hotels and clubs they'd been to on the West Coast: dinner banquets with steak and rabbit, fresh orange juice and eggs for breakfast, all kinds of meats and cheeses available buffet-style for men to assemble their own sandwiches.

Indulgence was the name of the game after their trial by fire aboard *Intrepid*. Fighting 18's aviators slept right through general quarters alarms since they did not have any planes or real responsibilities. They sunbathed all afternoon and had wine before dinner. Punchy Mallory, Boot Amerman, and "Fearless" Bill Herpich were roommates. They started off "arguing, bitching and raising hell" the day they boarded *Klipfontein* but soon found their old familiar friendliness returning. Mallory was feeling like his himself again, "care free [sic] and laughing all the time."[22]

With nothing to do, however, the men got jumpy any time the ship stopped on the way to Pearl Harbor. *Klipfontein* pulled into Eniwetok anchorage on 15 December to load water and other supplies. After just one day at anchor, Mallory and Amerman started to sling sarcastic remarks at one another. Roommates took their anxieties out on each other. Several of the men broke out in sores, including Bud Burnett, whose rash was so bad he had to be sent ahead to Pearl Harbor. Finally, after six days at Eniwetok, *Klipfontein* continued its leisurely trip to Hawaii.

Home was starting to feel like a reality. If the early days of gorging themselves and partying hard had been a response to worries that the rug was going to be pulled out from under them again, the last phase of their journey home brought out a more measured enjoyment of the simple things. The temperature finally dropped a bit, providing refreshment and the opportunity for men to enjoy the scenery above decks. Mallory began to wax poetically about the trip: "There is a sinking half moon and the ship is leaving a silvery wake that is beautiful to see. Even here in my cabin I can hear the waves splashing against the sides and the ship has a gentle pitch as we plow head on into the waves."[23]

For the first and presumably only time in their lives, the men got to celebrate Christmas Eve twice as *Klipfontein* crossed the International Date Line on 24 December. A temporary return to partying marked this special occasion. After nursing hangovers from the first Christmas Eve, the men spent the second night singing carols by the light of the moon. Two days later, the ship headed into Pearl Harbor. Windy Horn took the opportunity to make a "short snorter" souvenir out of a special one-dollar bill. The overprinted dollar was stamped HAWAII on the back in large horizontal letters that spanned the length of the bill. This currency entered circulation in 1942 in case the Japanese occupied Hawaii and ceased issue in late October 1944, long after it became clear that would never come to pass. It made a fitting memento from Horn's wartime service. He got a half dozen men in the squadron to sign the bill and dated it in marker, "Dutch 'Klipfontein' 12–30–44."[24]

There was only one stop left after Hawaii: a trip under San Francisco's Golden Gate Bridge.[25] On 31 December *Klipfontein* headed for the West Coast. Emotions built all afternoon. Cecil Harris fretted about press and publicity, wishing he could fly under the radar rather than receiving a hero's welcome. Mallory was feeling lonely. He had made friends and happy memories with the squadron. Now that all seemed to be coming to an end. As midnight drew nearer, the men drank and grew merry. Small parties throughout the ship conjoined into one big gathering of forty-five men packed shoulder to shoulder in one small room, singing, yelling, and wishing each other a happy new year.

The noise swelled as collective catharsis stripped the men of their inhibitions, allowing them to finally exorcise eighty-one days' worth of tension. But there was still one thing left to do. More than a dozen men were missing from the party: Wells McGurk, Jackson Vliet, Jim Neighbours, Walter Passi, Henry Sartwelle, Harry Webster, Wesley Keels, Ralph DuPont, Bill Ziemer, Harold Meacham, George Griffith, Arthur Mollenhauer, Bill Thompson, James Hedrick. The squadron's losses had to be acknowledged.

Freddy Wolff, Fighting 18's morale officer, stepped in to bring the raucous crowd to heel. The room fell silent as he raised his glass. He took a moment to look into the faces of his squadron mates, and then he said simply and poignantly, "To the boys who didn't come home."[26] It was a perfect toast. There were no other words that could encapsulate the intense emotion they felt thinking about their fallen comrades. Freddy brought his glass to his lips and drank deep. As the men around him followed suit, they emptied their glasses in absolute silence until the whole gathering had a chance to quietly acknowledge one another—a nod, a grimace, a sad smile. Then the New Year's celebration got under way again.

The men were given thirty days' leave to see loved ones and get their affairs in order before the squadron's reformation at Naval Air Station Astoria, Oregon, on 25 January 1945. Reports of their return home and their service in "Two-a-day Eighteen," one of the Navy's top-ranking carrier fighting squadrons, circulated in hometown papers. Leave was more relaxing for some than others. Lt. Cecil Harris barely had any time for himself. He had to make an appearance at Radio City Music Hall in New York as part of the Navy Air Training Services publicity campaign. He demonstrated how to aim machine guns while flying a plane and spoke with attendees about his experience at sea. He posed for the camera with a serious, determined look, but behind it all he probably couldn't wait to get home to his fiancée, Eva. Even after he made it back to his hometown of Cresbard, South Dakota, there was a welcoming committee at the local high school with friends, family, and local dignitaries, including the governor.[27]

A whopping twenty-four pilots returned to Fighting 18 for the second go-around. Fighting 18's war history noted with some pride that the squadron probably had the highest percentage of combat-experienced pilots with any reformed unit.[28] It was funny to think that they had entered the war as complete novices, engaged in some of the biggest air and sea battles in the Pacific with minimal combat experience, and were now training for a second deployment as battle-hardened fighter pilots at a time when Japanese air forces and surface fleets existed as mere shadows of their former selves.

Others, like Beetle Beatley, were sent to bomber-fighter squadrons, a new kind of squadron introduced in 1945 alongside a reduction in the size of dive bombing squadrons. The change allowed carrier air groups to maintain ground attack capabilities while augmenting their ability to provide air defense in the age of the kamikaze. Some men were assigned to newly formed fighting squadrons to ensure the distribution of combat experience across the fleet. Some were even lucky enough to be transferred together in small groups, like Fred Tracy and Rudy Van Dyke, and Punchy Mallory and Boot Amerman, who all wound up together in VF-151, a squadron that was stood up shortly after the men returned home.

The prospect of another combat tour and the usual dangers of training spurred men to marry while they had the chance. Nobody knew what tomorrow would bring. In fact, in those first few months of training alone, Snuffy Mayer was one of the first to have a close call. His plane's landing gear collapsed on impact with the runway during routine operations. The plane was badly damaged, but he walked away relatively unscathed.[29] Mayer happened to be among the six men who married either during their thirty-day leaves or at Naval Air Station Astoria. Holding separate wedding receptions proved too boozy for the men. They learned after two parties and ample headaches ladled from a punchbowl of French 75 that they should combine the rest of the receptions into one big ball.

Cecil Harris' wedding was the last major event before training began in earnest. The squadron's veteran pilots wanted to show Harris, who had worked himself ragged bringing them up to speed in Hawaii and had led so many missions off the deck of *Intrepid*, what his dedication meant to them.

They packed snugly into four cars and decorated a fifth for Cecil and Eva. Despite the chilly winter weather, they popped the tops off the convertibles and drove around town noisily celebrating their lead scorer. It was far and away the highlight of their time in Oregon, where rainy weather always seemed to put a damper on things.

Training in 1945 followed the same basic pattern it had in 1943 and 1944. The squadron moved to San Diego in April to begin practicing with the whole air group. Improved weather accelerated their movement through the training syllabus. The dangers of field carrier landing practice reared their head again. One of the new ensigns had his engine cut out after his first touch-and-go, causing his plane to roll over and crash on its back. He was badly injured but survived, later making a full recovery.[30]

The social situation also improved in California, though Ens. Spencer "Inspector" Scheckter, one of the squadron's newcomers, was the life of the party no matter where he went. Even in Astoria, he was able to work his charm at the clubs until he was up on stage with the band doing his best Gene Krupa impression on the drums. Ensign Scheckter looked like a Hollywood leading man, with dark features, a strong chin, and a broad smile with flashing pearly-white teeth.

He was a "tail end Charlie," someone who entered training too late to see major action in the war, but he was a talented aviator in his own right. He typically flew with the skipper, Lt. Cdr. Ed Murphy, and in group operations flew wing on Air Group 18's commanding officer, Cdr. Wilson Coleman. The selection meant a lot to Scheckter, who—like most of the other new ensigns in the squadron—looked up to the combat veterans in a big way. He made friends with Intrepid stalwarts Frog Hurst, Laffy Naff, and Windy Horn and posed for photos with them in the California desert. Whenever the squadron's prior tour of duty was mentioned in local papers, Scheckter took his scissors to the pages and cut out the newsprint to file away for his scrapbook.[31]

Fighting 18 boarded the venerable USS Ranger (CV 4) on 21 May for carrier qualification. The stint aboard Ranger also presented an opportunity for members of Fighting 18 to test out Grumman's new F8F Bearcat fighter.

Battle-tested members of the squadron remembered transitioning from the F4F Wildcat to the F6F Hellcat in 1943, recalling how much better the Hellcat was than its predecessor. Even with that in mind, men reported that "the F6F seemed like a truck in comparison" to the F8F.[32] If Japanese aircraft had largely been inferior to the Hellcat by 1944, they could only imagine how one-sided things would be when the Bearcat entered service.

By 11 August the squadron's training syllabus was almost 90 percent complete. Bearcats were being delivered to replace the Hellcat, and carrier deployment seemed to be right around the corner. Fortunately for the men of Fighting 18, it never came to that: Emperor Hirohito broadcasted his surrender announcement just days later. Over the course of the next two months, the squadron's ranking lieutenants, including Lt. Cecil Harris, were discharged from active duty. The reservists still waiting to accrue enough points for separation from the Navy boarded *Ranger* in September for a trip through the Panama Canal.[33]

During wartime, carriers flowed westward from shipbuilding facilities on the Atlantic seaboard. Now, with the first postwar Navy Day around the corner, USS *Ranger* was heading east to give the people of New Orleans a show. Fighting 18's aviators arrived in October 1945 to stage mock attacks on their own ship as well as downtown New Orleans, thrilling onlookers in their shiny new Bearcats. Newspaper photographers and reporters were present when the men landed at Naval Air Station New Orleans. As one of the most highly decorated combat veterans remaining, Lt. Spider Foltz was interviewed about the Battle of Leyte Gulf, the anti-aircraft fire he braved, and his bomb hit on an enemy battleship.[34]

It must have been a surreal moment for Foltz. A year earlier, he and his squadron mates had been fighting for their lives thousands of miles from home. Back then, they were all living day-to-day. They were happy if they got to see the sun rise in the morning and were still there later to see it set. Now, the survivors had to figure out what came next in the relative surety of their lives.

EPILOGUE

SOON AFTER BILL ZIEMER WENT DOWN over Formosa on 12 October 1944, Wally Walworth wrote a letter to Bill's girlfriend and likely fiancé, Frances Leighton. It is clear from the letter that Wally believed Bill was still alive and hoped that he would be located by friendly forces before long. A number of Fighting 18 pilots who were shot down and listed as missing in action during their deployment turned up in one piece at a later date. That seemed to support Wally's conclusion. Frances thanked him for writing. She agreed, saying, "Somehow I have always felt that Bill will come back to me. Before he went away he promised that he would, and I have all the faith in the world in him."[1] She inquired about Egidio DeBatista and his broken leg and asked that Wally give him her regards. Then she closed out the letter.

October bled into November; fall leaves and Thanksgiving feasts gave way to Christmas carols and smoking chimneys. Still, there was no word about Bill's whereabouts. The only sign the family received was a bouquet of roses sent by the missing aviator. He had arranged the delivery before shipping out in case he was unable to make it home for the holidays. One of Bill's younger brothers, Howard, was cheered by their arrival. Amid the cold white December weather, here was a flash of color, of life. Then New Year's came and went, and the worry set back in.

Bill Ziemer was alive. He was being kept at Camp Ofuna, a secret interrogation facility south of Tokyo holding Allied aviators and other high-level officers captured by the Japanese. Through these cold months, in a tiny, unfurnished prison cell, he battled against the elements, maltreatment, and malnourishment to keep his promise to Frances. Men faced routine beatings for any rules infraction, real or perceived. Bill received a massive blow to the head for keeping onion peelings in his pocket. Sometimes he was beaten for no reason other than the satisfaction of the guards.

Through it all, he continued whispering through the wall to Lt. William Davidson Jr., the Avenger pilot in the adjacent cell. They encouraged one another and assured each other that they would make it out. Ziemer described his mother's checkerboard cakes and fruitcakes while their empty bellies rumbled, and the comfortable chairs in his parents' living room, soft and warm compared to the cold, hard floors of their unadorned six-foot-by-eight-foot cells. Memories of home kept them hopeful. There was something to look forward to if they could just hang on a little while longer.[2]

Winter slowly relaxed its grip. Men traded frostbite for tropical disease as temperatures rose in the spring of 1945. Food and medical supplies were extremely limited, not just out of avarice but because of the economic devastation wracking Japan. Bill had kept up his fortitude through the cold and the beatings. He was determined to see his loved ones again. He was tough; college football and growing up with four brothers ensured as much. Without adequate nutrition, however, Bill was rapidly losing weight. As the weather grew hotter, he developed beriberi and dysentery. His strength slowly ebbed as he grew sicker. His ability to take the beatings diminished. By August 1945 Bill had given all he had to give. He died just a month before Japan's formal surrender aboard USS *Missouri*.

His family was crestfallen. His squadron mates had trouble processing the news. Wally Walworth dutifully wrote to Frances Leighton to discuss their grave loss. It was hard to accept that he could have endured hell for ten long months only to die ten days before Emperor Hirohito's radio announcement that surrender was imminent. Frances traveled cross-county from California to mourn with the Ziemer family. While there, William Davidson visited to tell the family about his experience at Ofuna in the cell next to Bill's. It was good to get a sense of closure, even if it ended in heartbreak. Before leaving New Jersey, Frances made sure to spend time with Bill's brothers, taking photos and sharing memories. They closed a painful chapter in their lives and did their best to honor his sacrifice. Frances' sentiments no doubt echoed the

Ziemer family's and Wally's when she said, "I have him in my heart and no one can ever take him from me."[3]

Bill Ziemer's story would be the saddest in the saga of Fighting 18 if it were left there by itself, defined by his tragic death. But that is not how life works. His actions during his short time on earth left indelible marks on those around him. Like ripples in a pond, they continued to emanate long after he slipped beneath the surface. Howard Ziemer leapt headfirst into flight training after he learned Bill was missing. He rose rapidly through the ranks from machinist's mate to chief, chief to naval aviation pilot, and then finally jumped from enlisted man to officer. His remarkable career in the sea services spanned decades but can be traced back in large part to the example set by his older brother and the desire to honor his memory.

This pattern repeated itself from family to family. Wesley Keels was lost on the same day, and in the very same mission, as Bill Ziemer. Wesley's youngest brother, Orean, later joined the Air Force; another brother, Pat, named his firstborn son after Wesley. The Keels family connection to the Navy continued with another of Pat Keels' boys, Joel, who attended the U.S. Naval Academy.

Many Fighting 18 pilots survived World War II only to die in aviation accidents in the late 1940s and 1950s. They knew the risks inherent in flight duty, but their love of the air and their desire to serve kept them in the cockpit. After his tenure in Fighting 18, Richard Cevoli served as executive officer of VF-32, leading Thomas Hudner and Jesse Brown in the Navy's first racially integrated carrier division. He was killed in 1955 when his F9F-6 Panther jet crashed shortly after takeoff. Similar accidents claimed the lives of Winton Horn, Edgar Blankenship, and Leonard Woodward, all of whom stuck with the Navy after the war.

Two men became test pilots: former night fighter Bill Millar and Rudy Van Dyke, who had driven off Japanese fighters even after his guns ran dry. Bill Millar was one of Vought's senior test pilots flying the radically designed XF7U-1 Cutlass prototype. It was extremely dangerous work: all three prototype aircraft were destroyed in crashes suffered by Vought's test pilots. Bill's crash proved fatal. Rudy Van Dyke worked for the National Advisory

Committee for Aeronautics, the National Aeronautics and Space Administration's (NASA's) predecessor. According to NASA historians, Rudy flew faster and more frequently than almost anyone on earth in 1949 as part of supersonic speed testing at Ames Aeronautical Laboratory, just outside of San Francisco. In 1953 Rudy was piloting an F8F Bearcat when he went into a slow glide toward San Francisco Bay and crashed, possibly due to issues with his oxygen supply.

These men all had young children who never got to know their fathers. Many of those kids in turn had children who were curious about the grandfathers they never got to meet. In each case, this author witnessed a powerful desire to connect with the missing aviators, to understand them, and to honor them. From family to family, the song remained the same: they were gone but not forgotten.

Finally, there were those fortunate enough to survive their *Intrepid* deployment and subsequent service. They had the benefit of settling down to experience the civilian joys they had fought so hard to protect—though some, like Brownie Brownell and Punchy Mallory, flew right up until the end. The "flying bug" and the impulse toward service almost seems to have been genetic in some of these families. Boot Amerman has great-grandchildren at both Annapolis and West Point, mirroring the way he and his brother Roy ended up split between the services. Flaps O'Maley was berthed close to *Intrepid*'s Marine detachment in 1944. His son, Brian, wound up serving as a Marine Corps helicopter pilot. Clarence Blouin has a grandson who flies as a commercial jet pilot. The list could go on.

Cecil Harris remained humble about his accomplishments in the Pacific. He was the Navy's second-highest scoring ace of World War II and among the most decorated reserve pilots in history, and he had even been recommended for the Medal of Honor by Admiral Bogan and Admiral McCain. Like Jeep Daniels, Harris likely grappled with losses his squadron suffered during its deployment. Daniels later wrote, "I felt those guys were taken. I think they should have been as lucky as I was to return home to their families. . . . I have gotten over it, but I don't really understand it. I still have a problem with it."

The preceding work focuses heavily on daring air combat and thrilling stories of young men at war, but the reasons for writing this book derive more from my interest in who these men were: their hopes and aspirations, their hobbies, their demeanors, and all the rest. Some people are fortunate enough to have met their grandparents and great-grandparents. They retain glimpses of them in memory and in media. A great many do not have this luxury.

The greatest joy I have had in organizing and writing this volume has been learning about the human dimension of the pilots and attempting to wed those details with their military record. In this way, the ripples of their lives down through successive generations can find their way back to the source, bringing color and life to the black-and-white photographs and meaning to the static words in aircraft action reports. If I have achieved this feat even once in the preceding pages, I will count this endeavor a victory.

NOTES

PROLOGUE

1. USS *Intrepid*, war diary, November 1–30, 1944, 40, https://catalog.archives.gov/id /78704615.
2. Rene J. Francillon, *Japanese Aircraft of the Pacific War* (Annapolis, MD: Naval Institute Press, 1987), 377.
3. USS *Intrepid*, war diary, November 1–30, 1944, 42.
4. George Race, *The Kamikaze Corps*, 1. From the unpublished, unedited version of Air Group 18, war history.
5. "Pacific War Veteran Seeks County Post," *Daily Times* (Salisbury, MD), February 28, 1946, https://www.newspapers.com/article/the-daily-times-pacific-war-veteran-see /12354776/.
6. USS *Intrepid*, Report of Air Operations against Southern Luzon Island and Enemy Shipping in the Sibuyan Sea, Philippines, November 14–27, 1944, 21, https://catalog. archives.gov/id/78706712.
7. Race, 1.
8. VF-13, war history, 2, 3, https://catalog.archives.gov/id/77659248.
9. Air Group 18, war history, 23, https://catalog.archives/gov/id/77684444.
10. USS *Intrepid*, war diary, 40, November 1–30, 1944.
11. Capt. Cecil E. Harris, interview, August 7, 1968, Smithsonian National Air and Space Museum (NASM) sound archives collection.
12. USS *Hancock*, war diary, November 1–30, 1944, 10, https://catalog.archives.gov/ id/139777767.
13. USS *Intrepid*, war diary, November 1–30, 1944, 40.
14. Race, 1.
15. Forrest W. Aurentz, "Hellcat Ace in a Day," *Air Classics*, November 2003, 47, 48.
16. Charles Mallory, interview by Robert Gandt, November 3, 2007.
17. Edward Murphy collection, VF-18 Combat Accomplishments 1944, Enclosure B, 3.
18. Aurentz, 48; Air Group 18, war history, 23.
19. Race, 1.
20. USS *Intrepid*, war diary, November 1–30, 1944, 41.
21. USS *Cabot*, war diary, November 10–30, 1944, 5, 6, https://catalog.archives.gov/id /78703245.

22. USS *Intrepid*, Report of Air Operations, November 14–27, 1944, 18.

23. USS *Intrepid*, war diary, November 1–30, 1944, 41.

24. Race, 1.

25. USS *Intrepid*, war diary, November 1–30, 1944, 41, 42.

26. Details come from Charles Mallory collection, diary, 72–74. Scans of the diary were provided by Forrest W. "Woody" Aurentz, who received them from Mallory in conjunction with research for Aurentz's article, "Hellcat Ace in a Day."

27. Harold R. Thune, oral history, Intrepid Museum, March 15, 2017, 23, 24.

28. USS *Intrepid*, war diary, November 1–30, 1944, 46.

29. VF-18 Combat Accomplishments 1944, Enclosure B. The number of aces is also reflected separately in a typed document in the Mallory papers.

30. USS *Intrepid*, war diary, November 1–30, 1944, 47.

31. Mallory diary, 78.

32. John Forsyth, *Hell Divers: U.S. Navy Dive-Bombers at War* (Osceola, WI: Motorbooks International, 1991), 158.

33. Lyrics to the "Zoomie Song" were found on the reverse side of *Intrepid*'s Plan of the Day for September 6, 1944, in the Collection of the Intrepid Museum.

34. Air Group 18, war history, 25.

35. Mallory diary, 80.

CHAPTER 1. CROSSING PATHS AND EARNING WINGS

1. *Sheaf* (yearbook), Principia College (Elsah, IL), 1941, 86, 126, 158, https://principia.contentdm.oclc.org/digital/collection/PYB01/id/30821/rec/2.

2. Valerie Junge, *Flying Ace, Edward A. Ritter* (Tukwila, WA: Reischling Press, 2010), 89.

3. Robert Right Rea, *Wings of Gold: An Account of Naval Aviation Training in World War II* (Tuscaloosa: The University of Alabama Press, 2015), 22–23.

4. Air Primary Training Command, Regional Office, New York, National Archives roll 32664_b042963, 96; "Local Men Reported for Naval Aviation," *Brooklyn Daily Eagle*, June 15, 1942, https://www.newspapers.com/article/the-brooklyn-daily-eagle-local-men-repor/132632620/.

5. Dominick Pisano, *To Fill the Skies with Pilots: The Civilian Pilot Training Program, 1936–1946* (Chicago: University of Illinois Press, 1993), 60, 61.

6. "Ten NSTC Students Apply for CAA Course Which Begins Today," *Exponent*, October 1, 1940, Cecil E. Harris Collection, Beulah Williams Library Archives and Special Collections, Northern State University (Aberdeen, SD), 1, https://digitalcollections.northern.edu/digital/collection/p16707coll7/id/9008/rec/1).

7. Harris interview, Smithsonian NASM.

8. Biographical note, Harris Collection.

9. Harris interview, Smithsonian NASM.

10. Officer biography sheet, Harris Collection.

11. Orean Keels and Lillie Earle Keels-Fincher, interview by Michael Fink, August 14, 2022.

12. "Missing in Action," *Echo* (Pisgah Forest, NC), December 1, 1944, 14, https://newspapers.digitalnc.org/lccn/2014236906/1944-12-01/ed-1/seq-14/.

13. Muster Rolls of U.S. Navy Ships, Stations, and Other Naval Activities, Naval Reserve Aviation Base Atlanta, GA, roll 32863_255973, 363.

14. Wesley Keels collection, flight training notebook, class 2X, March 30, 1942.

15. "Flyer from Monroe Wins Commission," *Charlotte (NC) Observer*, January 17, 1943, 10, https://www.newspapers.com/article/the-charlotte-observer-flyer-from-monroe /132635617/.

16. Fritz Jauch, "Illini Hall Whips Delts, 32-25, for I-M Cage Crown," *Daily Illini* (Champaign, IL), April 9, 1941, 6, https://idnc.library.illinois.edu/?a=d&d=DIL19410409.2.71&e =-------en-20-DIL-21--txt-txIN-9+April+1941---------.

17. Bryant Walworth collection, letter from Robert Smith to Bryant Walworth, July 16, 1942.

18. Bryant Walworth, interview by Lee Walworth, August 1986.

19. Walworth collection, wartime diary, 1.

20. Walworth collection, wartime diary, 2, 3.

21. Walworth collection, wartime diary, 5.

22. Walworth collection, wartime diary, 10.

23. Walworth collection, wartime diary, 12-18.

24. Walworth collection, wartime diary, 19.

25. Walworth collection, wartime diary, 2, 24.

26. Walworth collection, wartime diary, 25-30.

27. SNV Valiant, National Naval Aviation Museum, https://www.history.navy.mil/content /history/museums/nnam/explore/collections/aircraft/s/snv-valiant.html.

28. Walworth collection, wartime diary, 37, 38.

29. Walworth collection, wartime diary, 40-44.

30. SNJ Texan, National Naval Aviation Museum, https://www.history.navy.mil/content /history/museums/nnam/explore/collections/aircraft/s/snj-texan.html.

31. Walworth collection, wartime diary, 49-54.

32. Walworth collection, wartime diary, 55.

33. "Comdr. Starkes Gets 3 Medals," *Honolulu Advertiser*, December 18, 1946, 5, https:// www.newspapers.com/article/the-honolulu-advertiser-comdr-starkes-g/132647714/.

34. Walworth collection, operational training–VR pilot completion report, June 21, 1943.

35. Charles Paul Amerman papers, printed map of Sea Island, St. Simons Island, Georgia, dated May 10-23, 1943, Collection of the Intrepid Museum.

36. "Lost in Crash, Lieut. Thomas P. Sorensen, Jr.," *St. Louis Post-Dispatch*, May 21, 1943, 20, https://www.newspapers.com/article/st-louis-post-dispatch-lost-in-crash/132941094/.

37. John B. Lundstrom, *The First Team and the Guadalcanal Campaign: Naval Fighter Combat from August to November 1942* (Annapolis, MD: Naval Institute Press, 2005), 146-50.

38. "Ziemer Captains Lafayette Team," *Wilkes-Barre (PA) Times Leader*, November 16, 1940, 1, https://www.newspapers.com/article/wilkes-barre-times-leader-the-evening-n /134290573/; "Two Sophs Listed for Lafayette," *Standard-Speaker* (Hazleton,

PA), October 3, 1941, 21, https://www.newspapers.com/article/standard-speaker
-two-sophs-listed-for-la/134290824.

39. "Father Talks Sons into Navy," *Asbury Park (NJ) Press*, May 27, 1945, 5, https://www
.newspapers.com/article/asbury-park-press-father-talks-sons-into/23914900/.

40. Weymouth High School (Weymouth, MA), yearbook, 1939, 30, https://archive.org
/details/weymouthhighscho1939unse/page/30.

CHAPTER 2. BECOMING A SQUADRON

1. Naval History and Heritage Command (NHHC), "Fighter Squadron Lineage," 12,
https://www.history.navy.mil/research/histories/naval-aviation-history/insignias
/naval-aviation-squadron-lineage/fighter-squadron-lineage.html.

2. James D. Hornfischer, *The Last Stand of the Tin Can Sailors: The Extraordinary World War
II Story of the U.S. Navy's Finest Hour* (New York: Bantam Books, 2005), 67.

3. Hornfischer, *Last Stand*, 69–70.

4. Roy A. Grossnick, *Dictionary of American Naval Aviation Squadrons*, vol. 1 (Washington,
DC: Naval Historical Center, 1995), 13.

5. NAS Whidbey Island, war diary, March 28 to April 3, 1943, https://catalog.archives
.gov/id/1341367501.

6. "San Diego County, California Weather Data," *Wisconsin Journal Sentinel*, June 1, 1943,
https://data.jsonline.com/weather-data/san-diego-county/06073/1943-06-01/?syear
=1895&eyear=2023#summary.

7. USS *Prince William*, war diary, May 1–31, 1943, 27, https://catalog.archives.gov/id
/134287077.

8. USS *Trathen*, war diary, May 28 to August 5, 1943, 55, https://catalog.archives.gov/id
/134311450.

9. Walworth collection, wartime diary, 61, 62.

10. Frederick Wolff collection, aviator's flight log book, August 1943 entries.

11. Officer biography sheet, Harris Collection.

12. Thomas Wright Jr. email, Harris Collection; Harris interview, Smithsonian NASM.

13. Fighting Squadron 27, Harris Collection, 2, 3.

14. Unofficial E. C. Simmons diary, Harris Collection, 4.

15. Simmons diary, Harris Collection, 5.

16. Fighting Squadron 27, Harris Collection, 3, 4.

17. Miscellaneous report on the fitness of officers, April 24, 1942–May 24, 1943, Harris
Collection.

18. Steve Ewing and John Lundstrom, *Fateful Rendezvous: The Life of Butch O'Hare* (Annapolis, MD: Naval Institute Press, 1997), 151.

19. C. B. Colby, "How the Hellcat Got That Way," *Popular Science*, December 1943, 72.

20. Colby.

21. Barrett Tillman, *Hellcat: The F6F in World War II* (Annapolis, MD: Naval Institute Press,
2000), 10.

22. Plane specifications for F4F-3 Wildcat, https://www.history.navy.mil/content/history/museums/nnam/explore/collections/aircraft/f/f4f-3-wildcat.html, and F6F-3 Hellcat, https://www.history.navy.mil/content/history/museums/nnam/explore/collections/aircraft/f/f6f-3-hellcat.html, NHHC.
23. Harris interview, Smithsonian NASM.
24. Thune, oral history, 4, 5.
25. VF-9, war history, 72, https://catalog.archives.gov/id/77658405.
26. Tillman, 48.
27. Tillman, 10, 11.
28. NHHC, "Fighter Squadron Lineage," 12.
29. Aircraft roster shows only fighter types left circa November 1. Commander, Western Sea Frontier, war diary, November 1–30, 1944, 311, https://catalog.archives.gov/id/139850542.
30. Murphy collection, VC-30 orders dated October 4, 1943.
31. Murphy collection, Commander Aircraft Atlantic Fleet, "Flight Operations U.S.S. Ranger," May 28, 1941, and Chief of Naval Operations, "Herbert Schiff Memorial Trophy Competition Standing," February 1, 1941.
32. Frank Foltz collection, officer biography sheet, May 26, 1961.
33. Thune, oral history, Intrepid Museum, 12.
34. "Social Events," *Sedalia (MO) Democrat*, September 26, 1943, 8, https://www.newspapers.com/article/the-sedalia-democrat-social-events/7183660/.
35. Walworth collection, training diary, 63.
36. Commander, Western Sea Frontier, war diary, October 1–31, 1943, 31, https://catalog.archives.gov/id/136046263.
37. J. R. Leeds, "Aviation Personnel Fatalities in World War II," Bureau of Naval Personnel memo, https://www.history.navy.mil/research/library/online-reading-room/title-list-alphabetically/a/aviation-personnel-fatalities-in-world-war-ii.html.
38. USS *Copahee*, war diary, November 1–30, 1943, 25, 26, https://catalog.archives.gov/id/136006387.
39. "Copahee," *Dictionary of American Naval Fighting Ships*, NHHC, https://www.history.navy.mil/content/history/nhhc/research/histories/ship-histories/danfs.html.
40. "Copahee," 31.
41. Walworth collection, training diary, 65.
42. Robert Brownell collection, letter to Lieutenant Barrick, December 24, 1942.
43. USS *Copahee*, war diary, 31.
44. USS *Crane*, war diary, November 1–30, 1943, 29, https://catalog.archives.gov/id/136030096.
45. Wolff collection, aviator's flight log book, November 1943 entries.
46. USS *Yorktown*, war diary, December 1–31, 1943, https://catalog.archives.gov/id/782724519.
47. Thune, oral history, Intrepid Museum, 13.

48. South Dakota Sports Hall of Fame, "Harold Thune–Inducted 2013," www.sdshof.com /inductees/harold-thune/.

CHAPTER 3. LEARNING THE ROPES

1. Oliver Jensen, "Truk, End of a Bogey," *Bureau of Naval Personnel Information Bulletin* 338 (Washington, DC: Bureau of Naval Personnel, May 1945), 26, https://media.defense .gov/2019/Apr/10/2002112313/-1/-1/1/AH194505.pdf.

2. Ian W. Toll, *The Conquering Tide: War in the Pacific Islands, 1942–1944* (New York: W. W. Norton, 2015), 405.

3. Toll, 404.

4. VF-9, war history, 10, 11.

5. VF-9, war history, 94–97.

6. VF-9, war history, 98.

7. VF-9, war history.

8. VF-9, war history, 109, 110.

9. USS *Monterey*, Report of Action, Air Group 30, Tinian Islands, Marianas, February 22, 1944, 7–11, https://catalog.archives.gov/id/78326447.

10. USS *Monterey*, Report of Action, 12.

11. Trapp, VC-66 informal history, 10.

12. James D. Hornfischer, *The Fleet at Flood Tide: America at Total War in the Pacific, 1944–1945* (New York: Bantam Books, 2016), 34; Toll, 398.

13. VC-66, Aircraft Action Reports, Operations against the Marshall Islands, February 6–21, 1944, 44–49, https://catalog.archives.gov/id/139754790.

14. William H. Adams, ed. *The Japanese Airbase on Taroa Island, Republic of the Marshall Islands, 1937–1945: An Evaluation of the World War II Remains* (San Francisco: U.S. National Park Service, 1997), 20.

15. Trapp, VC-66 informal history, 11, 12.

16. Wells McGurk collection, letter, C. A. Blouin to John S. McGurk, March 5, 1944.

17. McGurk collection, letter, C. A. Blouin to John S. McGurk, March 29, 1944.

18. VF-40, war diary, March 1–31, 1944, 2, 3, https://catalog.archives.gov/id/78559819.

19. Andrew Faltum, *Aircraft Carrier* Intrepid (Annapolis, MD: Naval Institute Press, 2022), 6.

20. Clark G. Reynolds, *The Fast Carriers: The Forging of an Air Navy* (Annapolis, MD: Naval Institute Press, 2013), 38, 39; Toll, 301, 302.

21. Faltum, 4, 9.

22. Faltum, 5.

23. Sortie count derived from Faltum, 16, 19; torpedo incident from Faltum, 24, 25.

24. Faltum, 26; NHHC, "Fighter Squadron Lineage," 12.

25. Anticipation of damage repair completion by air group personnel circa May 1944 indicated by Air Group 18, war history, 7.

26. "William Edward Ellis," NHHC, Modern Biographical Files.

27. Air Group 18, war history, 3; Gregory G. Fletcher, *Intrepid Aviators: The American Flyers Who Sank Japan's Greatest Battleship* (New York: NAL Caliber, 2013), 89.

28. E. G. Blankenship, scrapbook, Collection of the Intrepid Museum, 18, 44.

29. Identification of the unit was made possible by reference to its leader in Air Group 18, war history, 13; and Lt. Gen. William K. Jones, *A Brief History of the 6th Marines* (Washington, DC: History and Museums Division, U.S. Marine Corps, 1987), 105, 106.

30. Forsyth, 52.

CHAPTER 4. DEPLOYMENT DELAYED

1. Amerman, photograph collection, Intrepid Museum.

2. Blankenship, scrapbook, Intrepid Museum, 14–16.

3. Wolff collection, scrapbook photographs; National Park Service, National Register of Historic Places Registration Form, "Star of the Sea Church, Kalapana Painted Church Site #10–63–7380," https://npgallery.nps.gov/AssetDetail/039507b0-dfea-49b3-bb0c -fc861c299ec0.

4. Robert O'Maley collection, letters, May 8 and May 25, 1944.

5. O'Maley, letters.

6. VB-18, war-history, 10, https://catalog.archives.gov/id/77643136.7; Tillman, 10, 11; familiarization with -5 type from available log books, such as Wolff collection.

7. USS *Intrepid*, war diary, June 1–30, 1944, 3–4, https://catalog.archives.gov/id/78520108.

8. USS *Intrepid*, war diary, 5; Faltum, 27.

9. Ernest Allen papers, folder 5, Archives Branch, NHHC.

10. Wolff collection, scrapbook, "No Man's Complete without Courage," article, *Jacksonville Journal*, August 3, 1963, 5. Additional details from conversations with the Wolff family.

11. Wolff collection, aviator's flight log book, July 7, 1944 entry.

12. Fletcher, 104; "Little Hope Held for Missing Aviator," *Ephraim (UT) Enterprise*, August 4, 1944, 1, https://www.newspapers.com/article/the-ephraim-enterprise-little-hope-held /134345967.

13. USS *Intrepid*, war diary, July 1–31, 1944, 5, https://catalog.archives.gov/id/78577023.

14. NHHC, *Building the Navy's Bases in World War II*, vol. 2, part 3, chap. 26, 324, https: //www.history.navy.mil/research/library/online-reading-room/title-list-alphabetically /b/building-the-navys-bases/buidling-navys-bases-vol-2-chapter-26.html; Air Group 18, war history, 8.

15. Based on the presence of three carrier task groups circa August 29, 1944, in Commander, Task Force 38, Summary of Operations, August 28 to October 30, 1944, 244, https: //catalog.archives.gov/id/78648835.

16. Reynolds, 232.

17. Commander, Air Group (CAG) 18, Aircraft Action Report (AAR), Operations in the Palau Islands, September 6–8, 1944, 2, 6, 11, 16, 21, 26, 31, https://catalog.archives.gov /id/139750650.

18. Arnold S. Lott, *Most Dangerous Sea: A History of Mine Warfare and an Account of U.S. Navy Mine Warfare Operations in World War II and Korea* (Annapolis, MD: U.S. Naval Institute, 1959), 173.

19. Stephen C. Murray, "The Palauan *Kirikomi-tai* Suicide Bombers of World War II and the Siege of Babeldoab: A Reconsideration," *Pacific Asia Inquiry* 4, no. 1 (2013): 30, 34; "The Battle of Peleliu," Marine Corps University, https://www.usmcu.edu /Research/Marine-Corps-History-Division/Brief-Histories/Marines-in-World-War-II /The-Battle-of-Peleliu/.

20. Stan Fisher, *Sustaining the Carrier War: The Deployment of U.S. Naval Air Power to the Pacific* (Annapolis, MD: Naval Institute Press, 2023), 117; John Lawrence Donoghue, Intrepid Museum oral history project, 8, https://intrepid.emuseum.com/groups /oral-histories.

21. Donoghue oral history, 2–4.

22. Donoghue oral history, 6.

23. CAG 18, September 6–8, 1944, 28, 32.

24. CAG 18, September 6–8, 1944, 33.

25. "Harlan Rockey Dickson," NHHC, Modern Biographical Files.

26. CAG 18, AAR, Operations in the Philippine Islands, September 9–10, 1944, 24, https: //catalog.archives.gov/id/139750327.

27. CAG 18, September 9–10, 1944, 28, 29.

28. CAG 18, September 9–10, 1944, 26.

29. CAG 18, AAR, Operations against the Central Philippine Islands, September 12–14, 1944, 5, https://catalog.archives.gov/id/139751174.

30. CAG 18, September 12–14, 1944, 21.

31. Ray Coll Jr., "Dogfight over Formosa," *Honolulu Advertiser*, November 8, 1944, 5, https://www.newspapers.com/article/the-honolulu-advertiser-dogfight-over-fo /13633790/.

32. "Scholarship Winner," *Montclair (NJ) Times*, June 22, 1937, 5, https://www.newspapers .com/article/the-montclair-times-scholarship-winner/35713358/.

33. VF(N)-78, AAR, Operations in the Philippine Islands, September 9–22, 1944, 10, https://catalog.archives.gov/id/139754790.

34. VF(N)-78, September 9–22, 1944, 12–15.

35. Tillman, 123.

36. Commander, USS *Hornet*, Report of Operations Against the Palau and Philippine Islands, 108, 109.

37. Commander, USS *Hornet*.

38. USS *Bunker Hill*, Report of Air Operations against the Palau and Philippine Islands, August 29 to September 30, 1944, 422.

39. CAG 18, September 12–14, 1944, 23.

40. CAG 18, September 12–14, 1944, 27, 28.

41. Leslie Nichols, radio reports, December 5–6, 1944, Hoover Institution Library and Archives, https://digitalcollections.hoover.org/objects/51681/leslie-nichols-radio -reports-from-5-and-6-december-1944.

42. CAG 18, AAR, Operations against the Philippine and Palau Islands, September 13–17, 1944, 5, https://catalog.archives.gov/id/139751255.

43. USS *Bunker Hill*, August 29 to September 30, 1944, 512.

44. CAG 18, September 12–14, 1944, 24.

45. CAG 18, September 12–14, 1944, 29.

46. CAG 18, September 12–14, 1944, 29.

47. CAG 18, September 12–14, 1944, 27.

48. Richard Montfort, *Intrepid* diaries, September 13, 1944.

49. U.S. Secretary of the Combined Chiefs of Staff, *Octagon Conference, September 1944: Papers and Minutes of Meetings* (Washington, DC: Department of Defense, 1944), 34.

50. John Prados, *Storm over Leyte: The Philippine Invasion and the Destruction of the Japanese Navy* (New York: Penguin Random House, 2016), 80; William F. Trimble, *Admiral John S. McCain and the Triumph of Naval Air Power* (Annapolis, MD: Naval Institute Press, 2019), 159.

51. Reynolds, *Fast Carriers*, 244, 245.

52. Combined Chiefs of Staff, *Octagon Conference*, 228.

53. Combined Chiefs of Staff, *Octagon Conference*, 228.

54. CAG 18, September 13–17, 1944, 20.

55. CAG 18, September 13–17, 1944, 20.

56. "Keels Jr., Isaac Wesley," Scrapbook, Heroic Sons of Gold Star Mothers, Union County, NC, http://history.union.lib.nc.us/GoldStarMothers/keelsi.htm.

57. James P. Duffy, *War at the End of the World: Douglas MacArthur and the Forgotten Fight for New Guinea, 1942–1945* (New York: New American Library, 2016), 330, 331.

58. Dan Caldwell, "Remembering Peleliu," *Naval History Magazine* 14, no. 2 (April 2000), https://www.usni.org/magazines/naval-history-magazine/2000/april/remembering-peleliu.

59. CAG 18, AAR, Operations against Luzon, Philippine Islands, September 21–22, 1944, 5, https://catalog.archives.gov/id/139751278.

CHAPTER 5. ESCALATION

1. John T. Correll, "Disaster in the Philippines," *Air & Space Forces Magazine*, November 1, 2019.

2. "Navy's Second Ranking Ace Home on Leave," *Del Rio (TX) News Herald*, January 17, 1945, 1, https://www.newspapers.com/article/del-rio-news-herald-cecil-harris-ranking /5287518/.

3. Sandy Wells, "Innerviews: I Was Just Lucky," *Charleston (WV) Gazette*, November 11, 2002, 1C, https://www.proquest.com/docview/331226082.

4. CAG 18, September 21–22, 1944, 5.

5. Air Group 18, war history, 10, 12.

6. Air Group 18, war history, 13, 14.

7. Francillon, 378, 381.

8. CAG 18, September 21–22, 1944, 13, 14.

9. Francillon, 112.

10. CAG 18, September 21–22, 1944, 14, 15.

11. CAG 18, September 21–22, 1944, 14, 15.

12. Dallas C. Higbee, "A Dunbar Man Who Qualified as Expert in Aerial Combat," *Sunday Gazette-Mail* (Charleston, WV), November 7, 1965, 42, https://www.newspapers.com /article/sunday-gazette-mail-a-dunbar-man-who-qua/7141975/.

13. CAG 18, September 21–22, 1944, 14.

14. CAG 18, September 21–22, 1944, 8, 17.

15. Aurentz, 24, 25.

16. CAG 18, September 21–22, 1944, 18.

17. CAG 18, September 21–22, 1944, 23.

18. CAG 18, September 21–22, 1944, 24, 25.

19. CAG 18, September 21–22, 1944, 25.

20. CAG 18, September 21–22, 1944, 25.

21. CAG 18, September 21–22, 1944, 30.

22. CAG 18, September 21–22, 1944, 29, 30.

23. VF(N)-78, AARs, September 9–22, 1944, 17–20.

24. CAG 18, AAR, Central Philippine Islands, September 24, 1944, 16–19, https://catalog .archives.gov/id/139751319.

25. CAG 18, September 24, 1944, 27, 33.

26. CAG 18, September 24, 1944, 30. Though the pilot's name is not given, only one VF returned with damage on this date, and the damage listed corresponds to both Bryant Walworth collection, aviator's flight log book, and Lee Walworth, interview of Bryant Walworth, August 1986.

27. CAG 18, September 24, 1944, 30.

28. Air Group 18, war history, 12.

29. Thune oral history, Intrepid Museum, 20.

30. Charles Mallory collection, diary, 14.

31. Mallory diary, 15.

32. Mallory diary, 16.

33. Air Group 18, war history, 13.

34. Air Group 18, war history, 13.

35. Worrall Reed Carter, *Beans, Bullets, and Black Oil: The Story of Fleet Logistics Afloat in the Pacific During World War II* (Washington, DC: U.S. Government Printing Office, 1953), 225.

36. VF(N)-78, war history, 4, 5, https://catalog.archives.gov/id/77663361; USS *Independence*, Report of Air Operations against the Palau and Philippine Islands, August 29 to September 30, 1944, 1–3.

37. USS *Intrepid*, war diary, October 1–31, 1944, 2, 4, https://catalog.archives.gov/id/78663710.

38. "Gerald Francis Bogan," NHHC, Modern Biographical Files, https://www.history.navy.mil/content/history/nhhc/research/library/research-guides/lists-of-senior-officers-and-civilian-officials-of-the-us-navy/commander-first-fleet/bogan-gerald-francis.html.

39. Ray Coll Jr., "Profile of a Flying Admiral," *Honolulu Advertiser*, November 11, 1944, 14.

40. For more information, compare NHHC, Modern Biographical Files, "Robert Burns Pirie Sr.," https://www.history.navy.mil/research/library/research-guides/modern-biographical-files-ndl/modern-bios-p/pirie-robert-burns-sr.html; USS *Intrepid* cruise book (1963), 154.

41. William F. Halsey and J. Bryan, *Admiral Halsey's Story* (New York: McGraw-Hill, 1947), 204, 205; USS *Intrepid*, war diary, October 1–31, 1944, 9.

42. "VB-18 Attack and Raid on Ie Island," Collection of the Intrepid Museum.

43. CAG 18, AAR, Operations against the Ryukyu Islands, Formosa, Philippines, and the Japanese Fleet, October 10–30, 1944, 8, https://catalog.archives.gov/id/78715291.

44. CAG 18, October 10–30, 1944, 8, 13, 23, 32, 37, 46, 53.

45. Prados, *Storm over Leyte*, 124.

46. CAG 18, October 10–30, 1944, 9.

47. H. P. Willmott, *The Battle of Leyte Gulf: The Last Fleet Action* (Bloomington: Indiana University Press, 2005), 47, 48.

48. Willmott, 49.

49. Milan Vego, *The Battle for Leyte, 1944: Allied and Japanese Plans, Preparations, and Execution* (Annapolis, MD: Naval Institute Press, 2013), 47; David C. Evans, ed., *The Japanese Navy in World War II: In the Words of Former Japanese Naval Officers* (Annapolis, MD: Naval Institute Press, 1986), 419. Reasons for this are discussed in David C. Evans and Mark R. Peattie, *Kaigun: Strategy, Tactics, and Technology in the Imperial Japanese Navy, 1887–1941* (Annapolis, MD: Naval Institute Press, 1997), 326.

50. Prados, *Storm over Leyte*, 131.

51. USS *Intrepid*, war diary, October 1–31, 1944, 10.

CHAPTER 6. FIRE OVER FORMOSA

1. Edward H. Sims, *Greatest Fighter Missions of the Top Navy and Marine Aces of World War II* (New York: Harper, 1962), 155, 158.

2. A good explanation of complications associated with Point Option and YE/ZB homing beacon navigation is laid out in USS *Essex*, Action Report, GALVANIC Ops, November 18–25, 1943, 40, 41, https://catalog.archives.gov/id/136020848.

3. Philip S. Heisler, "Flyers Menaced by Head-Hunters," *Baltimore Sun*, October 23, 1944, 1, 6, https://www.newspapers.com/article/the-baltimore-sun-flyers-menaced-by-hea/52704108/.

4. CAG 18, October 10–30, 1944, 58, 62; Sims, 158.

5. Office of the Chief of Naval Operations, Division of Naval Intelligence, Air Intelligence Group, "Airfield and Seaplane Bases in Formosa," 21, https://catalog.archives.gov/id/78450948.

6. USS *Bunker Hill*, AAR, Operations Against the Ryukyu Islands, Formosa, and the Philippines, October 10–22, 1944, 93, https://catalog.archives.gov/id/7864243; Sims, 158.

7. Air Group 18, war history, 13.

8. USS *Intrepid*, war diary, October 1–31, 1944, 12.

9. Sims, 160, 161.

10. Prados, *Storm over Leyte*, 134.

11. John Prados, *Combined Fleet Decoded: The Secret History of American Intelligence and the Japanese Navy in World War II* (Annapolis, MD: Naval Institute Press, 1995), 609.

12. Frank Hearrell collection, personal account of Frank C. Hearrell Jr; Commander, Air Group 18, October 10–30, 1944, 62.

13. NHHC, air target maps and photos, selected targets, Northern Formosa, Pescadores, October 1, 1944.

14. NHHC, air target maps and photos, 62; USS *Bunker Hill*, October 10–22, 1944, 93.

15. Harris interview, Smithsonian NASM.

16. Participation of VF-8 in the Marianas drawn from USS *Bunker Hill*, Report of Operations in Support of Marianas and Attack on Japanese Task Force, June 6–27, 1944, 2; USS *Bunker Hill*, October 10–22, 1944, 93.

17. USS *Bunker Hill*, October 10–22, 1944, 94.

18. Charles W. deMoss oral history, Collection of the Intrepid Museum, transcript 18.

19. Thune oral history, Collection of the Intrepid Museum, 17.

20. Burley's earlier mishap is described in Nichols, radio reports; CAG 18, October 10–30, 1944, 63.

21. CAG 18, October 10–30, 1944, 63.

22. VF18 Combat Accomplishments 1944, 1918–1945, entry UD-09D, box 322; Murphy collection.

23. Coll Jr., "Dogfight over Formosa," 5.

24. "Navy Fighter Pilot Becomes City's 1st Ace," *Santa Barbara News-Press*, October 18, 1944, 1, 2, https://www.newspapers.com/article/santa-barbara-news-press-navy-fighter-pi/134355712/.

25. This story appeared in newspapers across at least twenty-six states due to distribution by the Associated Press. The parent article is Philip S. Heisler, "First Clash with Japs Leaves Ensign an Ace," *Baltimore Evening Sun*, October 18, 1944, 1, https://www.newspapers.com/article/the-evening-sun-3-day-attack-on-formosa/52703584/.

26. CAG 18, October 10–30, 1944, 63; Sims, 162–64.

27. William Ziemer collection, letter, Mrs. L. C. Ziemer to son Arthur R. Ziemer, October 29, 1945.

28. CAG 18, October 10–30, 1944, 60.

29. James Newsome collection, letter from Egidio James DiBatista, undated.

30. CAG 18, October 10–30, 1944, 63.

31. USS *Yarnall*, war diary, October 10–30, 1944, 6.

32. Commander, Task Group 38.2, Air Operations, Ryukyu Islands, Formosa, and the Philippines, October 10 to November 3, 1944, 36.

33. Ikuhiko Hata and Yasuho Izawa, *Japanese Naval Aces and Fighter Units in World War II* (Annapolis, MD: Naval Institute Press, 1989), 396; Lundstrom, *The First Team: Pacific Naval Air Combat from Pearl Harbor to Midway*, 230.

34. Shigeru Fukudome, "The Air Battle Off Taiwan," in Evans, *Japanese Navy in World War II*, 347.

35. VF-7, war history, 22, https://catalog.archives.gov/id/77658304.

36. USS *Bunker Hill*, October 10–22, 1944, 159.

37. CAG 18, October 10–30, 1944, 70.

38. Forsyth, 69.

39. Forsyth, 69, 70.

40. CAG 18, October 10–30, 1944, 70.

41. Enemy Oil Committee, Fuels and Lubricants Division, *Petroleum Facilities of Formosa* (Washington, DC: Office of the Quartermaster General, 1945), 67, https://www.scribd .com/document/43228345/Taiwan-Petroleum-Facilities-1945; Chang Chih-yuan, "The Historic Preservation and Rebirth of the Shell Oil Company Storage in Tamsui Taiwan," paper presented at the International Association of Societies of Design Research, Hong Kong Polytechnic University, November 12–15, 2007, 4–6.

42. CAG 18, October 10–30, 1944, 68.

43. The site of these bombings has undergone substantial restoration and preservation and opened to the public in 2011 as the Tamsui Cultural Park. "Former Warehouse of Jiashi Foreign Company," Tamsui Historical Museum, machine translation by Google, https://www.tshs.ntpc.gov.tw/xcmapguide/cont?xsmsid=0I232583746428540053 &sid=0I233377846694452838&viewmode=info; Xie Dexi, "Stinky Oil Stack Legend," Tamsui Culture Foundation, machine translation by Google, http://www.tamsui.org .tw/83-3.html.

44. CAG 18, October 10–30, 1944, 67.

45. CAG 18, October 10–30, 1944, 71.

46. Kenneth P. Barden, diary, Collection of the Intrepid Museum, 15, 16.

47. Barden diary, 67.

48. USS *Intrepid*, war diary, October 1–31, 1944, 12.

49. VF-18 Combat Accomplishments 1944, Enclosure C.

50. CAG 18, October 10–30, 1944, 91.

51. USS *Intrepid*, war diary, October 1–31, 1944, 13.

CHAPTER 7. ON PATROL AND IN SUPPORT

1. USS *Intrepid*, war diary, October 1–31, 1944, 14.

2. Prados, *Storm over Leyte*, 49, 50.

3. USS *Intrepid*, war diary, October 1–31, 1944, 15.

4. USS *Cabot*, Rep of Air Operations, October 6–14, 1944, October 20–31, 1944, 5.

5. USS *Intrepid*, war diary, October 1–31, 1944, 15.

6. Ray Coll Jr., "A Gun Crew from the Mess in Action," *Honolulu Star-Advertiser*, December 13, 1944, 14, https://www.newspapers.com/article/the-honolulu-advertiser-a-gun-crew-from/13630707/.

7. Emily Hegranes, "Segregation in the Navy," *Naval History Magazine* 35, no. 1 (February 2021), 8, https://www.usni.org/magazines/naval-history-magazine/2021/february/segregation-navy; Eugene Smith Jr., Intrepid Museum oral history project.

8. CAG 18, October 10–30, 1944, 111–15.

9. CAG 18, October 10–30, 1944, 124, 125.

10. Commander, Task Group 38.3, Report of Carrier Air Ops against Formosa, October 12–14, 1944, 7, https://catalog.archives.gov/id/78705547.

11. USS *Franklin*, Report of Action with Japanese Aircraft Southeast of Formosa on October 13, 1944, 1, 2, https://catalog.archives.gov/id/139760123.

12. Samuel Eliot Morison, *History of United States Naval Operations in World War II*, vol. 12, *Leyte: June 1944–January 1945* (Annapolis, MD: Naval Institute Press, 2011), 95, 96.

13. CAG 18, October 10–30, 1944, 127–30.

14. Morison, 95, 96; Toll, 169–72.

15. CAG 18, October 10–30, 1944, 132–35.

16. USS *Intrepid*, war diary, October 1–31, 1944, 19.

17. David L. Boslaugh, *Radar and the Fighter Directors*, unpublished manuscript, circa February 2018, https://ethw.org/Radar_and_the_Fighter_Directors. Details about CXAM sets at Pearl Harbor come from chapter six, subheading "First Encounters"; details regarding *Hornet* as the first American ship with a dedicated radar plot are in chapter five, subheading "Early Experience with the CXAM."

18. Boslaugh, chapter 6, subheading "Status of Identification Friend or Foe in the U.S. Navy, May 1942"; Office of the Chief of Naval Operations, *CIC Magazine* 1, no. 7 (September 1944), 22–23.

19. *CIC Magazine* 1, 35.

20. Office of the Chief of Naval Operations, *CIC Magazine* 2, no. 2 (November 1945), 3–5.

21. Description of CIC taken from *CIC Magazine* 2, no. 2, 3–7.

22. Tell Studios, *The Life and Legacy of Bill Daniels* (Denver, CO: Daniels Fund, 2012), 17–22.

23. Roy Burnett collection, biography by his daughter, Kate Johnstone. Story also referenced in fax sent from Bill Daniels to Kate Johnstone, February 1, 1999; CAG 18, October 10–30, 1944, 144.

24. CAG 18, October 10–30, 1944, 140.

25. USS *Intrepid*, war diary, October 1–31, 1944, 19; *CIC Magazine* 1, no. 9 (December 1944), 19–21.

26. CAG 18, October 10–30, 1944, 146–50.

27. George Naff, interview by Heather Steele, World War II History Project, July 16, 2011, 18–23.

28. Air Group 18, war history, 16.

29. Prados, *Storm over Leyte*, 144; Commander, Task Group 38.1, Report of Air Operations against the Ryukyu Islands, Formosa, and the Philippines, October 2–29, 1944, 16, https://catalog.archives.gov/id/78716147.

30. Mark Stille, *Leyte Gulf: A New History of the World's Largest Sea Battle* (Oxford, UK: Osprey, 2023), 109.

31. Prados, *Storm over Leyte*, 148.

32. Bertram Vogel, "Japan's Wartime Hocus-Pocus," *Proceedings* 74, no. 4 (April 1948), https://www.usni.org/magazines/proceedings/1948/april/japans-wartime-hocus-pocus.

33. Stille, *Leyte Gulf*, 109.

34. Willmott, 293, 294.

35. Prados, *Storm over Leyte*, 145; Morison, 103, 104.

36. Charles Mallory, diary, 32.

37. Commander, Task Group 38.1, 19, 20.

38. CAG 18, October 10–30, 1944, 151–54.

39. CAG 18, October 10–30, 1944, 156–59.

40. CAG 18, October 10–30, 1944, 159; Air Group 18, war history, 17.

41. CAG 18, October 10–30, 1944, 161–10.

42. Vego, 176.

43. Ray Coll Jr., "Waiting News in Ready Room," *Honolulu Advertiser*, November 12, 1944, 24.

44. CAG 18, October 10–30, 1944, 176–79.

45. Frank Olynyk, *Stars & Bars: A Tribute to the American Fighter Ace 1920–1973* (London: Grub Street, 1995), 4, 5.

46. CAG 18, October 10–30, 1944, 181–84.

47. Mallory diary, 39.

48. Willmott, 92–93.

49. Air Group 18, war history, 16.

50. "Artist-Fighter Pilot Kept Carrier's Morale High," *Brooklyn Daily Eagle*, December 30, 1945, 13.

51. Carl Solberg, *Decision and Dissent: With Halsey at Leyte Gulf* (Annapolis, MD: Naval Institute Press, 1995), 66.

CHAPTER 8. LEYTE GULF: IN THE SIBUYAN SEA

1. Thomas J. Cutler, ed., *The Battle of Leyte Gulf at 75: A Retrospective* (Annapolis, MD: Naval Institute Press, 2019), 117.

2. Trimble, 186.

3. Vego, 196, 248, 249.

4. Dissent on this point by Capt. Raymond D. Tarbuck, the ranking naval officer in MacArthur's staff, was ignored. Compare Marc D. Bernstein, "He Predicted Leyte Gulf,"

Naval History Magazine 15, no. 5 (October 2001), https://www.usni.org/magazines /naval-history-magazine/2001/october/he-predicted-leyte-gulf.

5. Commander, Third Fleet, October 23–26, 1944, 13.

6. Commander, Third Fleet, October 23–26, 1944, 16.

7. CAG 18, October 10–30, 1944, 200.

8. Mallory diary, 35, 39.

9. Willmott, 113.

10. Morison, 175.

11. Air Group 18, war history, 18; Donald Watts collection, grease pencil sighting report; Commander, Third Fleet, October 23–26, 1944, 18.

12. Amerman papers, citation for Air Medal; Donald Watts collection, citation for Distinguished Flying Cross.

13. CAG 18, October 10–30, 1944, 200.

14. deMoss, oral history, 23.

15. Prados, *Storm over Leyte*, 201; Willmott, 106.

16. Commander, Third Fleet, October 23–26, 1944, 18, 19; Morison, 175, 176.

17. Identification of ships comes from Willmott, 10; Ritter's participation comes from aviator's flight log book, Edward A. Ritter, Collection of the Intrepid Museum; CAG 18, October 10–30, 1944, 199, 200.

18. CAG 18, October 10–30, 1944, 200.

19. Commander, Task Group 38.4, 7, 8.

20. Morison, 178–83.

21. Prados, *Storm over Leyte*, 259–61.

22. CAG 18, October 10–30, 1944, 200.

23. Reynolds, 265.

24. Willmott, 72.

25. Willmott, 111, 112.

26. CAG 18, October 10–30, 1944, 202; USS *Cabot*, October 6–14, 1944, October 20–31, 1944, 14.

27. Forsyth, 12–14.

28. Fletcher, 242–45.

29. Fletcher, 246, 247.

30. Fletcher, 248–54.

31. Prados, *Storm over Leyte*, 203, 204.

32. CAG 18, October 10–30, 1944, 203; Forsyth, 16, 17, indicates these planes belonged to Lt. (jg) Benjamin Emge, whose engine was hit, and likely to Forsyth, based on description of damage to the plane's elevator.

33. Morison, 184.

34. Fletcher, 256; Forsyth, 15.

35. Prados, *Storm over Leyte*, 202, 203.

36. Hearrell collection, signed account of action.

37. Hearrell collection, signed account of action.; author interview with Chris Cox, May 2022.
38. Hearrell collection, signed account of action.
39. CAG 18, October 10–30, 1944, 217.
40. USS *Intrepid*, war diary, October 1–31, 1944, 37.
41. CAG 18, October 10–30, 1944, 207.
42. Thune oral history, Intrepid Museum, 20, 21.
43. World War II draft registration cards for Rhode Island, October 16, 1940–March 31, 1947, https://www.fold3.com/image/657956210.
44. Fletcher, 260; Prados, *Storm over Leyte*, 204.
45. Prados, *Storm over Leyte*, 203.
46. Willmott, 115.
47. Morison, 184.
48. USS *Intrepid*, war diary, October 1–31, 1944, 36.
49. Prados, *Combined Fleet Decoded*, 641.
50. Toll, 234.

CHAPTER 9. LEYTE GULF: ANTICLIMAX

1. Willmott, 133.
2. Willmott, 112.
3. Vego, 277, 278.
4. Prados, *Storm over Leyte*, 219, 220.
5. Willmott, 121.
6. Willmott, 121.
7. Willmott, 123; Reynolds, 258.
8. Solberg, 119.
9. USS *Intrepid*, war diary, October 1–31, 1944, 39.
10. CAG 18, October 10–30, 1944, 240.
11. CAG 18, October 10–30, 1944, 247.
12. Donald Watts collection, aviator's flight log book, entries for 10 and 18 October.
13. Morison, 322.
14. CAG 18, October 10–30, 1944, 240.
15. CAG 18, October 10–30, 1944, 233.
16. CAG 18, October 10–30, 1944, 240.
17. CAG 18, October 10–30, 1944, 240.
18. CAG 15, Report of Operations against the Philippine Islands, October 21–27, 1944, 64; Morison, 324.
19. Morison, 324.
20. C. Vann Woodward, *The Battle for Leyte Gulf: The Incredible Story of World War II's Largest Naval Battle* (New York: Skyhorse Publishing, 2007), 152.
21. Description of strike coordinator hand-off from Office of Naval Records and Library, Personal Interviews, Cdr. Theodore H. Winters Jr., https://www.fold3.com

/image/301984750/personal-interviews-page-1895-us-world-war-ii-war-diaries-1941-1945; CAG 18, October 10–30, 1944, 247; Prados, *Storm over Leyte*, 263.

22. Prados, *Storm over Leyte*, 263; Christmas color reference made in Commander, Air Group 19, Report of Operations against the Ryukyu Islands, Formosa, Philippines, and Japanese Fleet, October 10, 1944 to November 6, 1944, 374, https://catalog.archives.gov/id/139768009.

23. CAG 18, October 10–30, 1944, 244, 247; Morison, 324.

24. *Intrepid* searchers reported the ship's absence in their report. CAG 18, October 10–30, 1944, 240.

25. Mark Stille, *Imperial Japanese Navy Aircraft Carriers, 1921–1945* (Oxford, UK: Osprey Publishing, Ltd., 2005), 45, 47, 72.

26. CAG 18, October 10–30, 1944, 245.

27. Prados, *Storm over Leyte*, 265–67.

28. Possible identification of ship based on damage described by the pilot in CAG 18, October 10–30, 1944, 247, and consonance with historical record, e.g. Willmott, 158, 159, and Prados, *Storm over Leyte*, 264.

29. Willmott, 158, 159, 202.

30. CAG 18, October 10–30, 1944, 240.

31. Toll, 272.

32. Willmott, 297.

33. Prados, *Storm over Leyte*, 252.

34. Willmott, 174.

35. Willmott, 193.

36. Willmott, 193, 195.

37. Intrepid Museum, Richard Montfort *Intrepid* Diaries, entry for October 25, 1944; Mallory diary, 45.

38. Ray Coll Jr., "'Sunken' Warships of Fleet Rise, Claim 58 Enemy Vessels," *Honolulu Advertiser*, October 31, 1944, 7, https://www.newspapers.com/article/the-honolulu-advertiser-sunken-warships/24397194.

39. Trimble, 179.

40. CAG 18, October 10–30, 1944, 254–59.

41. CAG 18, October 10–30, 1944, 254, 259.

42. CAG 18, October 10–30, 1944, 256, 258.

43. DeMoss oral history, Intrepid Museum, 24, 26, 27.

44. Richard Cevoli collection, newspaper clipping, "Lt. Richard L. Cevoli Permanently Cited for Navy Cross," date unknown.

45. "Decorations and Citations," *All Hands Magazine*, August 1947, 55; Willmott, 224; CAG 18, October 10–30, 1944, 256.

46. CAG 18, October 10–30, 1944, 255.

47. CAG 18, October 10–30, 1944, 266; Mallory diary, 45.

48. Willmott, 148; Fletcher, 263.

49. CAG 18, October 10–30, 1944, 273.

50. George A. Griffith Jr. papers, Collection of the Intrepid Museum, VF-18 squadron commander Lt. Cdr. E. J. Murphy to Griffith's wife Karolyn, October 29, 1944.

51. A photograph of the event corroborates the details of the onlookers, from the Collection of the Intrepid Museum.

52. USS *Intrepid*, war diary, October 10–31, 1944, 47.

53. Griffith papers, letter from Lt. Don Watts to Griffith's wife Karolyn, October 30, 194.

CHAPTER 10. KAMIKAZES AND CLARK FIELD

1. Morison, 301–3.

2. Toll, 199–203.

3. USS *Intrepid*, war diary, October 1–31, 1944, 26, 46.

4. Donoghue oral history, 8, 9.

5. CAG 18, October 10–30, 1944, 277–280.

6. CAG 18, October 10–30, 1944, 277–280.

7. USS *Hancock*, Report of Air Operations against the Ryukyu Islands, Formosa, and the Philippines, Including Attacks on the Japanese Fleet, October 6–31, 1944, 179, 180.

8. Yasuho Izawa with Tony Holmes, *J2M Raiden and N1K1/2 Shiden/Shiden-Kai Aces* (Oxford, UK: Osprey, 2016), 107.

9. Francillon, 328–29.

10. CAG 18, October 10–30, 1944, 278–80.

11. CAG 18, October 10–30, 1944, 282–85.

12. CAG 18, October 10–30, 1944, 285.

13. CAG 18, October 10–30, 1944, 285.

14. CAG 18, October 10–30, 1944, 285, 286.

15. National Archives and Records Administration, Survival and Escape Information/Interviews, 1918–1945, interview with Ens. Dan A. Naughton, USNR, of VF-18 (*Intrepid*).

16. Naughton interview.

17. CAG 18, October 10–30, 1944, 272–86.

18. DeMoss oral history, 21.

19. DeMoss oral history, 21; CAG 18, October 10–30, 1944, 283.

20. USS *Intrepid*, war diary, October 1–31, 1944, 48.

21. Robert Hurst collection, "WWII Memories and Records," 6.

22. USS *Intrepid*, Report of Air Operations against the Ryukyu Islands, Formosa, and the Philippines, October 10–31, 1944, Including Action against Japanese Fleet, October 24–26, 1944, 3–4.

23. Hurst, "WWII Memories," 6.

24. Hegranes; Smith, Intrepid Museum oral history project, 6–8.

25. Smith, 3, 7.

26. Daniel Garas, "The Oerlikon 20mm: The Rights Tool for the Job," *Sextant*, March 18, 2019, https://usnhistory.navylive.dodlive.mil/Recent/Article-View/Article/2686834/the-oerlikon-20-mm-the-right-tool-for-the-job/.

27. USS *Intrepid*, October 10–31, 1944, 75.

28. USS *Intrepid*, October 10–31, 1944, 83, 84; USS *Intrepid*, war diary, October 1–31, 1944, 48, 99.

29. USS *Intrepid*, war diary, October 1–31, 1944, 99, 100.

30. USS *Intrepid*, war diary, October 1–31, 1944, 103–6.

31. USS *Intrepid*, war diary, October 1–31, 1944, 48, 99.

32. CAG 18, October 10–30, 1944, 292.

33. Aurentz, 46.

34. Aurentz, 47.

35. CAG 18, October 10–30, 1944, 290; Philip S. Heisler, "2 Zeros Downed by Baltimore Navy Flyer," *Baltimore Evening Sun*, November 17, 1944, 1, https://www.newspapers.com/article/the-evening-sun-2-zeros-downed-even/52701666/; Mallory diary, 50.

36. Aurentz, 47; Mallory diary, 52.

37. Photograph, Collection of the Intrepid Museum, which shows Lt. Crusoe's F6F-5 bureau number 70667 after its crash landing; USS *Intrepid*, war diary, October 1–31, 1944, 52; CAG 18, October 10–30, 1944, 290.

38. CAG 18, October 10–30, 1944, 294.

39. Francillon, 215.

40. CAG 18, October 10–30, 1944, 298.

41. CAG 18, October 10–30, 1944, 294–98.

42. Eric Hammel, *Aces against Japan II: The American Aces Speak*, vol. 3 (Pacifica, CA: Pacifica Press, 1996), 220, 221.

43. CAG 18, October 10–30, 1944, 304–6.

44. CAG 18, October 10–30, 1944, 297.

45. Hammel, 221–22.

46. Air Group 18, war history, 21; Robert De Vore, "Wing Talk," *Collier's Magazine*, May 19, 1945, 8.

47. De Vore, 8.

48. Hammel, 222.

49. USS *Cabot*, October 6–14, 1944, October 20–31, 1944, 8; USS *Intrepid*, war diary, October 1–31, 1944, 49.

50. USS *Intrepid*, war diary, October 1–31, 1944, 49.

51. CAG 18, October 10–30, 1944, 295–98, 305, 306.

52. Rex Loftin, scrapbook, "Plan of the Day 31 October 1944," Collection of the Intrepid Museum.

53. Mallory diary, 52.

CHAPTER 11. STRAFING AND SURVIVING

1. Trimble, 185.

2. Christian Heidgerd, "Admiral Thach: A Tactical Artist," *Naval History Magazine* 36, no. 2 (April 2022), https://www.usni.org/magazines/naval-history-magazine/2022/april/admiral-thach-tactical-artist.

3. Commander, Task Force 38, Report of Operations against the Philippines, Formosa, French Indo-China, South China, and the Ryukyu Islands, November 5, 1944 to January 2, 1945, 58–61.

4. Air Group 18, war history, 21.

5. Ernest Allen, papers, NHHC, Washington, DC.

6. Air Group 18, war history, 15.

7. Commander, Task Force 38, November 5, 1944 to January 2, 1945, 59–61.

8. Commander, Task Force 38, November 5, 1944 to January 2, 1945, 58; USS *Intrepid*, war diary, November 1–30, 1944, 12.

9. USS *Intrepid*, November 1–30, 1944, 28.

10. Commander, Task Force 38, November 5, 1944 to January 2, 1945, 6.

11. USS *Intrepid*, November 1–30, 1944, 29.

12. Commander, Task Force 38, November 5, 1944 to January 2, 1945, 59, 60.

13. CAG 18, October 10–30, 1944, 292.

14. CAG 18, Operations against Luzon Island, Philippines, November 5–6, 1944, 10, https://catalog.archives.gov/id/78677948.

15. CAG 18, November 5–6, 1944, 7–10.

16. Lt. Charles W. deMoss, interview, Robert L. Lawson collection, cabinet 12, drawer 1, VF-18 folder, National Naval Aviation Museum.

17. Charles deMoss, Intrepid Museum oral history project, 28, 29.

18. CAG 18, November 5–6, 1944, 12–15.

19. CAG 18, November 5–6, 1944, 19–23.

20. Commander, Task Group 38.2, November 5–6, 1944, 7.

21. Prados, *Storm over Leyte*, 193, 194, 327.

22. CAG 18, November 5–6, 1944, 25–28.

23. CAG 18, November 5–6, 1944, 30–33.

24. Vego, 332.

25. USS *Intrepid*, November 1–30, 1944, 12.

26. Edward Ritter collection, interview by Valerie Lasser, audio recording.

27. Mallory diary, 30.

28. USS *Intrepid*, November 1–30, 1944, 13; Roster of Officers, Air Group 18, October 1, 1944, Collection of the Intrepid Museum, 5.

29. USS *Intrepid*, November 1–30, 1944, 14, 17.

30. Air Group 18, war history, 7.

31. Air Group 18, war history, 22, 23.

32. USS *Intrepid*, November 1–30, 1944, 20.

33. USS *Intrepid*, November 1–30, 1944, 31–33.

34. CAG 18, Operations against Enemy Airfields and Aircraft on Luzon Island, Philippines, November 19, 1944, 2–5.

35. Mallory diary, 33.

36. CAG 18, November 19, 1944, 5.

37. CAG 18, November 19, 1944, 9–12.

38. USS *Intrepid*, November 1–30, 1944, 32.

39. Donald Watts collection, aviator's flight log book; Amerman collection, aviator log book, Intrepid Museum; CAG 18, November 19, 1944, 14–17.

40. Mallory diary, 33.

41. CAG 18, November 19, 1944, 17.

42. James Newsome collection, "Interrogation aboard USS *Currituck*," December 25, 1944.

43. Newsome collection, Edward J. Murphy, letter to Mrs. Margaret L. Newsome, November 20, 1944.

44. Newsome collection, John F. Herlihy, letter to Mr. and Mrs. Newsome, November 20, 1944.

45. Newsome collection, Murphy letter.

46. Newsome collection, Herlihy letter.

47. William Ziemer collection, letter from Mrs. L. C. Ziemer to Arthur R. Ziemer, October 29, 1945.

48. Naughton interview; Quentin Reynolds, "Wing Talk," *Collier's Magazine*, June 30, 1945, 8, 42.

49. DeMoss oral history, 29.

50. National Naval Aviation Museum, interview with Lt. Charles W. deMoss, Naval Air Station Sanford, Florida.

51. Newsome collection, "Interrogation aboard USS *Currituck*."

CHAPTER 12. THE DARKEST DAY, THE END IN SIGHT

1. Ed Ritter, cartoon, Collection of the Intrepid Museum.

2. Air Group 18, war history, 23.

3. Thanksgiving Day menu, 1944, Collection of the Intrepid Museum.

4. Air Group 18, war history, 23.

5. Mallory diary, 69, 70.

6. Morison, 357.

7. USS *Intrepid*, war diary, November 1–30, 1944, 40; Raymond T. Stone, *My Ship! The U.S.S. Intrepid* (South Salem, NY: G. P. Books, 2003), 170.

8. Stone, 170.

9. USS *Intrepid*, war diary, November 1–30, 1944, 40.

10. "Recommendations for Awards in the Case of," Cecil E. Harris Collection, Beulah Williams Library Archives and Special Collections, 2, 3.

11. "Recommendations for Awards in the Case of," 2.

12. "Recommendations for Awards in the Case of," 3.

13. "Recommendations for Awards in the Case of," 3.

14. USS *Intrepid*, war diary, November 1–30, 1944, 42.

15. USS *Intrepid*, November 14–27, 1944, 97.

16. Race, 2.

17. Richard Moot Collection, Bronze Star citation, courtesy of John Moot.

18. Race, 2.

19. Race, 3.

20. USS *Intrepid*, war diary, November 1–30, 1944, 42.

21. Mallory diary, 80.

22. Mallory diary, 86.

23. Mallory diary, 91.

24. Winton Horn collection, scans of "short snorters," courtesy of Teresa Sherman.

25. Mallory diary, 94.

26. Mallory diary, 98.

27. "Navy's Ace Shows How It's Done," *Des Moines Tribune*, January 18, 1945, 24, https://www.newspapers.com/article/des-moines-tribune-navys-ace-shows-how/55019157/.

28. VF-18 war history, 4.

29. VF-18 war history, 5, 6.

30. VF-18 war history, 8.

31. Spencer Scheckter collection, scrapbook.

32. VF-18 war history, 13.

33. VF-18 war history, 14; Scheckter collection, Canal Zone photographs.

34. Scheckter collection, undated newspaper clippings.

EPILOGUE

1. Bryant Walworth collection, letter from Frances Leighton to Bryant Walworth, November 23, 1944.

2. Ziemer collection, letter from Mrs. L. C. Ziemer to Arthur R. Ziemer, October 29, 1945.

3. Walworth collection, letter from Frances Leighton to Bryant Walworth, November 13, 1945.

FIGHTING SQUADRON 18 PERSONNEL

Lt.(jg) C. Paul Amerman

AMM1c William G. Arrington

PR1c James R. Barrow

ART1c Harry M. Bearden, Jr. † ☾

Lt.(jg) Redman C. Beatley

ART1c James E. Bice ☾

Ens. William F. Bland

Lt.(jg) Edgar G. Blankenship

Lt. Clarence A. Blouin

Lt. Robert E. Brownell

Lt.(jg) Franklin N. Burley

Lt. Roy O. Burnett, Jr.

Lt. Richard L. Cevoli

Lt. Alfred S. Cleveland ☾

Lt. Harry H. Cropper

Lt. Kenneth G. Crusoe *

Lt. Robert H. Davis

Lt.(jg) Charles W. deMoss

Lt. Anthony J. Denman

Lt.(jg) Egidio J. DiBatista

Lt.(jg) John L. Donoghue

Ens. Ralph C. DuPont, III †

Ens. William G. Eccles *

Lt.(jg) George J. Eckel

Lt.(jg) Frank E. Foltz

Ens. Howard Frost, Jr. ☾

ACRM Charles C. Gillaspie

Lt. George A. Griffith, Jr. †

Lt. Robert M. Gowling

Ens. Albert R. Groves *

ARM1c Edward A. Haberstroh

Ens. Arthur S. Haig, Jr.

Ens. Lloyd A. Hammer, Jr.

Y1c Charles O. Hammontree

Ens. L.S. Hardy, Jr. *

Lt. Cecil E. Harris

Lt.(jg) Melvin J. Hayter

Ens. Willis R. Hearne *

Lt. Frank C. Hearrell

Ens. James P. Hedrick † *

AOM1c Eugene R. Herbruck ☾

Lt.(jg) John F. Herlihy

Ens. William A. Herpich ☾

Ens. Winton D. Horn

AMM1c Fred W. Howell

AMM1c Joseph W. Hunter ☾

Lt.(jg) Robert L. Hurst

Ens. William K. Jackson *

Ens. O.L. Jacobsen *

AM1c Clayton F.D. Jeans

ACMM Irby Johnson

AMM1c K. Mark Jungnitsch

Lt.(jg) I. Wesley Keels, Jr. †

AMM2c Charles M. Laundy

Lt.(jg) Charles M. Mallory

ARM2c John L. March ℂ

Ens. Donald P. Matheson ℂ

Lt.(jg) John F. Mayer

AMM1c William McGowen

Lt.(jg) S. Wells McGurk †

Ens. Harold S. Meacham † *

AMM1c William McGowen

ACEM Louis H. Michaud

Lt. William H.B. Millar ℂ

Ens. Arthur P. Mollenhauer †

Ens. Howard H. Moore *

Ens. Robert J. Morris

Ens. William P. Mufich

Lt. Comdr. Edward J. Murphy

Ens. William H. Murray

Ens. George J. Naff

Ens. Daniel A. Naughton *

Lt. James B. Neighbours †

Lt.(jg) James M. Newsome, Jr.

Ens. Erick D.H. Nygaard *

AOM1c Eldon W. Odneal

ACRT Frank J. Olech

AMM1c Harvey C. Olson

Lt. Robert G. O'Maley

Ens. Walter L. Passi †

ACOM Lonnie A. Passmore

Lt. Harvey P. Picken

Ens. Joseph Pierce

AOM2c Charles H. Rader

Lt. Thomas J. Rennemo

Ens. Sterling J. Richardson *

Lt.(jg) Edward A. Ritter, Jr.

Lt.(jg) William H. Sartwelle †

Lt.(jg) Robert F. Simpson

Ens. C.D. Smith *

ACMM Sidney O. Snodgrass

Ens. W.E. Stephens *

Lt.(jg) Noel L. Thompson

Lt. William B. Thompson † ℂ

Ens. Bruce H. Throckmorton *

Lt.(jg) Harold R. Thune

Ens. Edward W. Toaspern *

Lt. Frederick W. Tracy

Lt. Comdr. John W. Valentine

Lt. Rudolph D. Van Dyke, Jr.

Lt.(jg) Bryant L. Walworth

AMM2c Allen R. Watson

Lt. Donald L. Watts

Ens. Harry R. Webster, Jr. †

Ens. John T. Williss *

Lt. Frederick C. Wolff

Ens. Leonard S. Woodward

Lt.(jg) Edward W. Young ℂ

Lt.(jg) William C. Ziemer †

Ens. John A. Zink *

† MIA/KIA   ℂ Former VF(N)-78   * Replacement pilot

BIBLIOGRAPHY

ARCHIVAL MATERIAL

NATIONAL ARCHIVES AND RECORDS ADMINISTRATION

Office of the Chief of Naval Operations, records relating to naval activity during World War II, Record Group 38.

OPERATIONAL REPORTS

Commander, Air Group 15. Report of Operations against the Philippine Islands, October 21–27, 1944, https://catalog.archives.gov/id/78677845.

Commander, Air Group 18: Aircraft Action Reports

Palau Islands, September 6–8, 1944, https://catalog.archives.gov/id/139750650.

Philippine Islands, September 9–10, 1944, https://catalog.archives.gov/id/139750327.

Central Philippine Islands, September 12–14, 1944, https://catalog.archives.gov/id/139751174.

Philippine and Palau Islands, September 13–17, 1944, https://catalog.archives.gov/id/139751255.

Luzon, Philippine Islands, September 21–22, 1944, https://catalog.archives.gov/id/139751278.

Central Philippine Islands, September 24, 1944, https://catalog.archives.gov/id/139751319.

Ryukyu Islands, Formosa, Philippines, and the Japanese Fleet, October 10–30, 1944, https://catalog.archives.gov/id/78715291.

Luzon, Philippine Islands, November 5–6, 1944, https://catalog.archives.gov/id/78677948.

Enemy Airfields and Aircraft on Luzon, Philippines, November 19, 1944, https://catalog.archives.gov/id/139784438.

Commander, Air Group 19. Report of Operations against the Ryukyu Islands, Formosa, Philippines, and Japanese Fleet, October 10 to November 6, 1944, https://catalog.archives.gov/id/139768009.

Commander, Task Force 38:

Report of Operations against the Philippines, Formosa, French Indo-China, South China, and the Ryukyu Islands, November 5, 1944 to January 2, 1945, https://catalog.archives.gov/id/139838786.

Summary of Operations, August 28 to October 30, 1944, https://catalog.archives
.gov/id/78648835.

Commander, Task Group 38.1. Report of Air Operations against the Ryukyu Islands,
Formosa, and the Philippines, October 2–29, 1944, https://catalog.archives.gov/id
/78716147.

Commander, Task Group 38.2. Report of Air Operations against Luzon Island, Philippines,
November 5–6, 1944, https://catalog.archives.gov/id/140073781.

Commander, Task Group 38.2. Report of Air Operations against the Ryukyu Islands, Formosa, and the Philippines, October 10 to November 3, 1944, https://catalog.archives
.gov/id/83560463.

Commander, Task Group 38.3. Report of Carrier Air Operations against Formosa, October
12–14, 1944, https://catalog.archives.gov/id/78705547.

Commander, Task Group 38.4. Report of Operations, Leyte Island, October 22–31, 1944,
https://catalog.archives.gov/id/78676202.

Commander, Third Fleet. Report of Third Fleet Operations against the Japanese Fleet, October 23–26, 1944, https://catalog.archives.gov/id/139892940.

Commander, USS *Hornet*. Report of Operations against the Palau and Philippine Islands,
Fold3.com.

USS *Bunker Hill*. Aircraft Action Reports, Operations against the Ryukyu Islands, Formosa,
and the Philippines, October 10–22, 1944, https://catalog.archives.gov/id/7864243.

———. Report of Operations in Support of Marianas and Attack on Japanese Task Force,
June 6–27, 1944, https://catalog.archives.gov/id/78539578.

———. Report of Air Operations against the Palau and Philippine Islands, August 29 to
September 30, 1944. Fold3.com.

USS *Cabot*. Report of Air Operations, October 6–14, 1944, October 20–31, 1944, https:
//catalog.archives.gov/id/78659280.

USS *Essex*. Action Report, GALVANIC Operations, November 18–25, 1943, https://catalog
.archives.gov/id/136020848.

USS *Franklin*. Report of Action with Japanese Aircraft Southeast of Formosa on October 13,
1944, https://catalog.archives.gov/id/139760123.

USS *Hancock*. Report of Air Operations against the Ryukyu Islands, Formosa, and the Philippines, Including Attacks on the Japanese Fleet, October 6–31, 1944, https://catalog
.archives.gov/id/139762310.

USS *Independence*. Report of Air Operations against the Palau and Philippine Islands, August
29 to September 30, 1944. Fold3.com.

USS *Intrepid*. Report of Air Operations against the Ryukyu Islands, Formosa, and Philippines, October 10–31, 1944, Including Action against Japanese Fleet, October 24–26,
1944, https://catalog.archives.gov/id/78655720.

———. Report of Air Operations against Southern Luzon Island and Enemy Shipping in
the Sibuyan Sea, Philippines, November 14–27, 1944, https://catalog.archives.gov/id
/78706712.

USS *Monterey*. Report of Action, Air Group 30, Tinian Islands, Marianas, February 22, 1944, https://catalog.archives.gov/id/78326447.

VC-66. Aircraft Action Reports, Operations against the Marshall Islands, February 6–21, 1944, https://catalog.archives.gov/id/83545739.

VF(N)-78. Aircraft Action Reports, Operations in the Philippine Islands, September 9–22, 1944, https://catalog.archives.gov/id/139754790.

WAR DIARIES AND SHIP, AIR GROUP, AND SQUADRON HISTORIES

Air Group 18. War history, https://catalog.archives.gov/id/77684444.

Commander, Western Sea Frontier. War diary, October 1–31, 1943, https://catalog.archives.gov/id/136046263; November 1–30, 1944, https://catalog.archives.gov/id/139850542.

NAS Whidbey Island. War diary, March 28 to April 3, 1943, https://catalog.archives.gov/id/134136750.

USS *Cabot*. War diary, November 10–30, 1944, https://catalog.archives.gov/id/78703245.

USS *Copahee*. War diary, November 1–30, 1943, https://catalog.archives.gov/id/136006387.

USS *Crane*. War diary, November 1–30, 1943, https://catalog.archives.gov/id/136030096.

USS *Hancock*. War diary, November 1–30, 1944, https://catalog.archives.gov/id/139777767.

USS *Intrepid*. War diary, June 1–30, 1944, https://catalog.archives.gov/id/78520108; July 1–31, 1944, https://catalog.archives.gov/id/78577023; October 1–31, 1944, https://catalog.archives.gov/id/78663710; November 1–30/44, https://catalog.archives.gov/id/78704615.

USS *Prince William*. War diary, May 1–31, 1943, https://catalog.archives.gov/id/134287077.

USS *Trathen*. War diary, May 28 to August 5, 1943, https://catalog.archives.gov/id/134311450.

USS *Yarnall*. War diary, October 1–31, 1944, https://catalog.archives.gov/id/78667884.

USS *Yorktown*. War diary, December 1–31, 1943, https://catalog.archives.gov/id/78272451.

VB-18. War history, https://catalog.archives.gov/id/77643136.

VF(N)-78. War history, https://catalog.archives.gov/id/77663361.

VF-7. War history, https://catalog.archives.gov/id/77658304.

VF-9. War history, https://catalog.archives.gov/id/77658405.

VF-13. War history, https://catalog.archives.gov/id/77659248.

VF-18. War history, https://catalog.archives.gov/id/77660629.

VF-40. War diary, March 1–31, 1944, https://catalog.archives.gov/id/78559819.

VT-18. War history, https://catalog.archives.gov/id/77678918.

OTHER

Air Primary Training Command, Regional Office, New York, V5 and SV5, June 30, 1942 to November 1, 1944.

Beulah Williams Library Archives and Special Collections, Northern State University, Aberdeen, SD. Cecil E. Harris Collection, https://digitalcollections.northern.edu/digital/collection/p16707coll7/id/9008/rec/1.

Muster Rolls of U.S. Navy Ships, Stations, and Other Naval Activities, January 1, 1939–January 1, 1949, record group 24, Naval Reserve Aviation Base, Atlanta, Georgia.

National Naval Aviation Museum: Robert L. Lawson collection, cabinet 12, drawer 1, VF-18 folder.

Nichols, Leslie. Radio reports, December 5–6, 1944, Hoover Institution Library and Archives, https://digitalcollections.hoover.org/objects/51681/leslie-nichols-radio-reports-from-5-and-6-december-1944.

Survival and Escape Information/Interviews, 1918–1945, interview with Ens. Dan A. Naughton, USNR, of VF-18 (*Intrepid*), entry UD-09D, box 306.

VF18 Combat Accomplishments 1944, 1918–1945, entry UD-09D, box 322.

INTREPID MUSEUM COLLECTIONS
Amerman, Charles Paul
Barden, Kenneth P., diary
Blankenship, E. G., scrapbook
Bryant L. Walworth, papers
DiBatista, Egidio James "E. J."
Griffith Jr., George A., papers
Lofton, Rex, scrapbook
Montfort, Richard, *Intrepid* diaries
Ritter, Edward A., papers
Ziemer, William C., flight log book

SQUADRON FAMILY COLLECTIONS
Blouin, Clarence (Courtesy of Barbara Liese)
Brownell, Robert (Courtesy of Claire Brownell and Kelea Piper)
Burnett, Roy (Courtesy of Kate Johnstone)
Cevoli, Richard (Courtesy of Steve Cevoli)
Donoghue, Larry (Courtesy of Patricia Cashman)
Foltz, Frank (Courtesy of Laura Lee Barrera)
Harris, Cecil (Courtesy of Rebecca Harris)
Hearrell, Frank (Courtesy of Chris Cox)
Horn, Winton (Courtesy of Teresa Sherman)
Hurst, Robert (Courtesy of Cindy Schilder)
Keels, Wesley (Courtesy of Joel Keels)
Mallory, Charles (Courtesy of Woody Aurentz)
McGurk, Wells (Courtesy of Linde Cheema)
Mollenhauer, Arthur (Familysearch.org, https://www.familysearch.org/photos/gallery/album/411215)
Moot, Richard (Courtesy of John Moot)
Murphy, Edward (Courtesy of the Murphy Family)

Naughton, Daniel (Courtesy of Michael Naughton)
Newsome, James (Courtesy of Kent Newsome)
O'Maley, Robert (Courtesy of Brian and Pit O'Maley)
Ritter, Edward (Courtesy of Valerie Lasser)
Scheckter, Spencer (Courtesy of Anita Scheckter)
Walworth, Bryant (Courtesy of Lee Walworth)
Watts, Donald (Courtesy of Paul Watts)
Wolff, Frederick (Courtesy of Thomas Dyke)
Ziemer, William (Courtesy of Janis Grizzard and the Ziemer Family)

PUBLIC DOCUMENTS

Enemy Oil Committee, Fuels and Lubricants Division. *Petroleum Facilities of Formosa.* Washington, DC: Office of the Quartermaster General, 1945. https://www.scribd.com/document/43228345/Taiwan-Petroleum-Facilities-1945.

Jensen, Oliver. "Truk, End of a Bogey." *Bureau of Naval Personnel Information Bulletin* 338. Washington, DC: Bureau of Naval Personnel, May 1945. https://media.defense.gov/2019/Apr/10/2002112313/-1/-1/1/AH194505.pdf.

Leeds, J. R. "Aviation Personnel Fatalities in World War II." Bureau of Naval Personnel Memo. https://www.history.navy.mil/research/library/online-reading-room/title-list-alphabetically/a/aviation-personnel-fatalities-in-world-war-ii.html.

Naval History and Heritage Command. Air Target Maps and Photos, Selected Targets, Northern Formosa, Pescadores, October 1, 1944. https://www.history.navy.mil/research/library/online-reading-room/title-list-alphabetically/n/northern-formosa-pescadores.html.

———. *Building the Navy's Bases in World War II*, vol. II, part III, chap. 26. https://www.history.navy.mil/research/library/online-reading-room/title-list-alphabetically/b/building-the-navys-bases/buidling-navys-bases-vol-2-chapter-26.html.

———. *Dictionary of American Naval Fighting Ships.* https://www.history.navy.mil/content/history/nhhc/research/histories/ship-histories/danfs.html.

———. "Fighter Squadron Lineage." https://www.history.navy.mil/research/histories/naval-aviation-history/insignias/naval-aviation-squadron-lineage/fighter-squadron-lineage.html.

———. Modern Biographical Files, Navy Department Library

Bogan, Gerald Francis. https://www.history.navy.mil/content/history/nhhc/research/library/research-guides/lists-of-senior-officers-and-civilian-officials-of-the-us-navy/commander-first-fleet/bogan-gerald-francis.html.

Dickson, Harlan Rockey. https://www.history.navy.mil/research/library/research-guides/modern-biographical-files-ndl/modern-bios-d/dickson-harlan-rockey.html.

Ellis, William Edward. https://www.history.navy.mil/research/library/research-guides/modern-biographical-files-ndl/modern-bios-e/ellis-william-edward.html.

Office of the Chief of Naval Operations. *CIC Magazine* 1, no. 7 (September 1944). https://maritime.org/doc/cic/cic-44–09.pdf.

———. *CIC Magazine* 1, no. 9 (December 1944). https://maritime.org/doc/cic/cic-44-12.pdf.

———. *CIC Magazine* 2, no. 11 (November 1945). https://maritime.org/doc/cic/cic-45–11.pdf.

———, Division of Naval Intelligence, Air Intelligence Group. "Airfield and Seaplane Bases in Formosa." https://catalog.archives.gov/id/78450948.

U.S. Secretary of the Combined Chiefs of Staff. *Octagon Conference, September 1944: Papers and Minutes of Meetings.* Washington, DC: Department of Defense, 1944.

INTERVIEWS AND ORAL HISTORIES

Denman, Anthony J. American Fighter Aces Association oral history interview. 1989. https://archives.museumofflight.org/repositories/2/archival_objects/1494.

Harris, Capt. Cecil E. Interview, August 7, 1968. Smithsonian National Air and Space Museum Sound Archives Collection.

Intrepid Museum Oral History Project. https://intrepid.emuseum.com/groups/oral-histories.
Donoghue, John Lawrence. September 14, 2021.
deMoss, Charles W. August 15, 2017.
Smith Jr., Eugene. July 8, 2016.
Stone, Raymond T. June 14, 2013.
Thune, Harold R. March 15, 2017.

Keels, Orean, and Lillie Earle Keels-Fincher. Interview by Michael Fink, August 14, 2022.

Mallory, Charles. Interview by Robert Gandt, November 3, 2007.

Naff, George. Interview by Heather Steele, World War II History Project, July 16, 2011.

Thune, Harold R. Collection, Veterans History Project, American Folklife Center, Library of Congress.

Walworth, Bryant. Interview by Lee Walworth, August 1986.

BOOKS AND MANUSCRIPTS

Adams, William H., ed. *The Japanese Airbase on Taroa Island, Republic of the Marshall Islands, 1937–1945: An Evaluation of the World War II Remains.* San Francisco: U.S. National Park Service, 1997.

Boslaugh, David L. *Radar and the Fighter Directors.* Unpublished manuscript, circa February 2018. https://ethw.org/Radar_and_the_Fighter_Directors.

Carter, Worrall Reed. *Beans, Bullets, and Black Oil: The Story of Fleet Logistics Afloat in the Pacific During World War II.* Washington, DC: U.S. Government Printing Office, 1953.

Cutler, Thomas J., ed. *The Battle of Leyte Gulf at 75: A Retrospective.* Annapolis, MD: Naval Institute Press, 2019.

Duffy, James P. *War at the End of the World: Douglas MacArthur and the Forgotten Fight for New Guinea, 1942–1945.* New York: New American Library, 2016.

Evans, David C., ed. *The Japanese Navy in World War II: In the Words of Former Japanese Naval Officers*. Annapolis, MD: Naval Institute Press, 1986.

Evans, David C., and Mark R. Peattie. *Kaigun: Strategy, Tactics, and Technology in the Imperial Japanese Navy, 1887–1941*. Annapolis, MD: Naval Institute Press, 1997.

Ewing, Steve, and John Lundstrom. *Fateful Rendezvous: The Life of Butch O'Hare*. Annapolis, MD: Naval Institute Press, 1997.

Faltum, Andrew. *Aircraft Carrier* Intrepid. Annapolis, MD: Naval Institute Press, 2022.

Fisher, Stan. *Sustaining the Carrier War: The Deployment of U.S. Naval Air Power to the Pacific*. Annapolis, MD: Naval Institute Press, 2023.

Fletcher, Gregory G. *Intrepid Aviators: The American Flyers Who Sank Japan's Greatest Battleship*. New York: NAL Caliber, 2013.

Forsyth, John. *Helldivers: U.S. Navy Dive-Bombers at War*. Osceola, WI: Motorbooks International, 1991.

Francillon, Rene J. *Japanese Aircraft of the Pacific War*. Annapolis, MD: Naval Institute Press, 1987.

Grossnick, Roy A. *Dictionary of American Naval Aviation Squadrons*, vol. 1. Washington, DC: Naval Historical Center, 1995.

Halsey, William F., and J. Bryan. *Admiral Halsey's Story*. New York: McGraw-Hill, 1947.

Hammel, Eric. *Aces against Japan II: The American Aces Speak*, vol. 3. Pacifica, CA: Pacifica Press, 1996.

Hata, Ikuhiko, and Yasuho Izawa. *Japanese Naval Aces and Fighter Units in World War II*. Annapolis, MD: Naval Institute Press, 1989.

Hornfischer, James D. *The Fleet at Flood Tide: America at Total War in the Pacific, 1944–1945*. New York: Bantam Books, 2016.

———. *The Last Stand of the Tin Can Sailors: The Extraordinary World War II Story of the U.S. Navy's Finest Hour*. New York: Bantam Books, 2005.

Izawa, Yasuho, with Tony Holmes. *J2M Raiden and N1K1/2 Shiden/Shiden-Kai Aces*. Oxford, UK: Osprey, 2016.

Junge, Valerie. *Flying Ace, Edward A. Ritter*. Tukwila, WA: Reischling Press, 2010.

Lott, Arnold S. *Most Dangerous Sea: A History of Mine Warfare and an Account of U.S. Navy Mine Warfare Operations in World War II and Korea*. Annapolis, MD: U.S. Naval Institute, 1959.

Lundstrom, John B. *The First Team: Pacific Naval Air Combat from Pearl Harbor to Midway*. Annapolis, MD: Naval Institute Press, 1990.

———. *The First Team and the Guadalcanal Campaign: Naval Fighter Combat from August to November 1942*. Annapolis, MD: Naval Institute Press, 2005.

Morison, Samuel Eliot. *History of United States Naval Operations in World War II*, vol. 12, *Leyte: June 1944–January 1945*. Annapolis, MD: Naval Institute Press, 2011.

Olynyk, Frank. *Stars & Bars: A Tribute to the American Fighter Ace 1920–1973*. London: Grub Street, 1995.

Pisano, Dominick. *To Fill the Skies with Pilots: The Civilian Pilot Training Program, 1936–1946*. Chicago: University of Illinois Press, 1993.

Prados, John. *Combined Fleet Decoded: The Secret History of American Intelligence and the Japanese Navy in World War II*. Annapolis, MD: Naval Institute Press, 1995.

———. *Storm over Leyte: The Philippine Invasion and the Destruction of the Japanese Navy*. New York: Penguin Random House, 2016,

Rea, Robert Right. *Wings of Gold: An Account of Naval Aviation Training in World War II*. Tuscaloosa: The University of Alabama Press, 2015.

Reynolds, Clark G. *The Fast Carriers: The Forging of an Air Navy*. Annapolis, MD: Naval Institute Press, 2013.

Sims, Edward H. *Greatest Fighter Missions of the Top Navy and Marine Aces of World War II*. New York: Harper, 1962.

Solberg, Carl. *Decision and Dissent: With Halsey at Leyte Gulf*. Annapolis, MD: Naval Institute Press, 1995.

Stille, Mark. *Imperial Japanese Navy Aircraft Carriers, 1921–1945*. Oxford, UK: Osprey Publishing, Ltd., 2005.

———. *Leyte Gulf: A New History of the World's Largest Sea Battle*. Oxford, UK: Osprey Publishing, Ltd., 2023.

Stone, Raymond T. *My Ship! The U.S.S. Intrepid*. South Salem, NY: G. P. Books, 2003.

Tell Studios. *The Life and Legacy of Bill Daniels*. Denver, CO: The Daniels Fund, 2012.

Tillman, Barrett. *Hellcat: The F6F in World War II*. Annapolis, MD: Naval Institute Press, 2000.

Toll, Ian W. *The Conquering Tide: War in the Pacific Islands, 1942–1944*. New York: W. W. Norton, 2015.

Trimble, William F. *Admiral John S. McCain and the Triumph of Naval Air Power*. Annapolis, MD: Naval Institute Press, 2019.

Vego, Milan. *The Battle for Leyte, 1944: Allied and Japanese Plans, Preparations, and Execution*. Annapolis, MD: Naval Institute Press, 2013.

Willmott, H. P. *The Battle of Leyte Gulf: The Last Fleet Action*. Bloomington: Indiana University Press, 2005.

Woodward, C. Vann. *The Battle for Leyte Gulf: The Incredible Story of World War II's Largest Naval Battle*. New York: Skyhorse Publishing, 2007.

PERIODICALS

NEWSPAPERS

"Artist-Fighter Pilot Kept Carrier's Morale High." *Brooklyn Daily Eagle*. December 30, 1945. https://www.newspapers.com/article/the-brooklyn-daily-eagle-artist-fighter/7185775/.

Coll Jr., Ray. "Dogfight over Formosa." *Honolulu Advertiser*. November 8, 1944. https://www.newspapers.com/article/the-honolulu-advertiser-dogfight-over-fo/13633790/.

———. "Flattop Pilots and Crews in Action." *Honolulu Advertiser*. November 10, 1944. https://www.newspapers.com/article/the-honolulu-advertiser-flattop-pilots-a/13633324/.

———. "Roll of the Missing." *Honolulu Advertiser*. December 4, 1944. https://www.newspapers.com/article/the-honolulu-advertiser-roll-of-the-miss/13629997/.

———. "A Bit of Weather on a Flattop." *Honolulu Advertiser*. November 17, 1944. https: //www.newspapers.com/article/the-honolulu-advertiser-a-bit-of-weather/13632068/.

———. "Waiting News in Ready Room," *Honolulu Advertiser*. November 12, 1944.

———. "A Gun Crew from the Mess in Action." *Honolulu Advertiser*. December 13, 1944. https://www.newspapers.com/article/the-honolulu-advertiser-a-gun-crew-from /13630707/.

———. "Profile of a Flying Admiral." *Honolulu Advertiser*. November 11, 1944. https://www .newspapers.com/article/the-honolulu-advertiser-profile-of-a-fly/13633033/.

———. "'Sunken' Warships of Fleet Rise, Claim 58 Enemy Vessels." *Honolulu Advertiser*. October 31, 1944. https://www.newspapers.com/article/the-honolulu-advertiser -sunken-warships/24397194/.

"Comdr. Starkes Gets 3 Medals." *Honolulu Advertiser*. December 18, 1946. https://www .newspapers.com/article/the-honolulu-advertiser-comdr-starkes-g/132647714/.

"Father Talks Sons into Navy." *Asbury Park (NJ) Press*. May 27, 1945. https://www .newspapers.com/article/asbury-park-press-father-talks-sons-into/23914900/.

"Flyer from Monroe Wins Commission." *Charlotte (NC) Observer*. January 17, 1943. https://www.newspapers.com/article/the-charlotte-observer-flyer-from-monroe /132635617/.

Heisler, Philip S. "First Clash with Japs Leaves Ensign an Ace." *Baltimore Evening Sun*. October 18, 1944. https://www.newspapers.com/article/the-evening-sun-3-day-attack-on -formosa/52703584/.

———. "Flyers Menaced by Head-Hunters." *Baltimore Sun*. October 23, 1944. https://www .newspapers.com/article/the-baltimore-sun-flyers-menaced-by-hea/52704108/.

———. "2 Zeros Downed by Baltimore Navy Flyer." *Baltimore Evening Sun*. November 17, 1944. https://www.newspapers.com/article/the-evening-sun-2-zeros-downed-even /52701666/.

Higbee, Dallas C. "A Dunbar Man Who Qualified as Expert in Aerial Combat." *Sunday Gazette-Mail* (Charleston, WV). November 7, 1965. https://www.newspapers.com /article/sunday-gazette-mail-a-dunbar-man-who-qua/7141975/.

Jauch, Fritz. "Illini Hall Whips Delts, 32–25, for I-M Cage Crown." *Daily Illini* (Champaign, IL). April 9, 1941. https://idnc.library.illinois.edu/?a=d&d=DIL19410409.2.71&e =-------en-20-DIL-21--txt-txIN-9+April+1941---------.

"Little Hope Held for Missing Aviator." *Ephraim (UT) Enterprise*. August 4, 1944. https: //www.newspapers.com/article/the-ephraim-enterprise-little-hope-held/134345967/.

"Local Men Reported for Naval Aviation." *Brooklyn Daily Eagle*. June 15, 1942. https: //www.newspapers.com/article/the-brooklyn-daily-eagle-local-men-repor /132632620/.

"Lost in Crash, Lieut. Thomas P. Sorensen, Jr." *St. Louis Post-Dispatch*. May 21, 1943. https: //www.newspapers.com/article/st-louis-post-dispatch-lost-in-crash/132941094/.

"Missing in Action." *Echo* (Pisgah Forest, NC). December 1, 1944. https://newspapers .digitalnc.org/lccn/2014236906/1944-12-01/ed-1/seq-14/.

"Navy's Ace Shows How It's Done." *Des Moines Tribune*. January 18, 1945. https://www .newspapers.com/article/des-moines-tribune-navys-ace-shows-how/55019157/.

"Navy Fighter Pilot Becomes City's 1st Ace." *Santa Barbara (CA) News-Press*. October 18, 1944. https://www.newspapers.com/article/santa-barbara-news-press-navy-fighter-pi /134355712/.

"Navy's Second Ranking Ace Home on Leave." *Del Rio (TX) News Herald*. January 17, 1945. https://www.newspapers.com/article/del-rio-news-herald-cecil-harris-ranking /5287518/.

"Pacific War Veteran Seeks County Post." *Daily Times* (Salisbury, MD). February 28, 1946. https://www.newspapers.com/article/the-daily-times-pacific-war-veteran-see /12354776/.

"Scholarship Winner." *Montclair (NJ) Times*. June 22, 1937. https://www.newspapers.com /article/the-montclair-times-scholarship-winner/35713358/.

"Social Events." *Sedalia (MO) Democrat*. September 26, 1943. https://www.newspapers .com/article/the-sedalia-democrat-social-events/7183660/.

"Two Sophs Listed for Lafayette." *Standard-Speaker* (Hazleton, PA). October 3, 1941. https: //www.newspapers.com/article/standard-speaker-two-sophs-listed-for-la/134290824/.

Wells, Sandy. "Innerviews: I Was Just Lucky." *Charleston (WV) Gazette*. November 11, 2002. https://www.proquest.com/docview/331226082.

"Witnesses Failure to Identify Wrublewski." *Daily Times* (Davenport, IA). August 1, 1946, https://www.newspapers.com/article/the-daily-times-witnesses-failure-to-id /14156634/.

"Ziemer Captains Lafayette Team." *Wilkes-Barre (PA) Times Leader*. November 16, 1940. https://www.newspapers.com/article/wilkes-barre-times-leader-the-evening-n /134290573/.

MAGAZINES, JOURNALS, AND PAPERS

Aurentz, Forrest W. "Hellcat Ace in a Day." *Air Classics* (November 2003).

Bernstein, Marc. D. "He Predicted Leyte Gulf." *Naval History Magazine* 15, no. 5 (October 2001). https://www.usni.org/magazines/naval-history-magazine/2001/october/he -predicted-leyte-gulf.

Caldwell, Dan. "Remembering Peleliu." *Naval History Magazine* 14, no. 2 (April 2000). https://www.usni.org/magazines/naval-history-magazine/2000/april/remembering -peleliu.

Chih-yuan, Chang. "The Historic Preservation and Rebirth of the Shell Oil Company Storage in Tamsui, Taiwan." Paper presented at the International Association of Societies of Design Research, Hong Kong Polytechnic University, November 12–15, 2007.

Colby, C. B. "How the Hellcat Got That Way." *Popular Science* (December 1943).

Correll, John T. "Disaster in the Philippines." *Air & Space Forces Magazine* (November 1, 2019).

"Decorations and Citations." *All Hands Magazine* (August 1947). https://media.defense .gov/2019/Apr/10/2002112343/-1/-1/1/AH194708.pdf.

De Vore, Robert. "Wing Talk." *Collier's Magazine* (May 19, 1945).

Garas, Daniel. "The Oerlikon 20mm: The Right Tool for the Job." *Sextant* (March 18, 2019). https://usnhistory.navylive.dodlive.mil/Recent/Article-View/Article/2686834/the-oerlikon-20-mm-the-right-tool-for-the-job/.

Hegranes, Emily. "Segregation in the Navy." *Naval History Magazine* 35, no. 1 (February 2021). https://www.usni.org/magazines/naval-history-magazine/2021/february/segregation-navy.

Heidgerd, Christian. "Admiral Thach: A Tactical Artist." *Naval History Magazine* 36, no. 2 (April 2022). https://www.usni.org/magazines/naval-history-magazine/2022/april/admiral-thach-tactical-artist.

Murray, Stephen C. "The Palauan *Kirikomi-tai* Suicide Bombers of World War II and the Siege of Babeldoab: A Reconsideration." *Pacific Asia Inquiry* 4, no. 1 (2013): 30–57.

Reynolds, Quentin. "Wing Talk." *Collier's Magazine* (June 30, 1945).

Vogel, Bertram. "Japan's Wartime Hocus-Pocus." *Proceedings* 74, no. 4 (April 1948). https://www.usni.org/magazines/proceedings/1948/april/japans-wartime-hocus-pocus.

MISCELLANEOUS

"Keels Jr., Isaac Wesley." Scrapbook, Heroic Sons of Gold Star Mothers, Union County, NC. http://history.union.lib.nc.us/GoldStarMothers/keelsi.htm.

NATIONAL NAVAL AVIATION MUSEUM, AIRCRAFT ON DISPLAY.

F4F-3 Wildcat. https://www.history.navy.mil/content/history/museums/nnam/explore/collections/aircraft/f/f4f-3-wildcat.html.

F6F-3 Hellcat. https://www.history.navy.mil/content/history/museums/nnam/explore/collections/aircraft/f/f6f-3-hellcat.html.

F6F-5 Hellcat. https://www.history.navy.mil/content/history/museums/nnam/explore/collections/aircraft/f/f6f-5-hellcat.html.

SNV Valiant. https://www.history.navy.mil/content/history/museums/nnam/explore/collections/aircraft/s/snv-valiant.html.

SNJ Texan. https://www.history.navy.mil/content/history/museums/nnam/explore/collections/aircraft/s/snj-texan.html.

National Park Service. National Register of Historic Places Registration Form. "Star of the Sea Church, Kalapana Painted Church Site #10–63–7380." https://npgallery.nps.gov/AssetDetail/039507b0-dfea-49b3-bb0c-fc861c299ec0.

Sheaf (yearbook). Principia College, Elsah, IL. 1941. https://principia.contentdm.oclc.org/digital/collection/PYB01/id/30821/rec/2.

South Dakota Sports Hall of Fame Web site. "Harold Thune—Inducted 2013." www.sdshof.com/inductees/harold-thune/.

Trapp, Gerald. "VC-66 Informal Squadron History." https://cnrh.cnic.navy.mil/Portals/79/PMRF_Barking_Sands/Documents/VC-66%20UNOFFICIAL%20LOG.pdf?ver=TfVdmklDE7w6P7twzr1EPA%3D%3D.

INDEX

ABOUT THE AUTHOR

MIKE FINK is manager of development content at the Intrepid Museum. An avid researcher/historian, he has spent the past six years combing through archives and interviewing pilots and their families to uncover the incredible true story of "Two-a-Day 18," aircraft carrier *Intrepid*'s highest -scoring fighting squadron.